What the Modern Martyr Should Know:
Seventy-Two Grapes and Not a Single Virgin
The New Picture of Islam

Norbert G. Pressburg

Revised version of the book,
Good Bye Mohammed by Norbert G. Pressburg,
BoD Publishers, Germany
© Norbert G. Pressburg 2009 and 2010
Translation by Vincent A. Fisher

ISBN: 1468129031
ISBN-13: 9781468129038

It is not possible to prove the truth. But it is possible to prove a falsehood. And by doing so, we can approach the truth.

Sir Karl Popper

Contents

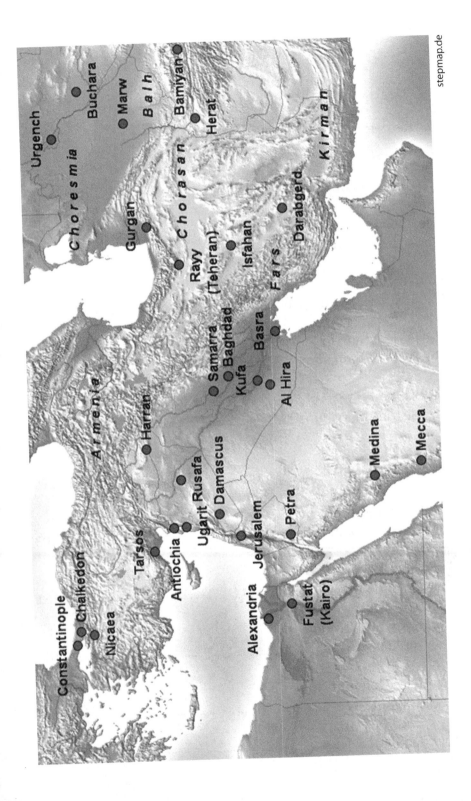

Preface

The Research on Islam Has Just Begun

The non-Muslim world experienced its first massive contact with the "followers of Muhammad" during the Crusades. The Holy Land, including Jerusalem—the birthplace of Christian beliefs—was occupied by "wrong-believers," and this was an unbearable thought for deeply religious medieval Europe. Christian pilgrims reported of harassment, atrocities, and the desecration of holy sites. The Holy Land had to be snatched from the "wrong-believers." The gateways had to be secured, and that's how the First—unsuccessful—Crusade began in 1096. More crusades followed, which left the Christian-Byzantine Empire weakened. That gave way to the rise of the Ottoman Empire, the greatest Islamic powerhouse in history. During its expansion, the Ottoman people made it to Vienna, Austria. This issue, however, was simply regarded as a problem of the Austro-Hungarian Hapsburg dynasty, and was pretty much ignored by the rest of Europe.

In contrast to, say, Buddhism, Islam has never been regarded as a respectable religion in the Western world. Here, one somewhat smiled a bit condescendingly at those peculiar habits: *No wine? No pork? Five prayers a day?* One smirked about polygamy, maybe even with some envy. The Turkish sultan was said to have had hundreds of women.

For a long time, hardly anyone really knew a whole lot about the religion of Islam, and actually, hardly anyone really cared. More intense contacts with this religion might have been expected with increased tourism in Islamic regions, but the focus of early visitors would more or less remain on relics of ancient cultures between the Nile and the Tigris rivers, and the oriental bazaars.

A romantic component was added to the Western view of Islam by the fairy tales of the *Arabian Nights*: the mysterious, exotic, medieval Baghdad with her legendary ruler Harun al-Rashid.

Islamic armies and flotillas threatened Europe several times, but in the eyes of the Western world, the Muslims kept their image as both destroyers of ancient buildings and sneaky rug sellers. Indeed, the "Orient" of that time was *interesting*—so long as one didn't have to live there. Arabia was conveniently far away, people there lagged behind the modern West anyway, and oil was of minor importance back then.

That changed in an instant, when, in 1973, the oil crisis sent a shockwave from the Middle East out to the world, stirring the minds of the West. It was the *Middle East* now—the exotic *Arabian Orient* was no more. Gasoline rationing affected just about everybody, but the problem still remained an economic one.

The events of the late twentieth and early twenty-first centuries, however, were of a different tenor. Violent anti-Westerners such as Muammar Gaddafi, Saddam Hussein, and Mahmoud Ahmadinejad rose to become the leaders of Arab states while claiming to be devout Muslims, effectively putting weapons of mass destruction into the hands of people who felt that committing even the most horrific murders were sanctioned by their Holy Book and the Prophet Muhammad. After terror groups such as Al-Qaida trained and dispatched Islamic bombers to Western metropolitan areas, monstrous, religiously motivated attacks were carried out on US targets on 9/11, and later in Tunis, London, and Madrid.

Troubling for many Westerners was the fact that, in many cases, the origins of these bloody deeds could be found not simply in the twisted minds of the actual perpetrators, but in the hate-filled public teachings of Islamic imams around the world, some of whom were subsequently arrested and convicted for their roles in the crimes.

Worst of all, however, was the fact that the horrific acts of violence that the rest of the world united to condemn were openly hailed by many Muslims, secretly endorsed by even more of them, and celebrated by some Islamic clerics as the beginning of the global, final jihad.

Many non-Muslims began to wonder, *What kind of a book is this Holy Book that backs such atrocities? What kind of Prophet calls for such horrific deeds? What kind of religion calls for nonbelievers to convert or be killed?*

Though a few young adventurers have been attracted to the camps of these bearded warriors, of the vast majority of people in the West and around the globe feel have come to resent and fear Islam, giving rise to a new term, *Islamophobia*. The jihadists' bloody attacks have meant a catastrophe not only for the targeted countries, but also for the Islamic world itself.

At the same time, "moderate" Muslims claimed that such atrocious deeds contradicted the "real" Islam because they violated the peaceful, pro-toleration teachings of the Qur'an. Interestingly, however, both moderate and radical Muslims were able to support their positions with quotes from the Qur'an. While there was absolutely no doubt to some that verses of the Holy Book called for production of nuclear weapons with which to smite Islam's enemies, others saw the exact same book as preaching tolerance.

This led to an even greater feeling of insecurity and confusion in the non-Islamic world. Who was right about the Qur'an? How could ideas that completely contradicted each other be derived from the same book? How was this possible?

When these questions suddenly arose, Christoph Luxenberg had already started work that would provide some astonishing answers. An expert in the field of ancient Semitic languages, Luxenberg provided an interpretation of the Qur'an that was based on the idea that the Qur'an was not a purely Arabic work but, rather, included a mixture of Syro-Aramaic elements. His findings, which he presented in a book available only in German, were considered so significant that they even made headlines on the front page of the March 2, 2002, *New York Times*. His theory held that parts of the Qur'an were written before the time of Muhammad, and composed in Aramaic, rather than Arabic. Because they had been unaware of this fact, early

Arabic scholars had produced catastrophic misinterpretations of the Qur'an's text.

In addition to Luxenberg's work, scientists in other fields have disputed substantial parts of the traditional idea of Islamic history. For a long time now, many scientific thinkers have called into question both the origin and reliability of the sources of the Qur'an and even the historicity of Muhammad.

Gustav Weil (1808–1889) was the first author who critically dealt with the historical aspects of this issue. From a historian's perspective, he regarded as useless all the information about the Prophet's life, deeds, and sayings, since it had only been orally passed on for generations. Around the same time of Weil's work, biographies of Muhammad by Ibn Hisham (?–834 A.D.) and at-Tabari (?–922 A.D.) were translated into several European languages.

From 1856 to 1861, William Muir (1819–1905) published the four-volume *Life of Mahomet*, in which he described the completely legendary nature of Islamic records and dismissed as worthless sources that had been based on storytellers.

Ignaz Goldziher (1850–1921), who was *the* old master of Islamic studies, published his two-volume *Muhammedanische Studien (Muslim Studies)* in 1889 and 1890. He came to the conclusion that the Hadiths—a purported contemporary collection of Muhammad's sayings and anecdotes about him—were pure fakes produced during later time periods.

The Italian expert on early Islamic studies, Leone Caetani (1869–1935), came to the same conclusions. In addition, similar findings were provided by the Belgian author, Henri Lammens (1862–1937), who spent his life in Lebanon and was fluent in both the old and the modern languages of the Middle East.

According to Nikolai Alexandrovich Morozov (1854–1946), a Marxist and former Soviet scientist on Islamic studies, the Qur'an was completed no earlier than the eleventh century. It was as late as the Crusades that Islam actually started forging its own identity. Morozov's colleague Lucian Klimovich spoke of Muhammad and the caliphs as mystical figures that had been created in later times. Back in the early twentieth century, his work *Did Muhammad Really Exist?* (1930) might have not been accepted for publication outside of the atheist Soviet Union in such clear words.

The French Qur'an translator and Arabic literature expert Regis Blachere (1900–1973) tried to reconstruct Muhammad's life but realized that there were no sources that would make this possible. The traditional texts he considered as mere legends and the Qur'an itself gave no information about this topic. American historian John Wansbrough (1928–2002) declared that Islam was a mutation of what was originally a Judeo-Christian sect.

There have also been Muslim scientists who have critically dealt with the historic sources of Islam. One of them was Dr. Suleiman Bashear (1947–1991), former professor at the University of Nablus. During one of his lectures, upset students threw him out through the window on the third floor; later, the publication of his *Introduction to Another History* (in Arabic) came at the cost of his job in 1984. In it, he dared to argue that certain traditions were simply invented to transfer the origin of Islam to Mecca.

However, though numerous scientific research studies seeking to discover the truth about Islam and its founder have repeatedly produced results that differ significantly from traditional Islamic teachings, the average person has remained ignorant of this fact, largely because nearly all issues regarding Islam were regarded as irrelevant by most non-Muslims until the towers of the World Trade Center collapsed on September 11, 2001. Until that day, Islam's critics had expressed these concerns rather discretely, almost in a bashful way.

The classical "Orientalists" continued to set the tone, and in their minds, the traditional version of Islam's history remained sound. They were either unable or unwilling to realize that in using Islamic sources, they were only dealing with secondary sources. But primary sources alone can form the basis for serious historical research. In addition, verification of any primary source's authenticity must be the very first step when carrying out scientific work. However, basic scientific requirements have not been met by these classical Orientalists, and there was not much at all to be expected from the Muslims dealing with such issues.

When researching texts such as the Qur'an, historians must try to get as close as possible to the original texts. Where did the texts derive from? Who wrote them? When were they written? In which language? Which type of scripts were used? Evaluations of those issues can only be carried out by using primary sources. Interpretation of the *contents* is not the point—that falls in the field of religion. What the true historian is interested in is the historical facts concerning the creation of the primary sources. And yet, when one reads the work of the Orientalists, it quickly becomes clear that they treat secondary sources as if they are primary sources. This amounts to a declaration of scientific bankruptcy.

The early history of Islam never happened as it has been presented in traditional Islamic accounts. Research regarding the question of what really happened has only just begun. The story about the origin of Islam, the Prophet, and the origin of "his" book, will have to be rewritten. And we are only at the beginning of this journey.

This book serves to provide the reader with the current state of knowledge regarding historical Islam. The findings are very revealing already. There is still a long way to go, but it is already clear that the picture regarding the origin of Islam, based on facts and only facts, will look nothing like the traditional image we have known.

❖ ❖ ❖

The Traditional Qur'an:

The Flawless Copy Directly Derived from Heaven

"The Qur'anic style is undoubtedly beyond human; we see a contemporary plan that no human could have created."
—*Muhammad Abdullah Draz, Qur'an scholar, Cairo .*

For the devoted Muslim, the Qur'an is the Holy Book, in which God disclosed His revelations through the Prophet Muhammad.[1] According to traditional interpretation, the Prophet sought retreat in a cave on the Hira Mountain near Mecca, where he received the so-called Meccan Suras. Later, he obtained additional Suras in Medina. They were all directly derived from God by oral communication and transmitted by the angel Gabriel to Muhammad. Later, Muhammad conveyed them to his companions, who memorized them and wrote them down.

Islam's foundational claim regarding the Qur'an is as follows:

The Qur'an is uncreated. Muhammad received the text by oral communication directly from God through the angel Gabriel and conveyed it to posterity absolutely, precisely, and 100-percent pure. Each and every word is correct, authentic, and unchangeable, holy, and eternally valid. Nothing on earth exists, not in the past, present, or future, that was not found in the Qur'an. Furthermore, the version of the Qur'an by Caliph Uthman represents the only authentic Qur'an, in exactly the way it was conveyed by the Prophet Mohammed. And finally, the Cairo version of 1924 completely corresponds to the Uthman Qur'an and is, therefore, the identical copy of the original that is kept in Paradise.

---

1 *Mohammed* or *Muhammad* are the most common transliterations, but *Muhamad* is closest to the Arabic spelling. The letter transliterated as *h* is actually the guttural *ch*.

This is the dogma that is still in place today and to which the Qur'an must live up. This dogma has to be kept in mind throughout the reading of this book.

The Qur'an consists of 114 suras (or chapters), which are further divided into verses. The number of verses in each individual sura varies; Sura 108 contains just three verses, while Sura 2 contains 286. According to traditional belief, Muhammad conveyed these suras to his followers orally over a span of twenty-three years. Various people were said to have memorized the verses, some of which were put down in writing on animal bones, pieces of leather, leaves, or whatever was at hand. No systematic collection of individual sayings was produced during Muhammad's lifetime. Thus, Muhammad never got to see his book. This is perhaps a negligible point, however, since—according to Islamic records—Muhammad was illiterate and could not read or write.

Given the haphazard fashion in which the Prophet's teachings were recorded, losses had to be expected. During his own lifetime, the Prophet himself occasionally revoked suras or changed them—some verses disappeared altogether. Ubay (died 649), stated that Sura 33 (al-Ahzab) initially consisted of 200 verses, but that only 73 of them could be found. The Prophet's favorite wife, Aisha (612–678), reported that she had kept some verses under her bed, and that they were later eaten by a goat.

Soon after the Prophet's death, according to Islamic tradition, his literary companion, Ibn Thabit, began compiling the texts, but soon several different versions of the compilation existed. More were to come. Following the orders of the third Caliph Uthman (regency 644–656 A.D.), and with the cooperation of selected helpers from the Quraysh tribe, Ibn Thabit produced yet another version, in which mistakes had been eradicated. This version was then reportedly sent to the four Islamic capitals—Medina, Damascus, Kufa, and Basra. This is called the *Uthman Qur'an*, which, according to orthodox Islamic tradition, represents the only valid version.

However, this version was not accepted by everyone. The Shi'a, for instance accuses Uthman of suppressing some authentic suras and forging others for purely political motives—in order to get rid of the prophet's son-in-law Ali, who the Shi'a sees as the only rightful caliph. The Shi'a introduced their own idea of the true, original Qur'an; it was published as the *Abdullah bin Masud* version.

In 1924, the *Cairo Qur'an* appeared on the scene and is considered by the Islamic mainstream to be based on the versions by Ibn Thabit and Uthman. *Cairo Qur'an* supporters believe that this version contains the exact information that God gave Muhammad, without a single error or omission.

Reading the Qur'an is difficult or impossible, many passages make no sense to the reader. (Readers are hereby invited to go ahead and find out for themselves.) Here, the standard response by Muslims is, that it their Holy Book only merely *seems* to be confusing to modern readers because the Qur'an was originally written in Arabic, and can only be read and understood in its original language. Curiously, the book is not any more comprehensible when reading it in Arabic. Even to Arabs, the Qur'an only becomes understandable in connection with further commentaries.

The thousands of Qur'an commentaries contain thousands of sub-commentaries. Some passages of text are interpreted in dozens of different ways. The classic tenth-century verse-by-verse commentary by at-Tabari stretches over thirty volumes. At-Tabari is one of the most respected commentators, but even he offers multiple interpretations for the same passage, and there are other commentators who present yet other completely different readings.

According to God's own statement in the book, the divine message was sent to earth in "clear Arabic." But since the Qur'an's message is clearly *not* clear, one is tempted to ask, "Where does all this confusion come from?"

The traditional answer goes something like this: "Of course, Allah's words can not be understood by humans just like that." But that has never prevented Qur'anic scholars from trumpeting their own interpretation as the one true word of God.

But the problems with God's "clear message" to Arabs does not stop there. For instance, though the Qur'an itself claims to have been given to Muhammad in Arabic, the text itself contains a great number of non-Arabic words, derived from the Syro-Aramaic, Persian, Greek, and Hebrew languages. Examples of such foreign-derived words include the frequently used term *jehenam* (meaning "hell" in Persian), or *taurah* (meaning "torah" in Hebrew), or *logos* (meaning "word" or "message" in Greek). The Qur'an consists of an especially large number of Aramaic words.

The problem in logic is an easy one to discern: if the Qur'an as originally revealed by Gabriel to Muhammad was given in Arabic, and if the Cairo Qur'an contains this revelation perfectly, preserved word-for-word as it was revealed to the Prophet, then God's word "in Arabic" should contain only Arabic words. To claim that it contained anything else would be offensive to every devout Muslim. However, it has been established beyond doubt that the Qur'an contains words derived from a number of non-Arabic languages that were spoken at that time in this region. Though even Arabic linguists confirm that there are non-Arabic terms in the Qur'an, many Islamic leaders continue to deny this fact. They claim that only purely Arabic terms could have been used in the Qur'an, because of God's own statement.

Abdullah Draz (1894–1958), Qur'anic interpreter at Cairo al-Azhar University, strictly ruled out any possibility that the imperfections of the Holy Book's human handlers could have in any sense tainted the perfect revelation of God's word. Even Muhammad himself, he argued, could not have diluted the purity of God's words with his own imperfect comprehension of them, or by inserting into the revelation his own personal reflections upon them. That was because Muhammad had had no ideas about this subject, Draz argued; he was illiterate, and thus was only God's instrument. How could an ignorant person like him have ever contributed his opinion on matters about which he had never read or heard discussed. While he might have been able to see the error in worshipping idols, Muhammad could never have known the truth about the rightful belief. Even if he was a strong rational thinker, unless they had been divinely revealed to him, Muhammad could have never known anything about the historical events he describes in the Qur'an - and yet, the Qur'an has many passages that correspond to the ones described in the Bible. Obviously, this Qur'anic scholar couldn't imagine that Muhammad might have had knowledge about the Bible. Although the Qur'an shares many similarities with the Bible, there are also many differences. For instance, Islam recognizes the existence of Jesus but does not acknowledge his death at the cross.

In addition, the sequence of events gets out of order from time to time: In a carefree move in Sura 19, the Qur'an relocates Haroon's sister Maryam (Aaron's sister Miriam) from the Egyptian-Pharaonic area of the Old Testament to the Roman times of Palestine and mutates her into the mother of Jesus:

> "O sister of Haroon [Aaron, the brother of Moses in the Old Testament]. Your father was not a bad man nor your mother an unchaste woman" (Sura 19:28). In response, she merely pointed at the baby. They said: "How can we talk to a baby in the cradle?" (Sura 19:29). And he [Jesus in the cradle] said: "I am indeed a servant of Allah. He has given me the Book and made me a Prophet" (Sura 19:30).

It would hardly cross many Muslim's mind to doubt these or any other Qur'anic statements, regardless of the historic evidence and practical impossibilities.

Moreover, the Qur'anic reader cannot but notice the lack of both logic and connection in many verses. Obviously, some verses have been placed out of context, and there are numerous contradictions found in them. In Sura 16:67, for example, wine is a gift of God, but in other places (e.g. Sura 2:219), drinking is declared a first-order prohibition for

Muslims. But then again, in Sura 47:15, wine is promised in Paradise to the believers (*"Rivers of water, milk, and wine; delicious to the ones who drink"*), but which understanding of wine is the believer supposed to apply at the end?

The presence of numerous discrepancies is well-known, and those passages are referred to as *abrogated* and *abrogating* verses. That means that one verse can be abrogated or annulled by another one. Depending on scholarly opinion, there are up to 500 such verses that contradict others.

Example 1:

Verse 2 of Sura 73: *"Stand in prayers the whole night except for a small part of it..."* is abrogated by Verse 20 of the same sura: *"God knows that you stand in prayers nearly two thirds of the night, or one half, or one third of it...."* It is interpreted that the night prayer may be significantly shortened.

Example 2:

Sura 4:7: *"Men will have a share in what their parents and their relatives leave, and women will have a share in what their parents and their relatives leave..."*

This passage is abrogated by Verse 11 of the same sura:

"God commands you concerning your children: that the share of a boy shall be twice that of a girl. In case there are only girls, two in number, their share will be two thirds of the estate; but if there is only one girl, her share will be one half of the estate.... God has issued this ordinance."

This suggests a modification of the inheritance claim.

Example 3:

Sura 2:190: *"Fight in the cause of God those who fight against you but do not exceed the limits. God does not like the ones who carry it too far."*

Abrogation is found in Sura 2:191: "...*and kill them [the unbelievers] wherever you find them.*" Additional abrogation appears in Sura 9:5: "*When the holy months are over, then kill the unbelievers wherever you find them, seize them, besiege them, and prepare for them each and every ambush.*"

Qur'an 2:190 only speaks of *fighting*; Sura 2:191 speaks of *killing*. Qur'an Sura 9:5 repeats the order to kill but puts a timely limit on it. The faithful may kill unbelievers, but war must rest during the time of Ramadan.

The Qur'an contains one such contradiction after another, yet the devout Muslim has no problem with this, since everything is possible for God. Sura 2:106 explains, "*For whichever verses we abrogate, we substitute them with better or equivalent ones. Do you not know that Allah has full power over everything?*"

It is common practice that later suras—the so-called Medinan Suras— are given priority because they are the most recent ones. But who would really know which were the later suras since they are simply numbered according to their length? The Medinan Suras are much more radical and focused on practical issues than the Meccan Suras— the latter of which chiefly contain theological material. Because the Medinan Suras are reckoned to have been composed later than the Meccan Suras, this often results in declaring that the more radical of two contradictory statements is the valid one, even if a more liberal passage is available.

It is hard to reconcile this mode of interpretation with the Qur'an's claim to be divine and perfect; but to a believer, this does not cause any problem because this method itself is covered by Sura 13:39, which explains, "*Allah abrogates and confirms what He pleases for He is the Mother of the Book.*"

Qur'anic verses are often semantically ambiguous—their meaning depends on how they are stressed. One verse, for example, says: "*There is no compulsion in religion*" (Sura 2:256).

Some scholars interpret this as granting people permission to freely choose their own religion. According to other interpretations, however, this verse is understood to mean, *"There is no compulsion in the religion."* This is taken to mean that Islam is the only possible religion within which a certain level of tolerance is possible.

The Qur'anic scholar Abdullah Draz goes on:

> *Each individual sentence is expressed in the most dignifying way, for which the smallest possible number of words was used, in order to express thoughts of greatest richness. Qur'anic speech is clearly beyond human because it breaks through the psychological law that intellect and emotion are always in inverse proportion to each other. From the structure of one sura, passing into the whole Qur'an, we see the all-pervasive plan which no human could have created.*

The all-pervasive plan consists of arranging suras in descending order according to their length. The longest suras are at the beginning; the shortest ones are found at the end (e.g., Sura 2 consists of 286 verses, Sura 4 has 175 verses, Sura 111 contains only five verses, and Sura 112 has only four verses).[2]

Because of this arrangement, any kind of chronological or topical relationship between suras is lost, resulting in an illogical jumble that challenges anyone who wishes to truly understand the text. Non-Muslim Qur'anic researchers have rather successfully reconstructed the suras' topical arrangements and logic order, allowing the meaning of many passages to be grasped for the first time. (Islamic clerics, however, have hardly acknowledged any of these findings.)

---

2 Sura 1, which is "The Opening Sura," does not actually represent a real sura because it addresses God and, therefore, cannot be God's words. However, when the imperative of "Speak!" is placed right in at the beginning of the sura, the believer's recitation of the rest of the sura becomes a divine command from God, and the words of the recitation itself—though addressed to God—are understood to have been composed by God himself. This kind of trick is found 350 times in the Qur'an.

The main argument of the believers for the divinity of the Qur'an lies at a completely different level, which is of the emotional kind: the rhyme-prose form of the suras and verses is considered to be absolutely perfect, and, in turn, the perfect aesthetics of the prose is seen as irrefutable proof of the divine origin of the Qur'an. The perfection of the verses is praised to the skies; every Muslim would certainly confirm their breathtaking lyric style—even if he doesn't understand them.

It would be useless to attempt to argue about the aesthetics of a language that is not one's mother tongue, but it is worth noting that history is rife with native-born Arabic public figures who have doubted that the Qur'anic language possesses much in the way of aesthetics—and they have often paid with their lives for saying so.

It has been well-known that there are numerous grammatical errors in the Qur'an. Ali Dashti[3] provides detailed lists of grammatical errors and syntactical impossibilities. He writes:

> The Qur'an includes incomplete sentences…there are foreign terms, expressions, and words that are unknown in Arabic but used anyway, and applied in ways that are different from their usual meanings. In the Qur'an, grammatical rules are ignored, regardless of whether it concerns the feminine or masculine gender, verb, noun, adjective, or adverbs. In addition, there are illogical and grammatically incorrect pronouns which in various places do not show any relation to each other.

All Muslims are supposed to read the Qur'an at least once in their lifetimes, and most of them have done so, beginning at ages ranging from three to six years. Normally, a teacher reads one verse aloud in Arabic, and the student repeats it. After some time, the student is able to say the verses on his own. If one asks the student about the

---

3 Ali Dashti (1896–1981), an Iranian, studied theology and history in Nedjaf. He was a Shi'a clergyman and later became a journalist. A well-known opposition politician who was imprisoned several times, his last imprisonment by Khomeini was in 1979. He died in prison in 1981.

meaning of what he or she has just said, the student will be unable to answer; he or she has learned to recite, but not to understand the content.

In order to do so, the student would need special training in Qur'anic Arabic. This is because the Qur'an is not written in the same Arabic language that is in general usage among Arab peoples. In truth, there is no single, general Arabic language. Instead, there are various types of generally used Arabic languages such as Moroccan, Syrian, Egyptian, Yemeni Arabic, Gulf Arabic, and so on. These Arabic dialects can differ from each other significantly, but each of them also differs from the *Arabiya*, which is the High Arabic. The *Arabiya* represents the official Arabic language, but, in general, the common person only has a rather imperfect command of it. Egyptian president Gamal Abdel Nasser, known for his great oral skills, was famous for starting his speeches in *Arabiya* but switching at critical passages to the *Ammiya*, the language of the common people. And at these moments, the public's feeling was running high.

But the Qur'anic language also differs from the *Arabiya* and cannot be understood by anyone other than the ones belonging to the inner circle of Qur'anic scholars. Even a Saudi, who is a person from the land of the Prophet, cannot cope with the Qur'anic language. Egyptians, Iraqis, and Moroccans have somewhat rudimentary linguistic intelligibility with it; non-Arabic Muslims completely lack any understanding. How much of the contents of the Arabic Qur'an does a Turk, Afghan, Pakistani, Iranian, Maldivian, or Indonesian understand? Literally nothing—even if they are able to recite it.

Muslims are not expected to actually understand the Qur'an, however, because the believer learns about its contents from imams or prayer leaders, who in most cases have received their interpretations in just the same fashion. This system has led to the incorporation of local traditions and explains both the presence of many different, diverse views within the faith and the reason why crowds of Muslims can be incited so easily by their religious leaders.

For instance, in 2005, news spread among Muslims that blasphemous cartoons insulting the Prophet had been published in a Danish newspaper. As a result, especially after Friday prayers, hundreds of thousands of Muslims flocked to the streets, set buildings on fire, and injured and even killed people. And this happened despite the fact that not a single one of the demonstrators nor their prayer leaders had themselves ever seen any of these cartoons. This sort of group mentality is inevitable, because Muslims are not taught to form their own opinions on matters of faith after a personal examination of the facts; rather, the correct opinion is the one already held by their leaders.

While there is no formal highest authority in Islam, Cairo's al-Azhar University has long been considered *the* authority regarding Qur'anic interpretations.

Let's summarize the traditional Islamic understanding regarding the origin of the Qur'an: there are 114 suras, each of which consists of up to 286 verses—an amount that would fill a thousand-page book. Such a volume was orally transmitted to Muhammad by the archangel Gabriel, which Muhammad (though illiterate and unschooled) flawlessly passed on to his followers. His followers memorized the suras or wrote them down and passed them on; no error or mistake occurred on their way through the centuries. From these perfectly conveyed, perfectly remembered, perfectly transcribed, perfectly translated words is derived the Qur'an of today—itself perfect in all ways.

Over the years, critics have pointed out what seem to be some insurmountable obstacles to anybody attempting to hold to the traditional Islamic line in the modern age. To start with, following Muhammad's supposed revelation, several significantly different "official" revisions and adaptations of his teachings surfaced. Furthermore, the Qur'an's "perfect and pure Arabic" contains numerous flaws and non-Arabic terms…and despite its claims of clarity, cannot even be understood by native Arabic speakers without the use of explanatory commentaries. Finally, many suras are obviously displaced; and the master arrangement of the suras according to their length adds to the general incoherence of the text.

Despite all of this, faithful Muslims assert to this day that every single word in the present canonical Qur'an—the standard version produced in 1924 in Cairo—represents God's word, without error, eternally valid and unchangeable. In the next chapter, we'll take a look at what science has to say about this claim.

❖ ❖ ❖

The Book that Contains Olive Oil:

The Qur'an and Science

Don't they [the skeptics] study the Qur'an? If it was by someone other than God, they would find many discrepancies in it.
—*Qur'an, Sura 4:82*

Rudi Paret (1901–1983), well-known Qur'anic translator, writes in the introduction of his German translation: "We have no reason to assume that there is a single verse in the whole Qur'an that was not by Muhammad." This statement is remarkable in that it comes from a person who had to deal with the Qur'an's contradictions, discrepancies, ambiguities, errors, illogic, and linguistic inconsistencies on a daily basis during his translating work.

Similar statements are made by Tilman Nagel, who writes, "Science has to keep to whatever can be assumed as proven, namely that the words in the Qur'an came from Muhammad."[4] He then proceeds to elaborate for an incredible thousand-plus pages upon this more-than-doubtful premise.

How could these two scientists come to such conclusions? Simply, they reflect the opinion of traditional scientists in Middle Eastern studies. While great works were carried out in the field of Islamic studies during the nineteenth century, with a few exceptions, no glorious work was produced until near the end of the twentieth century. Typically, for those twentieth-century researchers, credibility of sources seemed to be the least of their concerns. They, for example, translated the Qur'an into foreign languages so brilliantly that some foreign-language translations are probably closer to the original meanings than the Arabic source itself. In some cases, the creation of new translations themselves resulted in new interpretations of certain verses, but when this happened, the authors were quick to show that

---

4 Tilman Nagel, *Mohammed* (München: Oldenbourg, 2008).

the Arabic author (!) must have been wrong regarding certain issues. (I will present some examples of this sort of occurrence later in this book.)

At this point, any scientist should have sensed that something was amiss, since the original work the translators were "correcting" was supposed to be the true divine message in purest Arabic. Both the denial of obvious inconsistencies and the unbelievably sloppy handling of sources have ruined the reputation of the classic "Orientalists," and their low methodical standard in the field of Islamic research has become legendary.

According to tradition, Muhammad founded a new religion by spreading revelations between AD 610 and AD 632. During his lifetime, only oral transmissions existed. According to traditional Islamic teachings, it is said that Caliph Uthman, who was Muhammad's third successor, wrote down the material in the so-called *Uthman Qur'an* twenty years after Muhammad's death. This version was supposed to be the final authority regarding both orthography(!) and contents (!). And then—says the tradition—within just a few years, Muhammad's book and religion spread over Syria, Arabia, Iraq, Persia, Central Asia, Egypt, and North Africa. It was truly an epochal, high-speed event...if that's really how it happened.

But who says that is how it happened? Based on what sources?

None. Contemporary evidence supporting the traditional Islamic version of events is completely absent. There is no evidence suggesting the existence of a possible *Uthman Primary Qur'an*. The first completed version of the Qur'an known to exist was produced in the second half of the ninth century, and the known fragments of Qur'anic manuscripts do not date back to the alleged lifetime of Caliph Uthman. There is no historic evidence to even confirm the existence of the legendary producer of the *Primary Qur'an*, the mysterious Caliph Uthman. It was almost two centuries after the alleged Uthman-events that the first reports about Muhammad and his book began to circulate. Most of the reports were written *three* centuries later.

The scientific community, however, has knowledge of material that originated before the time of the Prophet and eventually reappeared in the Qur'an. According to estimates by Qur'anic researcher Günter Lüling, this pre-Muhammadic material accounts for at least 30 percent of the Qur'an's contents.[5]

What? There are Qur'anic scripts that existed before the founder of Islam was even born?

In 1890, Theodor Nöldeke[6] provided a catalogue listing numerous errors and peculiarities that he found in the Qur'anic language. He mentioned overlaps with the Syro-Aramaic language, but didn't discuss them in detail. In 1927, Alphonse Hormizd Mingana, Iraqi-born researcher on handwritten texts, was the first to point out that the Qur'an-Arabic was mixed with Syro-Aramaic on a large scale. Later, Lüling confirmed these findings and provided more details.

Numerous passages in the Qur'an, the so-called "dark spots," are incomprehensible even to Arabic interpreters. The various interpretations produced over the years by Islamic scholars for these puzzling spots have often differed significantly from each other.

According to traditional Islamic doctrine, Arabic is the language of God, so anyone who couldn't read those passages was understood as simply not having command of God's perfect Arabic. This explanation might satisfy the believers, but it was not convincing to scientists. A researcher on Semitic language and linguistics, Christoph Luxenberg[7], investigated some of the "dark spots." He started reading those unclear passages in the language that was in use at the time of Muhammad, Syro-Aramaic, and he came up with astounding results.

Sura 19 ("Surat Maryam") represents one of those passages. This sura begins by mentioning how Mary conceived Jesus, describes Mary's

---

5 Günter Lüling, A *Challenge to Islam for Reformation*, Delhi: Motilal Banarsidass Publishers, 2003.
6 Theodor Nöldeke, *Geschichte des Qorans*, Facsimile of the 1909 edition, Elibron Classic Series, Adamont Media Corporation, 2005.
7 Pseudonym of a professor at a German university. He is an ethnic Arab.

desperation about the birth of her son out of wedlock, and states that she therefore wished to be dead.

In Verse 24 of this sura, the traditional translation reads: *"And he [Jesus] said to her from beneath: 'Do not grieve. Your Lord has provided a brook at your feet.'"*

In Syro-Aramaic, however, the verse reads: *"Then he [Jesus] said to her after giving birth: 'Do not be sad, for the Lord has made your birth legitimate.'"*

A formerly peculiar sentence makes sense now. (One should not be surprised about the very verbal Jesus-baby, as he was called to help out at several places in the Qur'an. And that's something one should keep in mind—we find same in the Gospels of Thomas.)

Another example deals with the issue regarding virgins in Paradise, the so-called *houris*, who are being promised to the martyrs by the dozens. Luxenberg also sees these houris in a different light.

In the Qur'an, the translation of Sura 44:54 reads, *"and shall wed them [the believers] with houris that have big eyes."*

In the authorized Arabic version, this verse is *wa-zawwagnahum bi-hur inin* and can be translated from classical Arabic as "be married," according to Luxenberg. But it could only be translated in such a way if diacritical marks are placed above the *r* and below the *h*. (The diacritical mark defines how the letter is to be read.) However, diacritical marks didn't exist in the early texts. And without these marks, the word becomes *rawwah-na-hum*, which means "to let [someone] have a rest" in Arabic.

There is no doubt that *hur* represents the plural form of the feminine *hawra*, which means "white one." In Arabic, the word *in* has no meaning; therefore, Arabic Qur'an workers defined the word *in* as the plural form of *ain* (eye, fountain, well), despite the fact that, done correctly, it would have to be *uyun* or *ayun*.

From that, *hur in* would mean "white eyes." But given the context, this would not make any sense in Arabic either (in Sura 12:84, "white eyes" was transformed into "blinded"). Therefore, the Arabic interpretation of the Qur'an gives the version of "big-eyed white ones." That was transformed into "houris with big eyes," and from this, the "virgins of Paradise" were born.

In using Qur'anic as well as non-Qur'anic sources, Luxenberg was able, however, to show that the alleged "white ones" in the Paradise-related passages undoubtedly refer to grapes. The Syro-Aramaic word *in*, which is unknown in Arabic, means "crystal-clear, shiny, splendid, jewel-like appearance" in Aramaic. That means that *hur in* does not refer to any creature or person—certainly not to any houris—but rather, refers to shiny, jewel-like grapes.

And finally, the term *bi* does not appear in these passages as the Arabic word for "with," but rather as the Aramaic word for "under." Thus, the believer does not become the mate of houris, but takes a rest under the *hur in*—meaning that he takes a rest under the grapes.

From that, Luxenberg's corrected translation of Sura 44:54 is, *"We will provide a comfortable place for them under the jewel-like grapes."*

This obviously is a significant difference in meaning from the traditional interpretation, with rather substantial consequences for the "martyrs."

In various verses, the houris have kindled the imagination of the interpreters. In Sura 2:25, for example, the Arabic translation reads, *"There will be chaste spouses waiting for them in Paradise."* But in reality, the sura merely promises *"all kinds of pure fruit."*

From Sura 38:52, the Arabic Qur'an interpreters derived the age of the houris. At first, they were said to be of "equal age." Then they became "young." After that, they were "eternally young." In later interpretations, they were assigned the age of "thirty-three years."

None of this is found in the Qur'an. The key here is the word *atrab,* which is gibberish in Arabic and, therefore, was assigned a meaning by interpreters. The Aramaic root means "juicy," or "flesh of fruit."

The traditional interpretation of Sura 38:52—*"Beside them there shall be chaste* [thirty-three-year-old, eternally young] *houris of equal age, who have their eyes lowered"*—becomes, in the correct Aramaic translation,*"There will be low-hanging, juicy fruit for them."*

The Qur'anic workers top their efforts with the interpretations of Suras 55:56 and 55:74, in which they declare the houris as virgins. In further interpretations, the houris even stay virgins forever, even after having been at the believers' disposal:*"Therein* [in the gardens of Eden] *will be chaste females* [the *houris*] *with their eyes lowered, whom neither man nor jinn has deflowered before"* (Sura 55:56).

Interpretation of the expression *lam yatmithunna* as "deflower" was introduced by the Qur'anic interpreter at-Tabari and has been kept in usage without questions asked, despite the fact that, without any doubt, the Syro-Aramaic root simply means "to dirty,""to contaminate," or "to stain."

Thus, the sentence means, *"Therein are low-hanging fruit that no one has touched before."*

With regard to the traditional interpretation, Luxenberg writes,

> *Coming up with the term "deflower" in the interpretation really is the limit. At this point, everyone who reads the Qur'an with a minimum of comprehension has got to throw one's hands up in surprise. Not only the lack of knowledge could be blamed; it also takes a lot of impudence to not only create something like that when dealing with a holy work but to also incorporate such allegations in the Qur'an.*

One might add that the dirty minds of the bearded interpreters seem to have gone crazy.

But the Arabic Qur'an goes on and on in the same manner. Having learned now that the houris are beautiful, thirty-three years of age, and eternally chaste, in Sura 78:33, we find out another detail—they are busty: "[The pious ones are expected by] *houris with heaving breasts and a full cup of wine.*"

As a matter of fact, these heaving breasts are *luxuriant, juicy fruit,* as shown in detail by Luxenberg.

That means that the houris are completely derived from fantasyland. But they were apparently not satisfactory enough: there are also eternally young boy toys at the disposal of the pious ones in Paradise. Sura 76:19 promises that *"Boys with eternal youth* [wildanun muhalladuna] *go the rounds* [among the believers]."

Luxenberg shows that the term translated as "boys" actually means "juice" or "wine" in Aramaic. (Specifically, the term means "child of the wine grape"—referring to the product of the wine grape…juice or wine.)

Simply moving a single dot (a punctuation mark positioned below the letter instead of above it) changes *h* [the guttural *ch*] into *g*, so that the word *muhalladuna* regains its original Aramaic meaning, which is "ice cold" or "chilled." Thus, in contrast to eternally young boys, it is chilled fruit that *"goes the rounds."*

The mixing of Syro-Christian with Iranian ideas is very apparent in the Qur'an.

The symbolic fruit of the Syro-Christian Paradise par excellence was the grape, as has been shown a thousandfold. And this is what was called "Paradise" in the primary source materials of the Qur'an. In later versions, this initially rather modest Paradise gets blown out of proportion by typically Persian extravagance: the presence of big-eyed virgins becomes one of Paradise's trademarks; no Persian festive event would ever deserve to be called one without a garnish in the form of Hierodules—the boy toys—to perform musical art and other sorts of favors. The Persian term *fareedaiz* (Paradise) became the Arabic *faradoos*, and this Paradise is a sexist one that basically only serves male sexual fantasies.[8]

Disastrous mistranslations by Arabic authors have created a lecherous picture of Paradise that is in total contrast to the original and true message of the Qur'an. This warped vision has not only invited suggestive remarks by unbelievers, it has encouraged hundreds of thousands of hopeful jihadists to carry out bloody acts.

The next misreading—the "veil":

Everything that has to do with the "problematic head-veil matter," Luxenberg resolved by simply applying Aramaic terms. In the Qur'an, there is only a single passage that seems to refer to the head veil. Sura 24:31 reads in a traditional translation by Max Henning[9]:

> ... *let them draw their veils over their bosoms and not display their adornment except to their husbands, their fathers, their fathers-in-law...*

This passage Henning translates already into a rather freestyle version that commands women to *"draw their scarves over their bosoms."*

In the Arabic Qur'an, the literal translation of this passage is: *"they should draw their choomoor over their pockets."*

But what are these *choomoor*? And what is meant by *pockets* in this context? Working around the year AD 900—around three hundred years after the alleged time period of Islam's creation—the Persian at-Tabari[10] simply didn't understand the non-Arabic term *choomoor/chimar*. In his Qur'anic commentaries, without providing any explanation, he interpreted this term as "head veil," and then

---

8 Following this tradition, 9/11–leader Muhammad Atta included in the text about the preparation for his committing suicide detailed instructions to bandage his penis in order to symbolically protect it and to be ready for the virgins.

9 "Der Koran," *Reclam.,* 2006.

10 At-Tabari, *Tafsir al-Quran,* Vol. XVIII (Cairo,1968)

expanded upon this supposed command to require that a woman "cover hair, neck, and earrings." In the centuries since, the Islamic world has accepted the head-veil commandment as God's word.

Luxenberg, however, shows that this command was, in truth, merely at-Tabari's personal opinion. He argues convincingly that the dubious term *choomoor* (singular form of *chimar*) represents the misspelling of the Aramaic word *gmar,* meaning " belt" or "band." In addition, he points out that the word "draw" forms a known Aramaic idiom when used in combination with the terms "band" or "belt." Still used in Aramaic today, the phrase "to draw the band (belt)" refers to wearing a cloth belt around one's waist, but not over or around any "pockets."

The true meaning of this passage is therefore: *"They should strap their belts around their waistlines."* [11] In other words: women should close their dress with a band or belt when leaving the house.

Luxenberg opines, "Muslim women would have every right to reestablish the authenticity of the Qur'anic words and change the head veils, which have been forced upon them for centuries, back to cloth belts."

How can it be that Arabic authors have such tremendous problems in understanding texts that allegedly came in a "pure and crystal-clear Arabic to the people"? How can it be explained that nearly every single sura has to be interpreted in order to be comprehensible, and that many suras can easily be interpreted in a dozen different ways?

If one asks a professional linguist about the Arabic language, the linguist will most likely ask, "Which *kind* of Arabic?"

---

11 The mutation of the meaning of this term made its way into the Hadiths in a very remarkable way. Apparently, right after the revelation of this verse, the youngest wife of the Prophet, Aisha, and also other women, changed their cloth belts into head veils. Obviously, this Hadith displays the historical-etymological meaning-twister of the term *chimar* in quick motion, from cloth belt to head veil. For more, see Ibn Manzur, *Lisan al-Arab,* X, 355a. Beirut, 1955.

There have always been a number of Arabic dialects. In addition, there is the classic Arabic, the *Arabiya*. The Qur'an, however, was produced in even another kind of language: the Qur'an-Arabic, which can only be understood by the specialists. (The question of *how* comprehensible it is to them, considering the above-mentioned examples, is a question worth keeping in mind.) The uniting language of the era in which the Qur'an was composed was not Arabic, but Aramaic; its status was similar to that of Latin during the height of the Roman Empire. Because the Qur'an is influenced by Syro-Aramaic to such a significant extent, Luxenberg assumed the existence of a Primary Qur'an written in Aramaic. We can't know for sure whether this Aramaic Qur'an ever existed, but we know for a fact that the Qur'an is largely based on Aramaic texts.

People in ancient Arabia spoke Aramaic and/or the local dialects, but written texts were almost solely created in Aramaic. In addition, Greek was rather widespread among the well educated. The Arabic script evolved without doubt from the Aramaic script. During the sixth or seventh century, when Muhammad is believed to have lived, and during which the alleged transmission of the Qur'an took place, the traditional Qur'an-Arabic did not exist.

Semitic scripts only consisted of consonants. When pronouncing a word, vowels were placed according to common usage. If one were to apply this procedure to the modern English language, a single letter combination in writing might stand for a number of different words, depending on the context in which it was used. For example, the written word "lck" might stand for "lack," "lick," "luck," or "lock." If it stood for "lock," the word would still have multiple possibilities. It might mean the verb *lock* (as in, "We always lock our doors"), or the noun (as in "a lock of hair," or "I put a lock on my bicycle").

And that is with a three-letter combination. Now, what does *Lvndpc* mean? *Love and peace?* Or *Live in deep ice?*

But there is worse to come. The early Arabic alphabet consisted of just fifteen letters, only seven of which were clear symbols. Six of these fifteen letters had double meanings; one had three meanings; another had five. In early scripts, no difference can be made between f and q, j and kh, s and d, r and z, s and sh, d and dah, and t and z. The script only consisted of consonants and three half-vowels, the latter of which were not clearly defined at all; short vowels were pronounced according to context and common usage. This means that this type of consonant-only framework (*rasm*) was extremely ambiguous. Without previous knowledge, reading a text in order to understand it was practically impossible.

A little story may help to explain the point. Imagine that centuries ago, a Qur'anic scholar is walking the streets of Basra. Passing by a window, he hears someone reciting: "This is the book in which there is no olive oil…" This sounds somewhat familiar to the scholar, but also strange at the same time. He enters the house and discovers a young man who was just reciting Sura 2 of the Qur'an, which, however, correctly begins with "This is the book in which there is no doubt…"

The Arabic word for doubt is *rayba*; the term for olive oil is *zeita*. Without additional reading help in form of certain marks, these two words only consist of a set of consonants, which, in this case, are identical. Only the context could give these words their identity, their specific meaning.

Because this is a very unsatisfactory situation for the scholar, he tries to resolve this problem by making the script more precise—just as, in real life, Arabic philologists tried to make the rudimentary Arabic script more accurate. To do so, they used marks above and below the letters, which are the so-called diacritical dots. Later, marks indicating short vowels, letter doubling, lack of vowels, and sound stretching were introduced. These additional diacritical dots showed how the consonant framework was to be read: *lack, lick, lock, or luck; doubt or olive oil.*

There have also been reports about deaths after patients received the wrong medication due to misplaced dots on the prescription. Those additional diacritical dots, which made clear readability possible, did practically not exist in any of the early Qur'anic versions. The early Qur'anic texts only consisted of the *rasm* framework, which includes very ambiguous consonants and lacked any kind of vowels. Moreover, it was a common feature that Arabic and at times even Persian idioms and sayings were written in Aramaic scripts..

Consider, too, that in the olive oil story above, the correct interpretation is rather clear to the scholar—who, after all, knows Sura 2 by heart. Because of this, he is able to recognize the boy's error. This sort of clarification becomes far, far more difficult when dealing with texts with which one is unfamiliar, and even more so when these texts concerns abstract religious content that is not at all part of our everyday life or common heritage.

It is obvious that errors will have been produced by subsequently adding diacritical dots in order to clarify meanings in texts produced without any reading marks. Especially when some of the languages involved were largely incomprehensible to the copists centuries later. And here we also find the answer to the puzzling question of why the Arabic Qur'an workers produced these catastrophic errors: they were simply unable to comprehend the texts with which they were dealing. They fully understood neither the ancient languages involved, nor their mixed forms, and they were constantly confronted with texts that were extremely difficult to read due to basic script system. Because the written Arabic language only existed in a rudimentary form at this point, they had to define the rules for advanced reading. This was carried out in the ninth century by a group of editors that included such prominent and well-known members as at-Tabari. These people translated and interpreted texts, for which they also defined the grammatical rules.

Besides these systematic errors, there have been numerous erroneous versions and copies in the Qur'an's history. The spread of handwritten scripts itself resulted in differing versions, and in addition, writing errors occurred.

Let's take a closer look at Suras 50:12–14 and 26:176–177, which give a list of the individuals and groups who have been punished for disbelieving: in addition to Lut (the biblical Lot), the "People of the Thicket" (*Ashab al Aiykah*) and the "People of the Fountain" (*Ashab ar-Rass*) are also mentioned.

Al Aiykah means "thicket," and the expression "people of the thicket," as is it mentioned in the Qur'an, is confusing to Qur'anic scholars.

In the official Cairo version of the Qur'an, this term appears four times. In two of these four appearances, the term is accompanied by the grammatically correct article *al* (Suras 15:78 and 50:14), which results in *al Aiykah*. In the other two places (Suras 26:176 and 38:13), however, the article *al* is missing, which results in the term *Laiykah* instead.

Al Aiykah? Or *Laiykah?*

In the earliest available handwritten version (from Sana'a), the term *Laiykah* is found in the exact same place where the Cairo version speaks of *Al Aiykah*. Abu Ubaydah (ninth century) and Abu Hayyan al-Gharnati (fourteenth century) believed that *Laiykah* was the name of a place. Al-Gharnati considered the interpretation of this term in any other way as almost "falling away from the religion, which God will, hopefully, prevent from happening."

But precisely this blasphemous interpretation has been adopted for the current official version of the Qur'an. This puts Qur'anic scholars at jeopardy in two ways; they either have to admit that the "correct" version of the Cairo Qur'an is wrong or that the "incorrect" version is right. But neither of these options is possible because, according to official interpretation, the Qur'an has been passed on flawlessly from Muhammad to this day.

This above example again makes clear the great impact that the presence or absence of reading marks can have. Researcher Dr. Puin from Saarbrucken, Germany, has shown that *Laiykah* represents the interpretation that makes the most sense, because the texts simply refer to the well-known ancient Red Sea port named *Leuke Kome*. In a similar way the term *Ashab ar-Rass*, the "People of the Well" in the Qur'an, simply refers to the "Arsae people" who used to live north of Yanbu at the Red Sea coast, and had already been mentioned by the geographer Ptolemy under that name.

There is not even consistency when referring to the frequently mentioned Father Abraham. In the Qur'an, he is called *Abraham* fifteen times; another fifty-four times, he goes by *Ibrahim*. This points to the idea that parts of the Qur'anic text were derived from different sources.

In numerous handwritten fragments produced during early Islamic times (deposited in Leiden, Berlin, Paris, and Sana'a), corrections are found. Letters and even whole words had been erased and corrected, or had been replaced by new terms. The "palimpsests," well-known to hand script experts, are among them. The palimpsest is a parchment that, for reasons of economy, was washed clean from older scripts and reused again. By applying modern methods, the very first script can be made visible. In the Sana'a palimpsests, which were produced in the eighth century, it can be seen that great efforts had been made to place as many corrections as possible in the texts. When the number of corrections exceeded a certain limit, the pages were cleaned and reused. The first script differed greatly from the second one, mostly in orthographic changes, but also in significant modifications, including the use of different words or even the exclusion or addition of whole passages. It proves clearly the evolutionary origin of the Qur'an.

The occurrence of errors in handwritten copies is a well-known and perfectly natural feature—especially in Arabic texts where a misplaced, missing, or ambiguous dot can substantially modify the meaning.

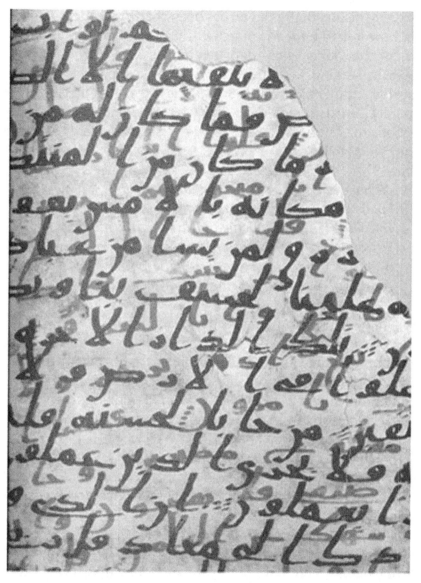

Foto Gerd Puin, from "Die Entstehung einer Weltreligion I", Berlin 2010

A page from Qur'an manuscript found in Sanaa, displayed in UV-mode. The two layers of the fonts can be seen clearly. The two versions of the manuscripts differ very much, they prove the editing work carried out on the Quran during the times

The entire history of the Qur'an has been characterized by arguments over how it is to be read correctly. And that is because the primary texts of the Qur'an were definitely not written in a clear Qur'an-Arabic. In reading the Qur'an by using Aramaic terms, Luxenberg provided another highlight. In Sura 97, he discovered that it consisted of purely Christian traditions. According to Luxenberg, this Sura tells the Christmas story. It consists of five verses, which are traditionally translated as follows:

> 1. We have sent him down in the night of destiny.
> 2. But how do you know that this is the night of destiny?
> 3. The night of destiny is better than a thousand months.
> 4. The angels and the spirit are coming down with permission by the Lord; they are all creatures of the logos.
> 5. It is (full of) blessings until the red dawn appears.

The summarizing commentaries by at-Tabari say:

> That night, the Qur'an was sent down to the lower heavens. Depending on purpose, God sent some of him down to earth until the Qur'an was completed. From beginning to end, the revelation took twenty years. The first part of the Qur'an was sent down that night.

Tabari was obviously of the opinion that by *"he/him,"* the Qur'an was meant. How did he get this idea, that which in no way could be concluded from this context??

Luxenberg made clear that the Aramaic term for "destiny" means "destiny by birth" but also "birth star" and "Christmas." Consequently, who or what was sent down on Christmas would have to be *Jesus*, not the *Qur'an*. At-Tabari must have noticed that somehow there was a star in play, because he let the Qur'an descend to the lower heavens, which are the spheres of the stars of the Qur'anic heaven.

Verse 3: Regarding the sura's third verse, *"The night of destiny is better than a thousand months."* Luxenberg suggests that the Aramaic term *leyla* (night) does not only represent the general meaning of "night," but also functions as a liturgical term in the sense of "nightly prayer," corresponding to the Latin term *nocturne*. In addition, the use of the word *months* is not based on the Arabic *shahr* (month) but, on the contrary, means the Aramaic liturgical expression *shara*, which denotes the term *vigilia* and, therefore, stands for the watch on the night before a significant religious event.

In Verse 4 of the same sura, "angels come down…they are all creatures of the logos." According to Luxenberg, the angels come down with "hymns" and are accompanied by the "spirit" - a reference to the well-known "choir of angels."

According to Luxenberg, this sura says,

1. We have let him (the baby-boy Jesus) come down in the night of destiny (night of the birth star, i.e., Christmas).
2. Do you know what is the night of destiny?
3. The night (the *nocturne)* of destiny is more merciful than a thousand *vigilias*.
4. In it, the angels, (accompanied by) the spirit, bring various hymns with them with permission of their Lord.
5. There is peace until the red dawn appears.

Luxenberg postulated that the talk was of "he/him" but not of "it," meaning "Jesus" instead of the "Qur'an," which results in a completely different context for this passage: the Christmas story. This idea had already been expressed by several researchers before Luxenberg, by the way. Moreover, Luxenberg set the record straight regarding the Qur'anic *tanazzalu* (angels), which is *tunazzilu* in its correct form— another case of misplaced dots. It's always the little things that cause the greatest problems.

Another "dark" passage is Sura 108. Luxenberg[12] is certain that it represents the misunderstood Aramaic version of the Epistle of St. Peter (Chapter 5, Verses 8–9), which undoubtedly is pre-Islamic in age. This text "belongs to the very fundamental principle which used to characterize the Qur'an

12   Christoph Luxenberg, *The Syro–Aramaic Reading of the Koran* (New York: Prometheus, 2007).

because, in its original form, the Qur'an was a Christian-liturgical book." According to Luxenberg, that applies to all of the information that has traditionally been assigned to the "first Meccan period."

Just like the information about Paradise or the head veil that later became a part of the dress code, the sending down of the Qur'an in the night of destiny makes clear that the traditional interpretation of the Qur'an is just wobbly all around. In many cases, the so-called interpretations simply reflect the personal opinions by members of the good-old-boys' club like at-Tabari and others—which, today, have made it to the status of God's word.

In addition, it is more than clear that knowledge of the Arabic language alone is absolutely insufficient in order to carry out Qur'anic research, because the basic language of large parts of the Qur'an is not Arabic but Aramaic. And it becomes increasingly apparent that the Qur'anic roots are Christian.

Moses is mentioned 136 times in the Qur'an; Mary is referred to 34 times; Jesus is brought up 24 times, but Muhammad is mentioned just 4 times (leaving open what *muhammad* simply means). In 1999, an Arabic coin from the year AD 766 was discovered in an archaeological site in Sweden together with Viking relics. That means the coin was minted one hundred thirty years after Muhammad's time—and was inscribed with *Musa rasul Allah* ("Moses is the messenger of God"). Because the names of Moses, Jesus, and Mary combined are mentioned an astounding 194 times in the theological part of the Qur'an, researchers have concluded that the theological part of the Qur'an is largely influenced by the Christian body of thought.

In its original version, there is no claim that the Qur'an represented an independent script in the form of a holy book of a new religion. In several suras, it is clearly expressed that the Qur'an was only *a part of a script* but that it never represented *the book* itself. For example, Sura 75:17 says, "*It is our responsibility to compile the lectionary by extracting it from the book and teach it.*" Sura 41:3 refers to "*a book which we transferred into an Arabic form."* Sura 5:68 commands, *"You people of the book, you have no ground to stand unless you observe the Torah and the Gospel and what was sent down to you by your Lord."* Suras 3:4, 15:1, 9:111, and others express similar ideas.

The original agenda of the Qur'an was to acknowledge and confirm the books of Torah and Gospel.

As already mentioned, Sura 2 begins with the words, *"This is the book in which there is no doubt."* Everybody who is able to read this Sura in its precise form knows that it does not say *this* but that it says *that.* There is, however, a difference between *this* and *that,* in the way that the term *that* denotes a distance. Here, once again, the clear reference is not to the Qur'an itself, but to another book.

The term Qur'an was derived from the Aramaic *Qeryan,* which means "lectionary." It represents a liturgical book that contains selected texts from the *script,* which includes mainly the Old and the New Testaments. It can be assumed that it derived from the Diatessaron, a liturgical book used by the Syrian Christians, in which they combined and summarized the four gospels into one shorter version. Frequently, there is the talk of "the gospel" in the Qur'an, despite the fact that there existed several gospels. Like the Diatessaron, the Qur'an represents a summary. That becomes evident in several places, as, for example, the line which deals with the warning of Lot's fate. This information merely represents a cross-reference of a certain event; there is no further explanation of the context. This means that the reader was expected to be familiar with the story from another source.

The Qur'anic structuring terms were directly taken from the Christian-Syrian Qeryan: Sura (Sura) and aya (Verse) are Aramaic. Additionally, there are also the typical symbols of Syrian liturgical books ❖ found in the Qur'an ❖ which are little crosses formed by four dots in order to separate the Verses. In its beginnings, the Qur'an cannot be understood as the Holy Book of Islam, as it has been customary, but rather as a term for a liturgical book of the Syro-Christian Arabs.

Over time, local traditions were added to the Christian standard model, which, for example, include the detailed legal evaluations in the so-called Medinan Suras. The message, which in its original form was theological in nature, was unrecognizably modified by later Arabic authors. They collected every written script and all information that had been passed down orally, but left a chaos of interpretations. This is a clear indication that the available texts had been produced in a language which was largely incomprehensible to them. Those exegetes were also grammarians. They basically created the Qur'an-Arabic and its script in their schools in Kufa and Basra.

What we find in the early Qur'anic scripts are both the texts of the Arabic Christians and their theology. But what we see in later Arabic works is the book of a different religion. Now the Qeryan had become the Qur'an—the Qur'an, in its own script and with its own contents was born. But it was derived from interpretations which could often not be extracted from the texts.

The production of more exegeses didn't come to an end—the authors had left too much room for different interpretations and at the same time created the need for additional adaptations. During the formation of Islam, a number of branches existed simultaneously that presented their own views on how to interpret the holy words. Numerous changes were made for theological reasons:

Traditionally, Sura 3:16 is read as "*God himself has testified ('shahida') that there is no God but He and so do [testify] the angels and those of knowledge…*" Because it doesn't give a good impression for God to testify on his own behalf or for him to put himself on a level with angels, the verb *shahida* was transformed into the plural noun *shuhada*, and *testify* became the *testifying ones,* the witnesses. Thus, the preceding Verse was transformed into:"the steadfast and sincere, truthful ones… are the witnesses of God and the angels are witnesses of this…"

In Sura 9 Verse 27, Mary vowed to fast for Allah (*sauman*); in another version she took a vow of silence (*samtan*); and yet in another version the vow had become to fast and to be silent (*sauman wasamtan*).

In one version of Sura 30, the defeat of the Romans (here the talk is of the Byzantine people) is described (*"ghulibat"*); in another version of the same sura, the Romans are declared victorious (*"ghalabat"*), giving the complete opposite statement.

The appearance of the Islamic rationalism movement, called *mutazila*, resulted in interpretations of a different dimension. During the regencies of the *Abbasid* caliphs in the ninth and tenth centuries, this movement became a very influential branch, and in the Persian east, *Choresmia*, it remained in practice until the Mongol invasion around AD 1220.

Following the general way of classic philosophy, the Mutazilites based their thinking mainly on rational reasoning. This concept they also applied to the Qur'anic exegesis, according to which the Qur'an had not been created for eternity but only for a certain situation. This interpretation by the Mutazilites didn't have much in common with orthodox teachings. During the time period of the Mutazilite Caliph al-Mamun (AD 786–833), the world was already viewed according to the Antiques-Arabica knowledge as being spherical in nature. In the orthodox teachings of the Qur'an the world had become flat again, and has officially remained so up to this day. The Mutazilites were ruthlessly fought by the orthodox groups and were eventually defeated by the Hanbalites. The Hanbali School represents the leading Sunni branch that more or less corresponds to what is called Islam today.[13]

By applying a combination of Neo-Platonism ideas and the search for their ideals in some kind of contemplation, the Sufism branch distanced itself even further from literal interpretations of the Qur'an. To them, the literal message of the Qur'an is meaningless; discovering the hidden idea behind the words is all that counts. This divine meaning is beyond the banality of a verse or a sentence. Therefore, the Sufi interpretation of the Qur'an works with symbols and allegories, which clearly show its Hellenic derivation.

---

13   The Egyptian theologian Ahmad Amin (1878–1954) wrote that the defeat of the Mutazila was the greatest disaster to the Muslims. In fighting the Mutazila, they committed a crime against themselves.

And certainly, the Shi'a has also tried to incorporate their views in the Holy Book: Sura 3 Verse 106's "*You are the best community (chejru ummatin)*" becomes "You are the best imams (*chejru a immatin*)." This manipulation was in accordance with the Shi'a idea of powerful imams (miracle powers have been attributed to imams up to this day; its main branch is called also *Imamism*) The Shi'a, believing that verses were missing in the Sunni Qur'an, included numerous additions which supported the positions of Ali and the imams.

As one can see, within a short period of time, different concepts of Qur'an interpretations developed and existed simultaneously. Because there was no official version, soon there would be hundreds of competing Qur'an editions. And they still exist to this day. But which of these versions is the real Holy Book now? Which is the one to be followed word by word?

In 1924, the al-Azhar University in Cairo published a version of the Qur'an which was supposed to be identical with the *Uthman Qur'an*. The *Uthman Qur'an* was named after the Third Caliph Uthman (regency AD 644–656), who, according to traditional belief, produced the first rightful Qur'anic version and had all the other ones burnt. According to Islamic dogma, the version of the *Uthman Qur'an* already possessed the correct grammar, including all the vowel signs and diacritical punctuation marks.

The problem, however, was that no Qur'an produced by Uthman had ever been shown to exist. Thus, for centuries, due to the Arab world's political domination by the Ottoman Empire, the Ottoman version was considered to be the correct one. Because this version significantly differed from the traditional interpretation, protests against it arose in Egypt, reportedly thousands of Turkish Qur'an copies were thrown into the river Nile, and the al-Azhar Qur'an school began creating its own version once the Ottomans were ousted from Egypt.

As a basic source, orthography books produced by the Spaniard al-Dhani (AD ?–1052) and al-Sigistani (AD?-928)were used to define how a *rasm* was supposed to be read. The Cairo scholars never examined the source of any of the texts; they simply postulated orthographic rules based upon their grammar. This resulted in interpretations which were closer to the traditionally accepted readings than the ones in the standard Turkish version, but they were not anywhere close to the seventh-century *Uthman Qur'an*. In addition, the linguistic hurdles of the ninth-century language definition had not been cleared either.

In other words, scholars cross-checked grammar and semantics using the rules that were defined by the producers of the language themselves. Then, after the Cairo scholars carried out some modifications, they announced that, by contents and language, this was now the version that was identical to the Uthman's original. This is circular reasoning at its best.

The *Uthman Qur'an* remains purely a fiction. By no means could they claim authenticity regarding the Prophet story for the *Cairo Qur'an*. From Damascus to Samarkand, various *Uthman Qur'ans* are on display as venerable relics. These versions show script types which clearly expose them as works from other time periods. They are, by the way, unavailable for examination by independent experts.

In 1924, this Cairo version of the Qur'an was declared to be the only adaptation from which further editions were allowed to be made for the Sunni Muslims.

Nobody has discovered an authentic *Uthman Qur'an*, but there are a number of early Qur'anic texts, and none of them bears hardly any reading rules, and none of them is written in the Qur'an-Arabic that is comprehensible to today's Muslims, and all of these ancient texts differ from each other. In the 1970s, for instance, Qur'anic fragments from the early eighth century were found in Sana'a, so far the oldest Qur'an scripts available. These show sura sequences that differ from the one in the official Cairo version. Even in texts from the tenth century, numerous Qur'an versions appear, all of which have sura sequences that differ from the official version.[14]

---

14 Bayard Dodge, *The Fihrist of al-Nadim* (New York: Kazi Publications, 1979)

There is no doubt that the Cairo version of the Qur'an could not be derived from any seventh- century version but that it is based on later works. There is no historical information on any *Uthman Qur'an* or on any *Caliph Uthman*. There are no historic traces of any of the first four caliphs.

Among the Islamic public and in Islamic literature, all of the discrepancies in Qur'anic passages as well as differences between individual Qur'anic versions are just completely ignored. "We know that the Qur'an we have today is exactly the one that was gradually transmitted to the Prophet fourteen hundred years ago. Therefore, neither the credibility nor the authenticity of the Qur'an need to be confirmed by historic evidence," is one of the statements issued by the Cultural Department of Iran.[15]

And that is just circular reasoning again, because it means, in other words: carrying out research on the Qur'an is unnecessary since we have already determined the results anyway.

Islamic scientists avoid carrying out research on the sources every time they fear to cross the timeline of the infamous *Uthman Qur'an*, because here the only purpose of research is to confirm their dogmas.

Recently, the Turkish scholar Tayyar Altikulac compared a modern Qur'an edition, which was regarded as the correct Qur'an version, with a handwritten script housed in the Topkapi Palace which had also been assigned to Caliph Uthman.

The investigation was carried out in a formal scientific manner. During the examination, a large number of discrepancies were revealed that showed that it was impossible for these two texts to be identical, proving that the handwritten script could not be considered Uthman's original, and that, at the same time, the modern text was no copy of the original. Despite all this, Altikulac stated that these texts were "similar" to each other and that, after all, the verses were only

---

15 Tabataba'i, Sayyid, Cultural Department of the Islamic Republic of Iran, Bonn, 1986.

passed on by a "capable tongue" (*fam muhsin*) who always knew how to correctly read them anyway.

It has always been a popular move to claim that content differences in written texts were unimportant because only the pronunciation was what really counted. The pronunciation, however, is something that cannot be identified so easily anymore. Yet there is no doubt about the fact that the Arabic oral traditions came with their written counterparts. The Turkish scientist must have felt somewhat uncomfortable after all, because he suggested that scholars "adjust the versions to each other" and then "prohibit any further investigations on them to be carried out."

That's some kind of scientific attitude.

But this lack of scientific vigor is not restricted to Islamic countries. Dr. Angelika Neuwirth, leader of the research project *Corpus Coranicum*[16] of the Berlin-Brandenburg Academy of Sciences and Humanities, Germany, stated that she and her team respected the "divine founding mythos of the Qur'an." Imagine if Darwin had done his research on evolution "respecting" the six-day creation story of the Bible

There has been Bible criticism for centuries. Awareness of the problems that arise when a book is distributed by handwritten scripts over a long time period has led to efforts to reveal the original nature of the religious faith. In order to carry this out, people have tried to find texts that were as close to the events as possible. For centuries, researchers, scholars, the ones inspired by religious faith, and adventurers, have combed through the Orient in the search for the original holy texts. During a research journey in 1844 paid for by the Russian czar, the Saxon aristocrat Konstantin von Tischendorf found a fourth-century handwritten Bible script in the Sinai monastery of St. Catherine.[17] Highly educated monks compared the various texts

---

16 See: http://en.wikipedia.org/wiki/Corpus_Coranicum.
17 He also found a writ of protection issued by the Prophet Muhammad for the monastery that was signed by the Prophet's handprint. This document turned out to be a forgery, but it nevertheless helped the monastery survive in its hostile environment.

and tried to identify their meanings. Nicolaus Cusanus (1401–1464), a cardinal of the Roman Catholic Church, suggested that the Qur'an be examined for material that derived from the gospels. Martin Luther didn't think much of this idea, because he thought the texts had been inseparably mixed already. From information like this, it becomes clear that the scientific corpus of the Church has always regarded the basis of the Qur'an as a Christian one; it also shows that it has been viewed as an essential aspect for Bible research to obtain and study texts that were as topical as possible.

This should go without saying in the research of every religion, but Qur'anic interpretation today remains based on the Cairo version, regardless of historical facts. As I've already described in detail, the Cairo version was created through the sorting and summarizing of ninth-century materials. Research that is based on an examination of the earliest sources available is a fundamental scientific process, but it does not exist in the Islamic world up to this day. A critical review using scientific methods, as should be expected even when dealing with historic questions of a religion, does not take place. Islam is the only "book religion" that treats itself to ignoring newly discovered texts and the latest research results. Every time they feel the heat, their strategy becomes to offer absurd explanations or declare any further discussion as unnecessary. This strategy has resulted in the situation where the experts on Islamic history are not among the Muslims but rather among the unbelievers.

In contradiction to the nice little legend, the Qur'an did not fall from the sky suddenly one day. Just like every holy book, the Qur'an has had a long journey, and has gone through many modifications. Early Syro-Aramaic texts, transitions from Aramaic to Arabic, the existence of the *Qeryan* of the Arabic Christians, Persian influences, local traditions, and various types of Arabic interpretations…all of these define the Qur'an. At this point, we already know that about 25 percent of the Qur'anic text represents complete mistranslations. Qur'anic research has only just begun, so the discovery of such a significant number of mistranslations in such a short amount of time justifies the suspicion that further inquiry should reveal that much more of the Qur'an consists of misinterpretations. After all, there are still numerous handwritten scripts that have not been examined yet, and the discovery of new findings can be expected.

The first printed version of the Qur'an was produced in 1802 in Kazan, Russia. This means that for over three-fourths of its history, the Qur'an was distributed and reproduced by handwritten scripts—with all of the predictable errors of transmission. No two handwritten texts of any kind of that length are ever identical to each other. This fact has nothing to do with the nature of the Qur'an; it is a fate shared by all those texts that have been transmitted over such a long time period.

The real issue is the claim that a text has remained identical and without any error—from Muhammad all the way to Cairo, 1924. The fact that this is *not* the case has been shown many times. But it remains the Islamic credo—and that is the central point of the critics if we talk of historical credibility.

Modifications, errors, falsifications, and misconceptions have been clearly identified. According to the Islamic teaching, every change or modification of the original Qur'anic text is a blasphemy. Following this doctrine, the official version of today's Qur'an is nothing but blasphemy.

❖ ❖ ❖

From the People, for the People:

Hadiths: Sayings and Actions of the Prophet

Nobody who carries out Islam studies in a respectable manner would ever get the idea to consider as sources sayings assumed to be from Muhammad and his followers, and use those to piece together history and the original teachings of Islam.

—Ignaz Goldziher

at the First International Congress on the History of Religions, Paris, 1900

In combination with the Qur'an, the Hadiths (plural of Hadith) form the most important religious scripts in Islam. Hadiths are sayings and actions of the Prophet: they contain statements of the Prophet he made regarding a large variety of issues, and the verdicts he announced. They give information about who was his most favorite wife, about his food preferences, and about all these many, many people he met, visited, talked to, dealt with, etc., etc. There was no event in Muhammad's life that was too little or unimportant to be put down in detail. In general, his sayings were put down as literal statements. Muhammad's tremendously colorful biography (*Sira*) is extensively captured in the Hadiths.

There are well over one million Hadiths. A set of six Hadith collections are canonized, meaning that they were officially accepted as authentic by the Sunni clergy (but not by the Shi'a clergy which presented their own collections of five sets). The authors of these six authoritative collections were al-Bukhari (AD ?–70), Muslim (AD ?–875), Ibn Maja (AD ?–886), Abu Dawud (AD ?–888), al-Tirmidhi (AD ?–892), and Nasa'i (AD ?–915). Occasionally, the earliest collection of biographic data by Ibn Ishaq (AD ?–ca. 770) is cited, which, however, has never been verified; whereas for unknown reasons, the collection by Ibn Hisham (AD ?–834) has not been canonized.

As mentioned above, the Prophet died in AD 632. That means that most of the Hadiths were put down in writing between one hundred fifty and two hundred fifty years after his death; some were even put down much later than that. Until then, they had been passed on orally, mainly by *quassas*, who are professional storytellers. And that's how the stories about the sayings and actions of the Prophet made it from bazaar to bazaar, from oasis to oasis, from one generation to the next, until they ended up on the desk of a writer.

Let's take a look at some of the Hadiths. All of the following ones were taken from the official collection of al-Bukhari. (The arrangement here is the one used by Reclam Publishing.) As a rule, only the first person providing a Hadith's information is mentioned. This makes the information seem to be much closer to the original source than it really was. It does not reflect the true history of how each saying was passed on, as what appears in the Hadiths to be second-hand information had to have passed through an additional five or six generations before it was written down. And that would make it a long chain of transmission, which one has to picture like this:

> That's how A told it and remarked that B mentioned that C had told him that D had remarked earlier that he had heard from E that F said that G had asked Aisha (one of Muhammad's wives): "What did God's Prophet like to eat?" And Aisha answered: "Verily, I can tell you that he liked candied fruit and honey, and he was especially fond of pumpkins."

Here are some sample Hadiths according to al-Bukhari:

(Numbering according to the "Reclam" Bukhari-Hadith collection, Stuttgart 1997)

II, 11
Narrated Ibn Abbas:
The Prophet said: "I was shown hell. And the majority of its inhabitants were women." Someone asked him: "Didn't they believe in God?" "They had been ungrateful to their life companions, not honoring the generous deeds they had been granted. When you treat such a woman nothing but nicely, but she discovers just a single flaw in you, she will tell you: I have not seen anything good in you."

II, 17
Narrated Abu Huraira, who said the messenger of God had told him:
Everyone who is sincere about his confession to Islam will be rewarded ten-fold to seven-hundred-fold for every good deed, whereas a bad deed will only be counted once.

III, 19
Narrated Abu Huraira:
I said: "Oh messenger of God, I hear so many Hadiths from you but often I forget them later." The Prophet answered: "Spread your coat." I did as I was told. Then, the Prophet moved his hands as if he was drawing something into my coat. Then he said: "Now put your coat back on." I did as he told me and have not forgotten anything ever since.

IV, 2
Narrated Hammam ibn Munabbih:
Abu Huraira said: "The messenger of God said: 'The prayer by an unclean person is not accepted until he exercises The Little Washing.'"
A man from Hadramaut asked him: "Oh Abu Huraira, what makes a man unclean?"
"When you are gassy, for example."

IV, 5
Narrated Anas:
When the Prophet sought a secluded place to relieve himself, he said: "Oh God, I seek shelter with you from the evil and unclean powers."

IV, 6
Narrated Abu Ayyub al-Ansari, who said the messenger of God had told him:
"When relieving yourselves, your faces or backs must not face the Ka'ba, but rather turn west or east."

IV, 24
Narrated Abu Huraira:
The messenger of God said: "Don't dare to urinate in stagnant water. You might need this water to wash yourselves later."

V, 3
Narrated Qatada:
Ana ibn Malik said: "During one night and one day, the Prophet dealt with all of his wives. And he had eleven." I asked: "Did he really have that much strength?" "Yes, he had the strength of thirty men."

V, 10
Narrated Ubay ibn Ka'b:
I asked the Prophet: "Oh, messenger of God, how is a man supposed to wash himself after he had intercourse with his wife but didn't have any ejaculation?" He replied: "He should wash all his body parts with which he touched his wife. After that he should carry out the Small Washing. Then he can do the prayer."

VI, 7
Narrated Asmaa Bint Abu Bakr:
A woman said to the messenger of God: "Oh messenger of God, what are we supposed to do if the dress has been stained by

menstruation blood?" He replied: "Remove the stains and wash the dress. You can then wear it again for the prayer."

VII, 1
Narrated Anas:
The Prophet said that he had met in the heavens with Enoch, Moses, Jesus, and Abraham, God's blessings may be with them, but he didn't provide any further details about their places of residence. He, however, mentioned that he saw Adam in the first heaven and Abraham in sixth heaven.

When Gabriel and the Prophet passed by Enoch, he said: "Welcome, oh sincere Prophet and pious fellow believer." "Then I met Moses. He said: 'Welcome, oh sincere Prophet and pious fellow believer.' After that, I saw Jesus. He also said: 'Welcome, oh sincere Prophet and pious fellow believer.' Eventually I met Abraham. He said: 'Welcome, oh sincere Prophet and pious fellow believer.'"

VIII, 38
Narrated Busr ibn Sa'id:
Zaid ibn Halid sent me to Abu Guhaim. I was supposed to ask him about what the messenger of God had said regarding passing by a praying person. Abu Guhaim said that the messenger of God had told him: "If a man, who is about to do such offense, knew about the punishment that was in for him, he would stop and wait for forty..." Abu Nadr added: "I don't know whether the Prophet was talking about forty days, months, or years."

IX, 11
Narrated Abu Huraira, the messenger of God said:
"The angels take turns day and night. During the morning and afternoon prayers they meet with you. And the angels which spent the night rise to heaven after the morning prayer. Though God knows best, He then asks them: 'What were my servants doing when you left them?' They answer: 'They were praying when we left. And when we returned in the afternoon, they were praying, too.'"

X, 14
Narrated Abdullah ibn Umar, the messenger of God said:
"The communal prayer is worth seven hundred and twenty times more than a prayer done alone."

XI, 4
Narrated Salman al-Farsi, the Prophet said:
"Everyone who takes a thorough bath on Friday, oils and perfumes his hair, then goes to the prayer and doesn't force himself between the praying people who have already taken their places, then carries out the prayer correctly, and carefully listens to the sermon, will be forgiven all of the offenses he did between this day and the previous Friday."

XV, 1
Narrated Abu Dharr:
The Prophet said: "My Lord gave me the good news that all members of my community who solely serve God and do not accept the idea of shared divinity, will be admitted to Paradise after their death." I asked him: "Does that also apply to people who committed adultery or stole?"—"Yes."

XV, 13
Narrated Abu Huraira:
The messenger of God said: "Every newborn has the natural tendency towards the rightful belief. It is their parents who raise them to be Jews, Christians, or magicians."

XVII, 5
Narrated Sa'id ibn Jubayr:
Ibn Umar used to treat his hair with oil. When I mentioned this to Ibrahim, he said: "What do you think about the Hadith that Al Aswad told me that Aisha said that: 'It still feels as if I could sense the smell of the perfume in the parting of God's messenger when he was taking holy orders.'"

XX, 15
Narrated Naf, the Maula of Ibn Umar:
When date trees are sold that have already been pollinated and no further agreements were made, the harvest belongs to the one who carried out the pollination.

XXIV, 3
Narrated Ibn Umar:
The Prophet prohibited eating two dates at once at a communal meal without asking the others for permission first.

XXVI, 7
Narrated Abu Sa'id al-Khudri:
The Prophet said to the women: "Is it not true that the testimony of a woman is only worth half of that of a man?" They replied: "Yes, Oh messenger of God."—"The reason for that is your intellectual deficiencies."

XXVIII, 18
Narrated Abdullah ibn Umar, God's messenger told him:
"I will fight the Jews until one of them tries to hide behind a stone. And this stone will yell, 'Come on here, this Jew is trying to hide behind me. Kill him.'"

XXIX, 5
Narrated Abdullah:
We were on a war campaign and had no women with us. Therefore, we said to the Prophet: "Wouldn't it be better for us to get castrated." He wouldn't allow us to do that but gave us permission to marry a woman for a limited time period."

XXIX, 7
Narrated Jabir bin 'Abdullah:
When we were getting close to our destination, the Prophet said: "Take your time and ride slowly so that you reach Medina not before sunset. The women should be given time to comb their hair and shave their genital hairs."

XXXIV, 15
Narrated Abu Huraira:
The Prophet said: "The evil eye is reality." And he banned getting tattoos.

XXXI, 14
Narrated Abdul Aziz:
Someone asked Anas: "Did the Prophet say anything about garlic?" "Yes, he said: 'A person who has eaten garlic shouldn't dare to get anywhere near our mosque.'"

Hundreds of thousands of Hadiths were written down at least two hundred years after the alleged events. It is only common sense to be skeptical regarding the authenticity of such large number of sayings that had only been passed on orally for centuries.

During the ninth century, a real Hadith-producing industry evolved. Hadiths were made to order and for money. People in power had Hadiths produced that would legitimize their positions. A certain al-Auja admitted to have made up four thousand hadiths.[18] Despite the fact that he was executed for this, the problem of forged Hadiths remained.

Abu Dawud, author of one of the official collections, stated that he kept "only forty-eight hundred" of half a million Hadiths because only those seemed authentic enough or somewhat authentic to him. Al-Bukhari, the most famous hadith editor, accepted "only seventy-four hundred" of six hundred thousand Hadiths as authentic. According to conservative estimates, there are around 1.5 million Hadiths. Even if only considering for reevaluation the Hadiths produced by the officially accepted six authors, it would mean that the authenticity of hundreds of thousands of Hadiths would have to be reconfirmed, keeping in mind that the earliest-written Hadiths date to one hundred fifty years after the time of Muhammad.

---

18 Mc Donald, *Development of Muslim Theology, Jurisprudence, and Constitutional Theory* (New York: Scribner, 1903).

A Hadith is traditionally considered "authentic" when it meets certain criteria:

The narrator
—has to be trustworthy and must have an impeccable reputation;
—must be flawless regarding religious belief and religious behavior;
—must be reliable with respect to having correctly understood the information;
—must have transmitted more than one Hadith.

The transmission must
—clearly show that the reported material was by Muhammad personally;
—have been passed on by an unbroken chain of trusted narrators;
—fit in Muhammad's time regarding its contents.

In addition, there are different categories into which Hadiths can be grouped regarding their level of truthfulness or potential level of usage. The quality of a Hadith can significantly differ in that it can have dogma-level status or be of "only" judiciary use, etc.

Hadiths are almost as important as Qur'anic Verses to Muslims, because they are God's word transmitted by the Prophet. Because their transmission was by common parlance, they are easy to understand by everybody and lack the reverential distance that one feels with the Qur'an. The editor of the introductory chapter of Reclam Publishing's Bukhari-Hadith collection writes, *"Non-Muslim readers will learn about many unfamiliar features that might appear strange and odd to them. They are about to approach the private spheres of an unknown culture."*

No contest on that. The reader of the Hadiths approaches private spheres—but not facts.

To a great extent, Hadiths contain day-to-day trivialities of life. They are, however, of great importance to the believer because the right course of action for any kind of situation can be derived from them. In every Islamic country, people can turn to numerous newspapers, radio programs, and TV shows that provide the appropriate Hadiths for their everyday problems.

But what they get are outdated answers to present-day questions—the basic problem of the Islamic way of thinking.

Only about five hundred passages in the Qur'an have legal relevance. In addition, there are a vast number of Qur'anic verses that often contradict each other, and, therefore, cause great problems during their attempted legal application. Because the Qur'an itself forms an incomplete legal system, for judicial purposes the actions, deeds, and sayings by the Prophet, his followers, and even by their descendants are included. Therefore, Hadiths form the most important basis of *shari'a* law, which is the judiciary system of Islam.

Many heads have rolled and numerous hands have been chopped off—all because of Hadiths.

The punishment for apostasy (defection from Islam) is the death penalty. And that is based on a single Hadith: "*Kill the one who changes to another religion.*" The Qur'an itself does not contain such a passage; but a single "statement," a Hadith, that appeared from who knows where, can decide a person's life or death.

There are different ideas about who could qualify as a transmitter of Hadiths. Basically, that would only apply to the Prophet himself; however, the Hadiths of his followers and even the Hadiths by their descendants and the companions of the followers have been accepted by most. The Shi'a only acknowledge the Fourteen Infallible Ones as Hadith transmitters. These are the Prophet, his daughter Fatima, and, additionally, twelve imams (the Twelve Imami Shi'a). One of the twelve imams lives according to tradition in hiding, and the Ayatollah Khomeini has already been given a quasi-infallibility status.

Besides the Shi'a, there are the Shafi'i, Hanbali, Maliki, and Hanafi branches of what is formally referred to as the Islamic School of Law. These various branches do not differ much in their legal approaches, but actually only hold opposing views regarding whose Hadiths are to be accepted as authoritative.

Shari'a Law is not about finding legal grounds by applying general legal principles but has to do with comparing Qur'anic verses with sayings and actions of persons who are regarded as models. And these are the conveyers of authorized Hadiths.

Qur'anic scholars are well aware of the problems regarding the Hadiths. There have always been projects dealing with adjusting or correcting them. In the name of the "Islamic science," *ilm al-rijal,* studies that focus on the narrators of the Hadiths have been carried out, with the goal to reevaluate "their life circumstances and scientific qualifications." In practical terms, it means that they are trying to find and exclude inauthentic hadiths and keep the correct ones. But what are the scientific criteria? One also has to raise the question again: what is "science" actually supposed to mean in the Islamic context? Clearly, it is being used in a way that does not correspond to the generally accepted definition.

The chain of the transmission of hadiths is called *isnad.* Looking at the history of Hadiths, it can be observed that efforts were made to always put a prominent name at the beginning of the chain in order to obtain credibility. The validity of a Hadith depends only on the *isnad.* Therefore, it is always the isnad that is subject to examination and never the Hadith itself.

Let's see...in order to get the Hadiths problem straightened out, we are talking about the necessity to reevaluate the following: the verification that chains of large sets of orally transmitted information were passed on flawlessly and truthfully, over five or six generations, by people who lived around fourteen hundred years ago; moreover, the biographies and impeccable characters of these people would have to be confirmed. Were we able to accomplish such a feat, one might call it a miracle, but the term *science* doesn't come to mind.

In terms of historical accuracy, the Hadiths are the equivalent of an extensive biography of George Washington, complete with word-by-word transcriptions of his speeches, that was put together based on oral stories passed along over several generations. Such a chain would sound something like this: "My great-grand-uncle told me that his father had said that a grandfather of a friend, whose grandfather used to know someone whose uncle served under George Washington, had said that he found out that…" What would be the level of reliability of such a text?

But this is what Hadiths are. This kind of information chain simply cannot be scientifically verified. After all, nothing could be said about the truthfulness of the messages. Everything that a naïve believer felt was a true saying by the Prophet became finally a Hadith.

The troubles caused by the unreliability of the Hadiths do not just bring into question individual passages, but the whole understanding of the Prophet's life and actions (*sira*). This is because Muhammad's life story is nothing else but the lining up of Hadiths in a biographical fashion.

This clearly shows the fundamental problem that Islam has with sources: word-of-mouth-stories are regarded as facts. The concept of source research does not exist.

Wikipedia, in the year 2011, does not mind saying: "*However, the Sira literature is technically different from Hadith literature as it is in general not as concerned with validation through the chain of transmitters.*"

Is the chain of transmitters supposed to be regarded as a seal of quality? If one considers the chain of transmitters as being capable of having "verified" the source of a Hadith, then, what, one wonders, is the definition of a "non-verified" source? A fairy tale comes into the room and leaves as a fact?

And: "...*According to the current state of research, except for a few passages, the Sira is basically an authentic historical source.*" But just the opposite is the case. Which scientist would seriously consider the *Sira*, meaning the Hadiths and their derivatives, as "authentic historical sources"?

Neither chains of oral transmissions that stretched over centuries nor results and references that were passed on by word of mouth could possibly provide enough information to draw even a rough outline about the living conditions of the people back then, or their way of thinking. "If one has no information from the seventh century other than the reports about it that were produced in the ninth century or later, he still won't know anything about the seventh century itself. He will only find out what people in the ninth century had to say about the seventh century."[19]

Due to the complete obscurity of their sources, one can safely say that Hadiths are not more than a collection of unverified stories. In no way do they meet the criteria for sources that could be considered historically reliable—with one exception: the Hadiths perfectly display the history of the development of Islam. Information regarding the changing ideas of the nature of the religion during its development, fights for position, internal dynastic battles, and the shaping of theological points of views all became part of the hadiths. Accordingly, regional characteristics in combination with different schools of thought—Damascus, Basra, Kufa, and Medina, Persian versus Arabic—significantly influenced the nature of the Hadiths because for each occasion and circumstance an appropriate Hadith was needed in order to justify and strengthen one's own position and, at the same time, weaken the position of one's opponents.

As is also seen in the Qur'an, the influence of local religions comes to the fore in the Hadiths, sometimes resulting in the appearance of a completely non-Islamic Prophet—as in the case where Jesus's famous Beatitude in Matthew 5:3 ("Blessed are the poor in spirit, for theirs is

---

19 Yehuda D. Nevo and Judith Koren, *Crossroads to Islam* (New York: Prometheus Books, 2003),

the kingdom of heaven,") becomes the Prophet saying that the vast majority of the inhabitants of Paradise will be the simple-minded ones...the ones who are poor in spirit. (The high-maintenance women, as we have noted, will form the majority of hell's inhabitants.) In another example, the canonical collection of Abu Dawud includes the narrator Abu-l-Darda's testimony that he has heard Muhammad saying a prayer starting with the familiar words,

> "Our Father who art in heaven, Hallowed be thy name. Thy will be done on earth as it is in heaven. Give us this day our daily bread; And forgive us our debts, as we also have forgiven our debtors..."

Hadiths have had a major impact on legal judgments. While in earlier teachings, such as the ones by Abu Hanifa and Malik bin Anas, the hadiths were not used—meaning no attention was paid to the "Prophet Muhammad", in later teachings, Hadiths became an essential part of the judiciary system. That meant a shift from legal principles to a justice system that was based on comparisons like "What did the Prophet say about this?" or "How did the Prophet handle this situation?" When no satisfactory answer could be found, the search was extended by looking into the lives of the Prophet's associates (not less than thirteen hundred of them) or his descendants (some ten thousand) for useful information. When still no answer could be retrieved, the course of action was to try to figure out, "What *would* the Prophet say?"

At this point, it became painfully clear that, without a matching Hadith at hand, one had reached the end of the "judiciary" road. The necessity for Hadiths gave rise to a production line of Hadiths and a forgery industry, which turned even what had started out as rather rational groups like the Hanifits into ambitious Hadith fabricators. The believers and their societies were at the end completely regulated by the Hadiths.

Together, the Hadiths and *Sira* (the Prophet's biography) form the so-called *Sunna*, which is the "tradition." That means that the Sunna consists of all Prophet-related transmissions combined. The Sunna consists of everything the Prophet said, what he did, and whatever was reported about him. Based on the Prophet's tradition, the Sunna regulated greeting ceremonials, how and what was to be replied to a person sneezing, the number of wives, beard-fashion, dress codes, and forbidden foods. The Sunna became the government and justice system. And finally, it became the overriding principle of all private and public life. As early as the third Islamic century, Qur'an and Sunna were considered equally important, and the maxim was "the Sunna is the Justice that rules over the Qur'an, but not the other way around." The leading law scholars al-Shaybani (ca. AD 750–803) and al-Shafii (AD 767–820) supported this idea, Ibn Qutayba (AD 828–885) created the thesis of the godliness of the Sunna. Being called *Salafi*, meaning "Emulator of the Tradition" (the Tradition of Muhammad), represented the highest honor for a believer in the ninth century. Even in the twenty-first century, the Emulators of the Tradition, known as *Salafists*, remain an influential branch of Islam.

It goes without saying that theology cannot develop in an environment in which emulation and adjustment are its highest virtues. And furthermore, the most basic Islamic motives were completely twisted around. The nature of the earliest Islam was characterized by the move toward clarity and simplicity, and, for that reason, it was very opposed to the Greek Christendom with its miracles and saints, which had been forced upon it. But as early as the third Islamic century, an excessive personality cult had become the trademark of the new religion Islam, meaning that its nature had completely changed into exactly what it had been so fiercely against in its beginning. In contradiction to both the Qur'an and the *Arabic Sunna*, a supra-figure, a perfect human that was flawless and beyond approach, was created. It was a superhuman who performed miracles and was shrouded in legend: Muhammad.

❖ ❖ ❖

The Perfect Human:

The Prophet Muhammad According to Traditional Reports

This is about a person with a magnificent character and his unusual, meaning supreme and exemplary, doings. Could you claim that there was any person you know, anyone in your family or among your friends with such character? Do you know of any human who never gets upset, never yells, or never shows any rage? Someone who is always patient, loving, and gentle?

I know of one single person like this. This is about the Prophet Muhammad—may Allah's blessings and peace be upon him. How much I wish I had had the pleasure of knowing this wonderful human and had lived during his time.

By the mercy of Allah, I have been granted to be a part of the Ummah of Muhammad—may Allah's blessings and peace be upon him. There is no greater mercy for me. Allah sent such a loving, merciful, and caring Prophet to us. He was a just person like no other and was always anxious to do good deeds. He was loved by his followers but, nevertheless, he was modest and even poor. Though he didn't own many things, he was thankful and content. Sometimes, he would fast or only eat one date a day. One time, while resting and reciting the Qur'an, the Prophet started weeping when he got to the passage which accentuates the statement by the Prophet Issa: "When you, Allah, pardon them, it is because you are most forgiving." Allah sent the angel Gabriel—may peace be upon him—down to him and he asked why he was weeping. The Prophet Muhammad—may Allah's blessings and peace be upon him—said that he was weeping for his Ummah. He was weeping for his Ummah. He feared for us. That's how important his Ummah was to him.

—Sister Nasreen in: http://muhammad.islam.de , 2009

According to Islamic tradition, and as is found in just about any reference, Muhammad was born in AD 570 in Mecca and died in AD 632 in Medina. He belonged to the Hashemite clan of the Quraysh tribe. His father was Abd Allah, who was a great-great-grandson of Qusayy, the founder of Mecca. His mother was Amina. In his early days, Muhammad was just a regular boy who tended goats and sheep. But the first incident was already about to happen. While he was traveling with a caravan to Syria at the age of twelve, a Christian monk he met along the way made the important prophesy that someday he would become an important man. In general, not much is known about his early years. There are just a few stories about him that praise his capabilities at leading caravans from north to south—a talent that would eventually attract the attention of the wealthiest woman of Mecca, called Khadija. At the age of thirty-nine, he got married to the fifty-five-year old Khadija. Together they had six children. This fact that Khadija gave birth at the age of sixty can be marked down as the first miracle.

Muhamad preaching. Eastern Persia (Uzbekistan, Turkmenistan), 13th century

The Arabia of that time was ruled by Bedouin tribes; only a few cities existed. Mecca was located at the crossroads of major trade routes and was therefore believed to be one of the most important metropolitan areas on the Arabian Peninsular. In addition to local tribes who worshipped many different natural deities, there were also Christian and Jewish communities. The Quraysh tribe, to which Muhammad belonged, was the most influential one. Their members lived in and around Mecca, and worshipped the principle deities of Allat and Uzza—the goddesses of the moon, the morning star, and fertility. The religious center was a black rock which was said to have been white originally but which gradually turned dark as a result of absorption of human sins. Today it is assumed that it is a meteorite, though it has been unavailable for scientific testing. Every year, pilgrimages to the holy rock were taking place, which represented important sources of income to Mecca. The pilgrims walked seven times toward the sun and around the holy rock, which was covered in precious linens. In addition, they practiced other ritual ceremonies. Because the goddesses were also deities of fertility, is it said that the pilgrims used to walk around the holy rock bare-naked in earlier times. Later, it became mandatory to wear special robes for the rituals. The crescent of the moon was the symbol of Allat and the morning star symbolized Uzza.

Now that Muhammad was Khadija's husband and therefore spared from financial problems, he turned to religion. He started wandering around the desert, fasting, and writing mystical verses. He would only return home occasionally to stock up on survival supplies.

In the blaze of day and during the clear desert nights, when the stars seem sharp enough to penetrate the eye, his very substance was becoming saturated with the "signs" in the heavens, so that he might serve as an entirely adequate instrument for a revelation already inherent in these "signs." It was then that he was undergoing preparation for the enormous task which would be placed upon his shoulders, the task of prophethood and conveying the true religion of God to his people and the rest of humanity.[20]

---

20 From: http://www.islamreligion.com; 2010.

One day during the holy month of Ramadan, when he was spending the night at Mount Hira (in some oral transmissions it is the Cave Hira), the archangel Gabriel appeared. Muhammad identified him as the same archangel who had come to Mary, the Mother Jesus. From now on, this night would be known to the Muslims as the "night of destiny."

The narrator Ibn Ishaq described this meeting according to Muhammad:

While I was sleeping, Gabriel came to me with a blanket made of silk brocade, in which there was book.

He said: IQRA. ["Read."]

I said: I don't read.

He strangled me with the scarf until I thought I was ready to die.

This procedure was repeated two more times until Muhammad started reading—the first Sura, Qur'an 96:1–5, had come to earth: *"Read. In the name of the Lord who created. He created man, out of a clot of congealed blood. Read. For your Lord is most bountiful. He who taught by the use of the pen taught man that which he knew not."* And he went on saying: *"But I awoke and it felt as if my heart had been inscribed."*

This incident had a severe emotional effect on him to the extent that he had thoughts of suicide. But then he had another experience:

"While I was on my way, I suddenly heard a voice coming from the heavens and recognized that it was the same angel who had come to me at Hira. Taken aback, I ran home and shouted: Cover me." [Due to this fearful experience, he developed a high fever—or was his intention to hide?]

And God revealed the words:

"Oh you who has wrapped yourself [in a garment or blanket], *stand up and warn, and praise the greatness of your Lord, and clean* [or purify] *your clothes, and keep yourself from the impurity of idolatry"* (Sura 74:1-5).

The revelations started coming in more and more frequently, and the pain associated with their occurrence increased. The unbelieving Quraysh people mocked him: *"Muhammad has been abandoned by his Lord."*

In order to prove them wrong, Allah sent down the Sura-Verses 93:1–5:

"By the morning and by the night when it is still. Your Lord has neither forsaken you nor does he hate you. Verily, the hereafter is better for you than the present. And verily, your Lord will give you and you will be well-pleased."

Every three to six months (different time periods are given by individual narrators), Muhammad received God's revelations. His followers paid painstakingly close attention to his words and grouped them accordingly. The words which were derived from the revelations would later form the Qur'an. The remaining words were put together as *Hadiths* (sayings) or *Sira* (biography). But first, Allah's revelations were either learned by heart or provisionally written down on whatever materials were at hand. The belief in one God formed the center around which all of Muhammad's preaching words revolved.

But his success was rather limited. His first group of believers only contained his wife Khadija, his friend Abu Bakr, his former slave, and an additional handful of followers. Though his group of followers was very small, the persecutions by the Meccan citizens and other Quraysh people increased—Muhammad dared to preach against their deities. There are very detailed reports about this difficult time period in Muhammad's life.

Eventually, the persecutions had reached such an unbearable level that Muhammad decided to go into exile to Abyssinia together with his small crowd of now-eighty followers. (According to some reports, Muhammad stayed in Mecca and only sent his followers to Abyssinia.) There, he was warmly welcomed by the Christian king Negus. The Meccan people, however, suspected Muhammad of joining forces with the Abyssinians and sent a delegation that demanded the extradition of Muhammad. In the hearing, Muhammad convinced the king by reciting verses from the Qur'an that he and his followers prayed to the same God.

The king was moved to tears and cried "Verily, that was written by the same God." And he was won over. The Muslims were not extradited but soon returned to Mecca of their own free will.

Back in Mecca, the group of Muhammad's followers steadily grew larger and so did the conflicts with the pagan Meccan people. Eventually, the Meccan inhabitants prohibited Muhammad's clan, the Hashmites, from having any contact with the locals and put this decree up on the Ka'aba, which, at that time, was still a pagan symbol. The following day, almost the entire decree had been eaten by white ants; only a little piece was left that said "Bismillah Allah"—another miracle had happened.

Hajj, a mandatory procedure for Bedouins, is the annual pilgrimage to Mecca in order to worship the holy rock and walk around the Ka'aba. This time, people from Yathrib, the ancient name of Medina, also joined the Hajj. Muhammad secretly met with them and brought them round to Islam in no time. In general, Medinan people were either Christian or Jewish, had a script, and were therefore much more open to the new religion than the antiquated Meccan people. On the occasion of the next Hajj a year later, the happy news could be delivered to Muhammad that his group of followers in Medina had grown to a sizeable crowd. That news didn't really help to improve relations with the Meccan people; they suspected this to be a conspiracy against them. The relations kept on deteriorating to the point that, night after night, small groups of the Prophet's followers decided to leave Mecca for Medina.

Muhammad stayed behind because he didn't want to take any action without God's orders. Eventually, Muhammad received the word. He told his cousin Ali to act as a decoy and stay in the Prophet's house, exchange his robe for Muhammad's, and lie down in the Prophet's bed. Muhammad himself sneaked off together with Abu Bakr. On race camels they headed for Medina.

All this took place on September 23, AD 622. It is called the *Hijra*—the Prophet's migration from Mecca to Medina, the beginning of the Muslim calendar.

During the trip, Muhammad built the first mosque in Islamic history in Quba. And soon, the loyal Ali had made it there, too.

The Prophet was enthusiastically welcomed in Medina. Here, right after building a mosque, he went back to taking care of revelations and teaching. His time in Medina would become the most fulfilling of his life.

Soon, difficulties would erupt between his followers from the early days, the Muhajiruns, and the new Muslims, the Ansari. Thanks to his diplomatic capabilities, Muhammad struck a deal between the two parties—the first community of believers, the Umma, was created. The rules of this community would, from then and up to today, form the model for Islamic communities and nations. Considering the uncompromising differences between these two groups, the idea that they were able to reach a deal at all is filed under "miracle" by some biographers.

But the problems just wouldn't go away. People with other beliefs, especially the Jewish, had always formed the majority in Medina, and the Prophet didn't get tired of trying to convince them of what was the correct religion. But they proved to be very resilient and had rock-solid reasons for that:

> *The Jewish people had greatly benefitted from the wrangling among the Arab tribes, for it was the unsteadiness in this region that gave them the upper hand regarding trade and supply. Peace among the Medinan tribes was a threat to Jews.*[21]

---

21 From: http://www.islamreligion.com; 2009.

Muhammad explained that he believed in the same monotheism and referred to the fact that Muslims faced Jerusalem during prayers, but the Jews denied the legitimacy of Muhammad's role as Prophet. The tension between these two groups increased. For that reason, Muhammad angrily turned his back on Jews and Christians. From now on, he would no longer refer to their prophets but, backed by new revelations, would only recognize the progenitor Abraham, stating, *"Abraham was neither Jew nor Christian, but he was the follower of the purest belief, an obedient servant of God, and he did not belong to the polytheists"* (Sura 3:67).

At the same time, he changed the direction that is to be faced during prayer (*qiblah*) from Jerusalem to Mecca, because it had been revealed to him that the Ka'aba, the pagan holy shrine of Mecca, had in reality been built by Abraham for the Muslims. The Sura *al-Baqarah* ("The Cow") gives this information. From now on, the Muslims couldn't trust the Jews any longer.

But there were more problems that needed to be resolved. Medinan inhabitants led by Muhammad's fiercest competitor, the infamous Ubayy, had supposedly converted to Islam—but they had only pretended. In secret, they were paid by the Jews and the Meccan people to fight the Prophet. Therefore, in the Medinan Suras of the Qur'an, the "Jews" and the "hypocrites" – those fighting the Prophet undercover - are often called to account.

The Hijra marks a clear line in the history of the Prophet, as can be seen in the Qur'an. The Suras get increasingly shorter and predominantly deal with judiciary and regulatory issues. These Suras also reflect Muhammad's problems with the Medinan unbelievers. Up to that point he had been a preacher, but from now on, he would be a warlord and statesman. He had become the leader of a small nation that soon would grow to the size of an Arabic Empire.

The situation in Mecca had further deteriorated. Muslims were now openly persecuted and tortured. But even worse than that was the fact that the Meccan inhabitants had forged an alliance with the hypocrite Ubayy and expanded their anti-Muslim activities to Medina.

That's when God granted the Muslims permission to raise their weapons against the unbelievers. [22]

The Muslims had been pacifists for thirteen years, but now they started going on little missions that were led by either the Prophet himself or by one of his subordinates. The goal of these missions was to track down and rob Meccan caravans on one hand, but on the other hand to forge alliances with other tribes. This way, the Muslims tried to put the Quraysh tribe under economic pressure so that the tribe would stop its persecutions of Meccan and Medinan Muslims.

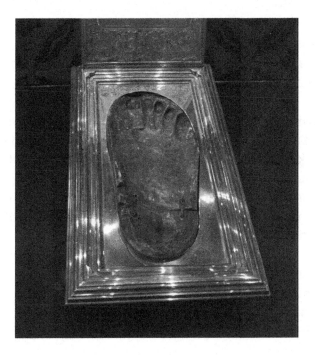

Alleged footprint of the Prophet Muhammad, that is is shown together with a beard hair, and a tooth, as well as the sword of David and Moses' stick in the Topkapi Museum in Istanbul. In fact we do not have any historic trace of Muhammad

---

22 Sura 22:39.

One day, the Prophet was informed of the approach of a large caravan from Syria. He called together his followers and said: "A caravan of the Quraysh tribe loaded with goods is on the way. Approach them. Maybe Allah will give you the goods as booty."[23]

It was another triumphant coup. Because the Muslim tactics proved to be very successful, the Meccan people decided to launch a counterattack by sending a thousand-man army to Medina. They decided that they finally wanted to get rid of this nuisance.

At the city of Badr on March 17, 642, "one of the most important battles in the history of mankind was fought."[24] The Meccan people were set against three hundred Muslims and their seventeen camels and three horses.

The Muslims were in despair, but then a message from God appeared to Muhammad which said, "*I will support you by sending a thousand angels*" (Sura 54:45).

Fortified with angelic support troops and inspired by this fact, the Muslims won the battle. All of Mecca was traumatized and stigmatized by this shock, and many tribes quickly converted to Islam, but the Meccan people, who were in alliance with the Jews and the hypocrites, just wouldn't surrender and showed up with three times as many fighters the following year. Another battle, the well-known battle at Uhud, ended in a tie. As a matter of fact, it was a close call because, during the battle, the Bedouins and the hypocrites under the command of Ubayy changed sides, but thanks to mastermind Muhammad, a catastrophe was prevented from happening. In another two battles, the Muslims were victorious. Eventually, the Meccan people agreed to a ten-year truce, which would become known as the famous Treaty of Hudaybiyya.

The Meccan people didn't keep to the treaty, however. Therefore, Muhammad had no choice but to attack and conquer Mecca two years later. A number of battles followed—sometimes led by him personally,

---

23 From: http://www.answering-islam.de; 2009.
24 From: http://www.islamreligion.com; 2009.

sometimes led by his reliable subordinates—and due to these, Islam was ultimately spread all over the Arabian Peninsula and Syria.

Muhammad also wrote letters to the Byzantine Emperor Heraclius, to the Persian king, and to the emperor of Abyssinia, with the invitation to convert to Islam. There are detailed descriptions of how the delivery of the letter to Heraclius in Jerusalem took place.[25]

Abdullah ibn Abbas narrates how Abu Sufyan ibn Harb described his encounter with the Byzantine Emperor in Jerusalem. (Despite the fact that Abu Sufyan was not a Muslim, he was entrusted with the delivery of the letter by the Prophet.)

> *The first question Heraclius asked me was:*
> *"What is his family's status amongst you?"*
> *I replied, "He belongs to a noble family amongst us."*
> *Heraclius further asked, "Has anybody amongst you ever claimed to be a Prophet before him?"*
> *"No."*
> *"Was any of his ancestors a king?"*
> *"No."*
> *"Do the nobles or the poor follow him?"*
> *"It is the poor who follow him."*
> *"Is the number of his followers increasing or decreasing?"*
> *"It is increasing."*
> *"Has any of his followers become displeased and, for that reason, renounced the religion?"*
> *"No."*
> *"Did you ever suspect him of telling lies before he claimed to be a Prophet?"*
> *"No."*
> *"Has he ever broken his promises?"*
> *"No. But it has been for some time now, that we are not sure anymore about his actions."*

---

25 Al-Bukhari, *Nachrichten von Taten und Aussprüchen des Propheten Muhammad*, (Stuttgart: Reclam, 1997).

(Abu Sufyan remarks that this was probably his only unfavorable answer.)
"Have you ever had a war with him?"
"Yes."
"What was the outcome of the battles?"
"Sometimes he was victorious and sometimes we were."
"What does he order you to do?"
"He tells us to worship God and God alone and to refuse to accept anyone else to share His divinity. Renounce all in which your ancestors had believed. In addition, he orders us to pray, to speak the truth, to be chaste, and to be charitable."

Heraclius was impressed by what he had just heard and replied by giving a long speech, in which he predicted that the Prophet would be the owner of his territory some day and closed with the words: "I knew that a Prophet was going to appear, but I did not know that he would be one of you. If I knew that I could reach him, I would do anything to meet him. If I was with him, I would wash his feet."

Then he requested him to read Muhammad's letter and read it aloud:

*"In the name of the most beneficent and most merciful God.
From Muhammad, the servant and messenger of God, to Heraclius, the Byzantine Emperor. Peace be upon him, who follows the right path.*

I invite you to convert to Islam. Become a Muslim and God will double your reward. But if you reject this invitation, you will be held responsible for the sins committed by your subjects. God the sublime, said: "O people of the scripture. Come together to a word common to you and us that serve none but God and refuse to accept anyone else to share His divinity, that none of us take other Lords in God's stead. But if they turn away, then say: 'Bear witness that we surrender to God's will.'"

There was a great hue and cry in the Royal Court, and the emperor sent the letter to his councilors in Constantinople for their opinions. They confirmed that the Prophet had come and that he truly was a prophet.

Then Heraclius spoke to the audience: "Byzantine People. Are you looking for happiness and the rightful leadership? Do you want your reign to continue on? Then you will have to follow the Prophet." Closely observing the reactions of the dignitaries, he lost all hope that they would ever convert to Islam. (Some have expressed the opinion that Heraclius only wanted to test the loyalty of his dignitaries.)

Nevertheless, the Byzantine Emperor Heraclius had his chance, and he wrecked it.

After his return to Medina from a pilgrimage to Mecca, Muhammad was busy preparing war campaigns against Byzantine, Syria, Persia, Egypt, and northern Africa. However, he unexpectedly got sick and died at the age of either sixty, or sixty-three, or sixty-five (depending on the chosen oral transmission). He was survived by wives that range in number from nine to twenty-three in different oral transmissions and by a larger number of slaves, and he left a great fortune.

Curiously, despite the large number of wives, he had no son. This would later cause great problems for the religious community. Immediately after Muhammad's death, fights over his inheritance broke out. His wives and his daughter Fatima were excluded from the inheritance. Ali, who was the first in line for the birthright, was killed by a rival party. This caused the first divide in Islam, because from then on, the "Party of Ali," the so-called Shi'a, would form an independent religious branch.

The present chapter only gives a very short summary of the Prophet's life. Traditional descriptions do not spare us a single detail of his biography and can easily fill whole libraries. Interestingly, there are substantial differences between individual descriptions. Therefore, an examination of the facts is overdue.

❖ ❖ ❖

Two Hundred Years of Silence:
The Historic Muhammad

Archaeology has no friends among the pious ones.

—*Volker Popp, Researcher on Islamic Studies and*
Numismatist

Muawiyya was the first caliph of the famous *Umayyad* Dynasty. In AD 641, nine years after Muhammad's death, he took up office. He belonged to the generation of glorious Islamic conquerors who allegedly subjugated all of the known ancient Orient and, within a few decades, incorporated it into an Islamic Empire. That's at least how traditional Islamic reports tell the story.

In Ta'if, located southeast of Mecca, there is an inscription by Muawiyya. In it, he refers to himself as *Amir al-Mu'minin*. According to Islamic tradition, the same title had already been used by Muawiyya's predecessor Ali, who was the son-in-law of the Prophet. Traditionally, it is translated as "Leader of the Faithful." Of course, only Muslims are considered the faithful.

There is yet another inscription by Muawiyya in the thermal springs of Hamat Gader (Israel), written in Greek:

> *In the days of God's servant Maavia, the commander of the protection providers, the hot springs were saved and restored… in the sixth year of the indication, in the year 726 of the founding of the city, in the forty-second year after the Arabs, for the healing of the sick, under the supervision of Johannes, the municipal authority of Gadara.*

The text begins with a sign of the cross. Back then, the use of religious expressions was common. But often, verbal expressions were replaced with signs, in this case, by a cross.

In addition to the presence of this symbol, which already seems rather confusing when used in connection with a Muslim ruler, historians noticed that the expression *Amir al-Mu'minin*, usually interpreted by Muslims as "Leader of the Faithful," means, however, in the Greek translation "*Commander of the Protection Providers*"—it is no reference to any *Leader of the Muslims*.

Tablet of Muawija, according to Muslim tradition the fifth of the caliphs, consecrated at the occasion of the renovation of the Roman thermal baths at Gadara (today Israel). The inscription starts with the sign of the cross, Muawiya calls himself in Aramaic Maavia

In the ancient Orient, the matter regarding the expression *Commander of the Protection Providers* is of central importance: all potentates justified their authority to be leaders by their function to fulfill a "protective purpose." Certainly, the respective person had to be capable of providing security to his subjects and to his subjects' belongings. But there was more to it than that: there was always a holy site involved in connection with the position of protection provider, and this holy site had to be protected as well. The defending and guarding of a holy shrine legitimized the execution of power. This concept was applied all across the ancient Orient, whether in Byzantine, Persian, or Arabian areas; a leader had no chance of being considered a legitimate ruler without providing protection.[26]

What was Muawiyya's holy site? His residence was Damascus and this city was host to the holy shrine of John the Baptist. During his time, the Baptist's head was the magnet attracting visitors. It was kept as a precious relic in the Crypt of St. John's Basilica. Many sources have told us that, together with Jerusalem, Damascus was the most important site for pilgrims in the seventh century.

Why did Caliph Muawiyya reside in Damascus and not in Mecca to execute his government business, when Mecca was considered the center of the Islamic world? There might have been practical reasons for this decision, but why did he not execute his reputable protective function over the number-one holy sites in the Islamic world, namely the Ka'aba in Mecca, and the Prophet's grave in Medina, which would have meant the highest level of legitimization for a Muslim caliph? Why was his choice, instead, the holy site of John the Baptist?

Muawiyya coins have been found also in Darabjerd in the Iranian Province of Fars, which used to be a part of his empire. The script on these coins corresponds to the Iranian tradition. Muawiyya didn't trade under his Arabic name, but under his Syro-Aramaic name of Maavia, just as it was put down in the inscription at Gadara. In Pahlavi, his title is *Amir-i Wlwyshnyk'n,* which means "Commander

---

26   The Saud Dynasty still has the title "Protector of the Holy Shrines," referring to Mecca and Medina. It represents the most important title the Saud Dynasty currently carries.

of the Protection Providers." And this is exactly what his official title was in Persian, Greek, and Aramaic. There is no evidence to support the interpretation that he was known as "Leader of the Muslims," a claim which, despite the fact that there is no proof for it, flits around in Islamic literature.

"At this point already," Popp states, "it becomes very clear the extent to which the Islamic usage of this title has blocked the approach to the specific Arabian elements of the early history of Islam."

The "Islam" label has been stamped on every bit of Arabic subject matter and forms a central thread through all the Islamic historiography, as we will see again and again.

Obviously, Maavia had no problem with manifesting himself in the languages of Aramaic, Persian, and Greek. After all, he lived in a Greek-Persian setting and was a native-born Syrian; therefore, his mother tongue was Aramaic. He was most likely fluent in Greek and Persian, too. His empire included today's countries of Syria, Iraq, and Iran. As the first Umayyad caliph, he is naturally considered a Muslim according to Islamic tradition.

In inscriptions found on memorials and coins, Maavia referred to himself as "God's servant" and "protector," but he never used the term "caliph," the title used for him today. In addition, the sign of the cross symbol has been found on several of his posthumous archaeological relics.

The inscription at Hamat Gader refers to a specific date three times:

1. the Byzantine tax year;
2. the time following the city's founding;
3. the time after the Arabs.

Since it was verified three-fold, there is no doubt regarding the date. The reference by Maavia to the forty-second year *kata Araba* ("after the Arabs") has, however, attracted special attention from researchers. In our calendar, the year 1 in the Arab calendar would correspond to the year AD 622. The Arab calendar's year 1 also represents the time of the Hijra, the escape of the Prophet in AD 622 from Mecca to Medina. Maavia makes no reference, however, to the time of the Hijra—that is, to the Islamic calendar. But doing so would have been the most natural thing in the world to a Muslim caliph.

The year AD 622 represents a significant year in Arabian history. It is the year in which the Byzantine Emperor Heraclius destroyed the Persian army. Due to the dictated peace that followed, Persia lost her western provinces from Mesopotamia to Egypt. At the same time, Heraclius continued a course of completely restructuring his empire. It was a process that would eventually lead to the giving up of Byzantine's permanent presence in Syria and Egypt. He left those territories to Arabian emirs who became tributary feudal lords. We know that Maavia was one of these feudal lords and that he had a very close relationship with the empire during the first half of his reign.

As early as AD 614, the Persians occupied Jerusalem. In AD 618, they took Egypt. They also appointed Arabian allies as governors. Not only did the Arab vassals in such western areas like Syria, Egypt, and Palestine survive the Persian catastrophe of AD 622, they also became warlords in their own respect—practically overnight. As a result of the Persian invasions, the Byzantine Empire had drawn back from areas that it had never really controlled and retreated to the region which forms the northern border of today's Syria. The *Limes Arabicus*, which was the southern and eastern border of the Roman Empire, had already been given up in the fifth century. Because the Byzantine Empire's northern border remained under constant threat, Byzantium knew it needed to stick to its primary interests; the unexpected but great victory over the Persians did nothing to change this decision. Thus, the Byzantines withdrew from the area, relieving the Arabs of the second power in the region. The Arabs now only had to fill the power vacuum that resulted from both the collapse of the Persian Empire and the Byzantine retreat. And so they did, very successfully. It was the beginning of the great Arabian Era that would last until the Mongols ended it in the thirteenth century.

That is the political side of the story, but it is incomplete without taking theological issues into consideration. In the years before its defeat by Byzantine troops, Persia had taken away from the Christian Empire Mesopotamia, Syria, Palestine, and even Cilicia, and carried away the Cross of Jesus from Jerusalem. Christians thought of Persia as the Antichrist, and, according to common belief at the time, total triumph of the Antichrist could only be followed by the end of the world. In addition, the *Katechon*, Greek for "the Defender against the Antichrist," had to appear as well as the last chance to avoid the Apocalypse.

After the glorious victory in AD 622, the title of "Defender against the Antichrist" could only apply to Byzantium and its allies! This victory turned everything upside down: the end of the world had been averted, the appearance of the biblical Gog and Magog (in the Qur'an: Ya'juj and Ma'juj), this last plague of mankind which had been locked away until the end of time by the *Dhul Qarnyan* (the Qur'anic name for Alexander the Great), was prevented from happening. But there was even more to it: Christ would return and establish justice. After a time of deep depression, the year AD 622 was the beginning of a new era, and that also applied to the Arab allies, without whom the victory would have never been possible. This is "the year of the Arabs" that is mentioned in the Hamat Gader inscription which begins with the sign of the cross.

The dates that are found on the coins of this time period also correspond to this calendar.

For centuries, this "year of the Arabs" (which followed the solar calendar) was in use until Muslims recreated the almanac so that the calendar became based on the legendary Hijra of the Prophet Muhammad. This newer Islamic calendar, however, was a lunar calendar. Subsequently, conversions from the solar to the lunar timetable were carried out, which eventually resulted in a total chaos for the dating of historical events. Confusion about the year has been a distinguishing mark of the Islamic tradition up to this day. There is practically not a single correct date in the first centuries of the Hijra timetable.

Recently, however, considerable doubts have arisen concerning the period after the Prophet. While the traditional view is that the Hijra/Hegira period commenced with Mohammad's flight from Mecca to Medina in 622, Robert M. Kerr of Wilfrid Laurier University (Waterloo, Canada), who has previously demonstrated based on script and language distribution that the Qur'an could not have originated in Mecca or Medina, has posited that this is just a later re-interpretation. According to the Islamic tradition, Caliph Umar ibn al-Chatab (NOTE: There is no historical evidence for his existence) introduced the Hijra/Hegira years in 638, shortly after the alleged death of the Prophet. However, the fact is that the first evidence for this supposed event being the beginning of a new era comes from the tenth century, otherwise when at all, we find mention of the *kata Arabas* as described previously. How then are the origins of the Islamic era to be explained?

The English word Hegira comes from the Arabic *higr*. As is customary in Arabic and other Semitic languages, this word is derived from a consonantal root, namely *HGR*. To such roots vowels can be supplied so as to create words. The most well-known derivation from this root is *Hagar*, who, according to biblical legend, gave birth to Abraham's first child Ishmael – the purported progenitor of the Arabs – in the Desert of Paran. In Late Antiquity then, in Greek, Latin and Aramaic sources, *Hagarenes* is a common term to denote Arabs. *Hagar* then means 'Arab'.

One of the meanings of this root in Arabic is "to separate, depart, emigrate", with a noun *higr* meaning "separation, departure, emigration." Robert Kerr has however noted that *HGR* is not a well-attested root, excepting Hagar, and that the meaning "to emigrate" given above is not attested in other Semitic languages, not even Aramaic, the language from which Arabic borrowed much of its technical (theological) vocabulary as Kerr has previously demonstrated. This is important since *higra* is first attested in the ninth century, to indicate an era even later.

Contemporary Christian sources as was noted use a derivation of the root *HGR* to indicate the peoples peoples also known as Arabs or Saracens. These sources even date events using this system, i.e. *kata*

Arabas, - that is the "era of the Hagarenes" especially since it is unlikely that Christians would date according to an Islamic era, something that not even "Muslims" at that time did. The question that remains then is why Muslims did not employ the term Hegira for over two centuries after it had been supposedly introduced as the binding Islamic way of counting years.

Robert Kerr's suggestion that the *Hagar*ene era mutated into the *Hegir*a era is convincing. *Higra* in Arabic was then originally just an abstract noun to indicate 'Arab', in this case as noted "the era according to the Arabs". When the Mohammedan legends were being formed in the ninth and tenth centuries, this uncommon Semitic root was not understood and reinterpreted so as to suit legendary events. Hence the key moment in the life of the alleged Prophet, and even of nascent Islam, has neither historical foundation nor linguistic support.

According to Islamic tradition, Maavia is a caliph, but historically, nothing that would indicate any connection with Islam is known about him. He paid his tribute to the Byzantine Emperor, and his interest in restoring Roman hot springs shows that he belonged to the Syro-Byzantine Mediterranean culture. It is obvious that he was not a Bedouin who came from the Arabian desert. He didn't know anything about a Muslim prophet called Muhammad who had allegedly lived in his empire just a few decades before him and on whose behalf he was, according to later Islamic historians, building an Islamic Empire. If he had been, one assumes that Maavia would have told us about it in his inscriptions or on his coins.

Maavia told us about the titles he had—but not a single time did he refer to himself as an Islamic "caliph." He gave us the date of a year—but did not use a calendar that began with the Hijra. He told us about the holy site under his protection—but it was not the Ka'aba in Mecca, it was the basilica in Damascus in which the head of Saint John the Baptist was kept as a holy relic. The coins from his time period show Christian-Judeo symbols like the crucifix, the Agnus Dei (the Lamb of God), the display of the relic of the head of John the Baptist, the Stone of Jacob, and the word "Zion." How Christian-Judeo symbols could possibly be used by an Islamic caliph remains the secret of traditional Islamic interpreters. Thus, based on archaeological results, there is no doubt that the Aramaic Maavia was a Christian ruler; he was no caliph or Umayyad. (Moreover, we don't know his real name; Maavia was only the name under which he ruled.)

Abd al-Malik started his own reign around the year 60 of the Arab calendar, which corresponds to the year AD 682. He was an Arab emir from Marw, a region in today's Turkmenistan. Back then, it was a Persian province, but the collapse of the Sassanid Dynasty after 622 brought the *Marwanids* (the emirs from Marw) into power in the eastern region. This change in power also had consequences for the Zoroastrians, in that the dominating religions in the area were now the Syrian and Nestorian branches of Christianity.[27] Understandably, then, the coins from Abd al-Malik's reign bear Christian symbols.[28] Nevertheless, needless to say, according to Islamic teachers, Abd al-Malik was a Muslim caliph.

With the Marwanids came also the *muhamad*. The term *muhamad* occurs first on Malik's coins. According to traditional interpretations, it, of course, refers to the Prophet Muhamad. The facts, however, tell a different story. As Christoph Luxenberg clearly shows, *muhamad* certainly does not represent an individual's name. In Arabic, as well as in Syro-Aramaic, the latter of which was the main language at that time, this term denotes a gerund and has the meaning "The One Who Is to Be Praised" or "the Praised One." *Muhamad* was a title, not a name. The *muhamad*-logo is found in many places. It was created in Persia and from there it spread all over the Arabic realm.

The same applies to the frequently used expression *abd Allah*, which means "God's servant" and serves as a modifier, not name. To the

---

27 In the eastern areas of the Persian Empire, there were also Buddhist influences. Signs of such influences were the Buddha statues of Bamiyan, Afghanistan, which were bombed and destroyed by the Taliban in 2001.
28 The dominant appearance of Christian symbols and signs on coins of the seventh and eighth centuries would be surprising only to people who accept Arabic history according to secondary sources produced in the ninth century, says numismatist Volker Popp.

Arabian Christians, the name for God has always been Allah; and this term hasn't got anything to do with the Islamic Allah.

Thus, the alleged "Islamic caliphs" Maavia and Abd al-Malik both held the designation of *Commander of the Protection Providers* as their highest title. Corresponding to the Byzantine tradition, they both referred to themselves as *servus dei* (Latin) or *abd Allah* (Arabic), meaning "God's servant." Their coins and inscriptions contained Signs of the Cross and other Christian symbols, and they denoted the beginning of the Arabs' independence ("the year of the Arabs") using a solar calendar, not the lunar Islamic calendar. *Abd al-Malik* honored a *muhamad*, one "that is to be praised," which is the word's meaning.

But who was the *muhamad*, who was the one that was to be praised?

The answer to this question is found in, surprisingly, a building in which no one would have ever guessed: in the Dome of the Rock in Jerusalem, which is the third-holiest Muslim site, right after Mecca and Medina. According to tradition, it was built on the site from which Muhammad ascended to the heavens on his white horse Buraq, that was equipped with wings and had a human face. According to his inscription, al-Malik completed the Dome of the Rock in the year 72 of the Arabs, meaning in the year AD 694. By In both its construction style and layout, it corresponds to a Byzantine-Syrian church with Roman-style pillars and a cupola, the latter of which represents an element that is typical of Roman-Byzantine stately buildings. The innermost area is largely preserved in its original state, especially the 240-meter-long inscription band that wraps twice around the Octagon.

The script band in the Dome of the Rock with the Kufic inscription of Abd al-Malik. The mosaics are of typical Roman-Byzantine style, but they are arranged forming Persian motifs

بسم الله الرحمن الرحيم لا اله الا الله وحده لا

سريط لا لا له الملك وله الحمد يحيي و يميت وهو

علي كل شيء قدير محمد عبد الله ودسوله

ارالله و ملكنه بطور على الله بابها الكبر امتوا

صلوا عليه و سلموا تسليما صل الله عليه و السلم

Transcript of the script-band (excerpt). The script is older than any know Qur'an. According to modern sciences the content is that of an Arab - Christian monotheistic faith

Traditionally, these inscriptions, attributed to Malik, the builder of the
dome, are read in a way that echoes basic Islamic ideas, despite the
fact that even just a quick-but-unbiased look at them would have to
raise red flags about this approach. Apparently, for the longest time,
nobody bothered to take an unbiased look—until linguist Christoph
Luxenberg came along. He translated the inscriptions by reading
them in the language that was used at that time—and triggered off
a tsunami in the field of Islamic research. By applying the language
of Syro-Aramaic that was used by the writer of the inscription, he
brought to light interpretations of key messages that differed from
the traditional Islamic translations.

The traditional translation of the inscriptions is:

> In the name of God, the Merciful, the Compassionate. There is no
> god but God alone, He has no associate. Unto Him alone belongs
> the sovereignty and unto Him belongs the praise. He quickens
> and He gives death. He has power over all things.

> Muhamad the son of Abd Allah, is his messenger. God and his
> angels shower blessings on the Prophet. You believers, ask for
> blessings on him and salute him worthily. Blessings and peace
> may be upon him and may God have mercy with him.

> You people of the Book, do not exaggerate in your beliefs and
> speak only the truth about God. The Messiah, Jesus, the son
> of Mary, was only a messenger of God and his word which he
> conveyed unto Mary, and a spirit from him.

> So believe in God and His messenger, and say not "Three." Cease it.
> It is better for you. God is only One God. His transcendent majesty
> needs no son. His is all that is in the heavens and all that is in the
> earth, and God is sufficient as protector.

> The Messiah is not too proud to be a servant of God, nor are the
> devoted angels. The one who is in high spirits and too proud, He
> will rally round Him.

God, bless Your messenger and Your servant Jesus, son of Mary. May peace be on him the day he was born, the day he dies, and the day of his resurrection. Such is Jesus, the son of Mary, that is the truth which you doubt. It befitted not the Majesty of God to spawn a son, Praise Him. When He decrees a thing He says to Him only: Be. And it is.

God is my Lord and your Lord. So serve Him. That is the rightful path.

God witnessed that there is no God but God. And the angels and the learned ones are witnesses to that, too. He provides justice. He is the only almighty and wise God. See, the religion of Allah is Islam. And the ones who have received the Book became disunited by disobedience after knowledge had come to them. And those who deny the signs of God, God is swift at reckoning.

The inscriptions in the Dome of the Rock are older than the oldest-known Quran'ic verses, older than any existing Qur'an copy. The writing is in an early form of Arabic script and therefore contains only a minimum of diacritical marks. Even just reading through the inscription in its traditional Islamic translation raises eyebrows. Primarily, the talk is of Mary, Jesus, and God. Each of the terms *Muhamad* and *Islam* is mentioned just once—without these, it would not cross anyone's mind that this was supposed to be an Islamic confession.

Here, Christoph Luxenberg steps in, translating the words by using the language of that time. Again, as we've previously seen with passages in the Qur'an, his translation quickly produces a context that makes sense.

Comparing the key passages gives the following results:

Traditional translation: "*In the name of God, the Merciful, the Compassionate…*"

Luxenberg:"*In the name of the loving and beloved God…*"

But right after that comes the first key difference in meaning:

Traditional translation: "*Muhamad, the son of Abd Allah, is His messenger…*"
Luxenberg:"*Praised is God's servant and His messenger…*"

In great detail, Luxenberg provides evidence that *muhamad* is a gerund and could, under no circumstance, be understood as a name—it would be a grammatical impossibility. Historians of other fields have also supported the idea that the name "Muhamad" would be a semantic impracticality, as this name has been shown to have never existed at any time before the birth of Islam. Numerous findings on coins corroborate that this term represented a title but not a name. (Again, the same applies to the expression *abd Allah*—"God's servant." It was an attribute, but it was no name at that time.)

In addition, abundant evidence that dates back to the early time period of Christianity has been found proving that this term was used when referring to Jesus. Sura 19:30 gives a clear example by stating that the baby Jesus in the cradle says of himself, "*I am God's servant* ["abd Allah"]…" No one would ever assume that Jesus claimed that his name was abd Allah. At the time the text was put down, *muhamad abd allah* was not *Muhamad, the son of abd-Allah*—that interpretation was dreamt up later—but it was *God's servant who was to be praised.*

But who is this *God's servant who was to be praised*?

The answer is found in the dome's inscription itself: it is *Isa bin Maryam*, meaning Jesus, son of Mary.

Traditional translation: "*The Messiah, Jesus, the son of Mary, was only the messenger of God…*"
Luxenberg: "*The Messiah Jesus, son of Mary, is the messenger of God.*"

Here, according to Luxenberg, the traditional Islamic translation of the inscription contains something else—an intentional error. The reading of sentence, "The Messiah Jesus, son of Mary, was *only a messenger of God"* cannot be explained merely as the result of the interpreter having read it incorrectly. It is an obvious and unjustifiable manipulation.

And the following passage in the inscription is of particular interest:

> So *believe in God and His messenger, and say not "Three"…God is only One God. His transcendent majesty needs no son. His is all that is in the heavens and all that is in the earth…*

Here, the builder of the Dome of the Rock and the author of the inscription, Malik, states that he opposes the idea of the Holy Trinity ("Three"), which is why he considers Jesus as the messenger of God but not as God's son.

The second key passage in the Dome of the Rock's inscription is represented by the following remark which, in its original form, says: "*in(na) d-din(a) llah(i) l-islam…*"

Traditional translation: *"See, the religion of Allah is Islam…"*

Din is interpreted as the term "religion," and "Islam" is referred to as the name of this religion. To Luxenberg and many others, this is a typical misinterpretation that was produced during later centuries. By both its form and meaning, the Arabic *din* is derived from the Persian *den*. The meaning of the term *den/din* at that time corresponded to "the truthful, the rightful" but does not relate to the Latin *religio*, the religion. While the term *religio* denotes a formal relationship with God, the term *din* refers to the spiritual component which enables one to do the right thing, including recognizing the rightful religion. Hence, the relationship of the words is not that the term *din* means the word religion but rather that religion represents the consequence of the *din*.

During Malik's time, the term *islam* was not yet used as the name of a religion. There is no known contemporary record of any origin or source in which the term *islam* was used in this sense. In Malik's time, the word *islam* stood for "correspondence," or "concurrence." It refers to the concurring or corresponding nature of the scripts, namely the Old Testament and the Gospels. And in order to achieve concurrence regarding the holy scripts, or, in other words, in order for one to "recognize what is rightful and not get confused about it or distracted from it," the *din* was needed.

It was only after the individual scripts had been combined into one Arabic Gospel, which later became the Qur'an, that *islam* could be called *Islam*, a religion. But that was certainly not the situation during Malik's time. Today's common ideas about "religion" and "Islam" are not found in Malik's message. Therefore, the correct translation of the second key sentence is:

"By the rightful thing God means the concurrence of the scripts...."

And it goes on:

"...because the ones, to whom had been given the Book, got in conflict [contradiction] *with the revealed knowledge by arguing..."*

This statement expresses the standpoint of opposing the numerous reinterpretations and re-constructions of the original concept that had been carried out during several ecclesiastical assemblies. As a consequence, the primary message not only became watered down, but each new version was dominated by the view of the Imperial Church.

"...and say not 'Three'"—this points to the big issue of that time: What is the nature of Jesus? Is Jesus a human, a God, or both? The Monophysites ("one nature") viewed Jesus as a person who only had one nature, namely the divine one. This represents the position of the Coptic Church for example. While according to the Dyophysism (Greek dyo = "two"), Jesus had two natures, a divine and a human one, Monothelitism followed the idea that Christ had a human nature but no human free will; instead, he only had God's controlled will. The Monarchians viewed Jesus as a person who certainly had a close

relationship with God, but believed that this, however, did not make Jesus divine in nature. This idea corresponds to the concept of a prophet (*rasul*) and a messenger of God (*kalifat Allah*). Many rejected this conception of Jesus-as-prophet as heresy. The Greek Orthodoxy and others also viewed Jesus as being both divine and human in nature and installed a spiritual force, a "Holy Spirit," that functioned as mediator between these two natures. This "trinity concept," which was a creation possible within classical-ancient understanding, solved logical problems while at the same time making it possible to retain the One God concept. By its nature, it was actually the result of logical, modern, Greek–style thinking.

The whole discussion was essentially about semantics wherein ideas and concepts got mixed into a blur and, consequently, couldn't lead to a precise definition. For current theology, those issues don't play much of a role anymore, but they were the main subjects of Christian theological discussions for centuries. The various fractions were arguing over these questions at several ecclesiastical assemblies, and that is what eventually led to the splitting off of the branch of Oriental Christians.[29] In contrast to both the Imperial Church of Byzantine and the Roman Church, the Arabian Churches did not adopt the dogma of the Trinity. Therefore, Abd al-Malik warned in his message of the "Three" that God does not need a son or a conveying spirit in order to reach humankind.

With the following sentence, Abd al-Malik completes his statement of belief by using the well-known subjects of Jesus's birth, his death, and his resurrection:

"Lord, bless your messenger and servant Jesus, son of Mary. Salvation be upon him on the day he was born, on the day he dies, on the day of his resurrection...."

The complete statement by Abd al-Malik given in AD 694 was as follows:

---

29 Namely Nicaea (AD 325), Constantinople (AD 381), Ephesus (AD 431), Chalkedon (AD 451).

In the name of the loving and beloved God. There is no God but God alone, He has no associate; unto Him alone belongs the sovereignty and unto Him belongs the praise. He gives life and He gives death, He is almighty.

Praise be upon God's servant and his messenger. God and His angels shower blessings on the Prophet. You believers, speak [words of] blessings and salvation upon him. God bless him, Salvation be upon him and God's love.

People of the Book, don't be misguided in your judgment and speak only the rightful thing about God. For Jesus Christ, son of Mary, is the messenger of God and his word that he conveyed to Mary and his spirit of Him. So believe in God and His messenger, and say not "Three." Reject it. It is better for you. God is only One God—praise be upon him—How could He have a son when all that is in the heavens and all that is in the earth is His. And God alone is sufficient as support.

Christ will neither consider it beneath him to be God's servant nor the one of God's closest angel.

But the ones who disregard to serve Him and behave overbearingly, those He will summon before Him.

Lord, bless Your messenger and servant Jesus, son of Mary, word of truth, over whom they argue.

It is not God's due to adopt a child, praise be upon Him. When He decrees a thing He says to Him only: Be. And it is. God is my Lord and your Lord. So serve Him; that is the rightful path. God reminded that there is no God but Him and the angels, as the learned ones truthfully confirm: There is no God but Him, the mighty and wise. By the rightful thing God means the concurrence of the scripts: because the ones to whom had been given the Book got in conflict with the revealed knowledge by arguing. And those who deny God's words written in the Book, God will swiftly call to account.

This inscription is the statement of faith by Abd al-Malik—a typically monarchical, meaning a strictly "one-god"—statement of belief, of the Christian-Arabic Church. But at the same time it was in opposition to the belief system of the Imperial Byzantine Church. Heraclius had his statement of belief in the Trinity installed in his Basilica, the Hagia Sophia in Constantinople. Now, Abd al-Malik put up his statement of faith in his basilica, the Church at the Temple Mount in Jerusalem.

Abd al-Malik was an Arabic Christian, but he was not a caliph and not a member of the Umayyads.

Just the fact that *muhamad* is a gerund and certainly not a name, as has been proven by coin inscriptions and texts, is a discovery that has major consequences.

Muhamad, the praised one is nothing else but the Arabic version of the Greek *Kraestos* and the Latin *Christus*, the *anointed one: Kraestos, Christus, muhamad:* they are all one and the same, namely Jesus.

Muhamad abd-Allah means "the praised servant of God." Reading this expression as "Muhammad is the servant of God" would be as absurd as interpreting the phrase *benetictus qui venit in nomine domini* ("Praised be the one who came in the name of the Lord") as "Benedict, who came in the name of the Lord."

According to Islamic tradition, these inscriptions are verses from the Qur'an. But in fact they are older than all of the known Qur'anic fragments.

The current chapter is actually dedicated to the historic figure of Muhammad but, so far, no information about his person is available. There are no historic traces of him. We absolutely don't know anything about him. But on the other hand, there are libraries full of religious books which elaborate on the subject "the Prophet Muhammad according to traditional reports."

The earliest references to Muhammad were made one hundred fifty years after the mythical year of his death, and the largest number of such references was produced between two hundred and three hundred years after the alleged event. They are all based on oral transmissions. Even when one has to settle for such kind of information instead of proof when dealing with persons who are long gone, oral transmissions with no other but religious background are not sufficient. In the Qur'an, there is basically no mentioning of Muhammad. In addition, there is complete consensus regarding the idea that the Hadiths and the Sira (the Prophet's biography), the latter of which were derived from the Hadiths, are, without question, not authentic sources.

There are numerous archaeological relics from that time period: coins, inscriptions, buildings, literature. But not a single trace or a single remark is found that would at least remotely indicate the existence of a prophet from Mecca called Muhammad. But his army conquers Jerusalem, Heraclius' holy city, right under Heraclius' nose. But Heraclius never had a clue. His successors lose Syria and Egypt to Muhammad and, again, they never noticed that. The same happened to the Iranians and all the others who did not have a clue that all of their lands had been taken away by Muhammad himself or in his name. Moreover, millions and millions of subjugated people belonging to various religions didn't say a word about the Prophet Muhammad, about a person who is said to have completely reshaped all of the ancient Orient, politically and religiously—in just a few years. How is one supposed to explain this?

The personification of Muhammad occurred in the literature of the ninth century for the first time. According to Dr. Abdallah Moussa at the Sorbonne, no references to the term *Muhamad* denoting it as an individual name can be found before the Islamization period. Up to that point, he thinks it is unlikely that the term *Muhamad* was used as a name.

The mentioning of the root MHMD is already found on little clay-tablets from the thirteenth century BC in Ugarit, the ancient city in nowadys Syria. The term *muhamad(un)* referred to the highest purity level of gold. Later, the meaning of this term gradually changed into *chosen, praised*, a connotation which it would keep during the following centuries. The term *Ahmad* was derived from the same root. Consequently, in the Qur'an the terms *muhamad* and *ahmad* are used synonymously.

The first religious manifestation of the title appeared in the east of the Persian Empire, from which the first coins with the *muhamad*-logo were reported. In this region, which today belongs to Turkmenistan and Afghanistan, *muhamad* was known as the "Praised One," the "servant of God" (*abd-Allah*), and the "speaker [messenger] of God" (*kalifat Allah*). There is no sign, not a single trace that would indicate the presence of a *Muhammad* on the Arabian Peninsular during that time.

We can state with great confidence that *muhamad* the "Praised One" was created in the very eastern region of the Persian Empire. And based on an overwhelmingly amount of evidence, the "Praised One" was Jesus. Abd al-Malik brought this *muhamad abd-Allah*, the "praised servant of God" with him to the western territories in his empire where he built a monument for him in Jerusalem at the Temple Mount. That is the place to which he is supposed to come back as *mahdi*, the Savior, on the Day of Judgment. There are numerous coins on which this scene is depicted (for more information see chapter 7).

"Muhamad" was a title before it became a name, as is also reflected in the Islamic scripts. According to Ibn Saad[30], the original name of the Prophet was Qutham. Later, he had six additional epithets: Muhamad (*the Praised One*), Ahmed (*the Praised One*), Kahtim (*the Seal*), Hashir (*the Enlightener*), Akib (*the Last Prophet*), and Makhiy (the *Forgiver of Sins*). This clearly represents a title concept. In 1869, Aloys Sprenger already pointed out, [31] "In these traditions, the term *muhammad* appears in the nature of the other titles, as an epithet of the Prophet but not as an individual name."

---

30 Ibn Saad (AD ?–845), *"Kitab al-tabarakat al- kabir"*
31 Aloys Sprenger, *Das Leben und die Lehre des Mohammad nach bisher grösstentheils unbenutzten Quellen Vol. I-III* (Reprint of the 1923 original. Charleston:,Nabu Press, 2011).

According to Volker Popp, the *Paraclete* of the New Testament is also characterized by the attribute concept. The term *Paraclete* is derived from the Greek *Parakletos* ("called to help," "helper") and denotes the *Comforter* or *Consoler*. Jesus repeatedly promised a Paraclete to his disciples as a comfort to them for the time period of his temporary absence. In Jesus's native language, which is Aramaic, the term for Paraclete is *mhamda*. In having the same consonant roots MHMD, the Aramaic *mhamda* can easily be read as *muhamad* in Arabic, fits as such easily in the Gospels, and could be understood as a prophecy. Just replace *mhamda* with *muhamad*:

John 14:16. "...and He (my Father) will send to you another *muhamad*...."

14:26. "But the spirit, the *muhamad*, which will be sent by my Father in my name, will teach you all things...."

John 16:13. "...It is good that I go because if I don't go the *muhamad* will not come to you. But as soon as I am gone I will send you the *muhamad*."

Despite the fact that in Christian theology the term Paraclete refers to the Holy Spirit, the transformation from *mhamda* to *Muhamad* is a small one and can easily take place in a heretic milieu. There was a great potential for a process like this to happen in a time period that was characterized by the longing for the predicted Arabic prophet.

One of these prophecies we find also in the Qur'an, when Jesus, son of Mary, in Sura 61:6, says: "O children of Israel, indeed I am the messenger of Allah to you confirming what came before me of the Torah and bringing good tidings of a messenger to come after me, whose name is Ahmad."

Ahmad comes from the same MHMD root; *mhamda* (Aramaic), *muhamad* (Arabic), or *ahmad* (Arabic) mean the same thing: muhamad the "praised one".

The question regarding the historic figure of the Prophet *Muhamad* has been answered of its own account by taking the *muhamad*-detour. The Hadiths, as well as the Prophet's biography which was derived from them, disqualify as historic sources to prove Muhammad. And, among the scientific community there is, in general, consensus about it. The Qur'an says next to nothing about the Prophet. But to go ahead anyway and consider the Qur'an as proof of the Prophet's existence can only be regarded as sheer mockery of science, logic, and methodology.

There are no nonreligious sources for Muhammad. And this feature is supposed to be considered plausible regarding a personality who is said to have completely overturned, recreated, reshaped, and remodeled the political and religious landscapes of half of the ancient world, and all of that in just a few years? Not a single person among the millions and millions of contemporary witnesses would talk about it? How is one supposed to imagine this? In order to believe such a thing, just as some Islamic historians do with such matter-of-factness, truly takes a miracle. And we are back to the quality of Hadiths.

We have no evidence regarding the existence of a prophet called Muhammad who allegedly lived from AD 570 to 632 (or so) and who is said to have preached the Qur'an. But in contrast, there is a lot of evidence that proves the muhamad-Jesus concept.

There might have been well a religious figure, maybe a preacher, who lived in the Arabic desert. But his name was certainly not Muhammad and his vita did not even remotely correspond to the anecdotal-biography of the Prophet. It seems possible that he might have left us his handwriting in the Medinan Suras but that would not provide us with any knowledge about this person. There might as well have been a team or even a religious sect behind the label "Muhammad."

The denying of the physical existence of the Prophet Muhammad might come as a shock. But the shock subsides quickly when one takes a closer look at the history of the origin of the Qur'an: the idea that a single person was the exclusive source has to be written off.

There is no doubt that the story of the Qur'an is a long and complex one, and that it therefore has "many architects."

It is certainly impossible to prove the nonexistence of a person. But it is, however, possible to verify the information that exists about a person. And, for Muhammad, the attempt at verification has failed. Up to this day, we still have nothing, not a single proof in our hands, as scientists like Weil, Goldziher, Blachere, Luxenberg, and others have demonstrated. Beyond the religiously motivated assumptions, there is not even the slightest trace of a real-world Prophet in sight.

This is not about bringing down a prophet, but rather about untangling the cluster of Jewish, Christian, and Islamic ideas, or simply: the Semitic concept regarding a rescuer, savior, redeemer, judge, or prophet. It is always about the same package of expectations—only wrapped in different names and traditions.

The person "Muhammad" is not essential for the development or emergence of either the book or the teachings. Many Muslims, (very) old and young ones, agree on that. The formation of Islam is first of all a process-related but not a person-related event, even if the configuration of a religion seems to require the involvement of persons who could function as messengers and identification figures.

After going through a long and twisted endeavor, the longing that the Arabic Christians had for a script of their own eventually led to the development of the Qur'an. Simultaneously, the transformation from *muhamad* to *Muhammad* took place. The occurrence of Muhammad was a necessity in order to justify their own revelations—finally they had revelations of their own. And after all, their own Arab Prophet from the House of Abraham had been predicted anyway—he was promised from the highest authority. The whole complex of traditions was more and more transferred to the Arabian Desert, until Muhammad, the Prophet of the Arabs from the Quraysh tribe was born—two hundred years after his "birth."

❖ ❖ ❖

Excursus:

The Church at the Temple Mount

On a rock plateau of around three hundred by four hundred fifty meters that lies to the east of the old city of Jerusalem, there are a few buildings, the al-Aqsa mosque, and the Dome of the Rock. But most of the plateau is vacant. Back in the seventh century, this area was just a rubble field: remains of the Temple of Herodias, remains of a Jupiter Temple, and remains of the history of one thousand years of religious activities. Despite its inhospitable appearance, this area is tied to religious emotions like hardly any other place: they say that this is the place where Abraham was ready to sacrifice his own son, and it is the site of the Temple of Salomon.

Based on the information in the inscription, the "Dome of the Rock" was finished in the year 72 of the Arabic calendar: "this holy monument was built in the year 72 by God's servant, the Imam al-Mamun, the Highest Protection Provider. May God accept it and may it please Him, Amen. You Kings of the world, praise God."

According to the timetable that was commonly used, the time according to the Arabs, *kata Arabas*, the year 72 corresponds to the year AD 694. But other dates have also been mentioned as the conversion from the solar to the Hijra-lunar calendar resulted in inconsistencies.

There is total agreement about the fact that Mamun did not build the monument. He just had the name of the true creator, Abd al-Malik, removed and replaced by his own name over a hundred years after al-Malik. But he kept the year of 694. There is no doubt: Abd al-Malik was the creator of the building, and this project was finished in AD 694.

Dymon Lynch

The Dome oft the Rock is built on the supposed place oft the temple of King Salomon over the rock, where Abraham was about to sacrifice Isaac, accoring to legend. In the 11th century the rock became in Muslim tradition the place, from where Muhammad ascended to heaven on his horse Buraq

The choice of the site had an obvious meaning: it was the location of the Temple of Salomon. Its architectural style was of the typical Syrian-Byzantine church design. One of the basic features of this design is a cylinder that rests on pillars. It either is a one-story construction or, depending on the height of the building, has an additional colonnade. The cylinder is covered by a cupola. Further structures were added as needed. The cylinder of the Dome of the Rock encloses a rock formation which is said to be the place of Isaac's sacrifice. Two sets of colonnades are arranged in an octagonal way around this site. The pillars used had been built in various ancient styles and are even of differing lengths. From that it becomes clear that materials were reused that had been parts of former buildings and ruins. Originally, this building was most likely of an open structure style. The believers came together on large areas that surrounded the building and from there they were able to follow the ceremonies inside. Apparently, it was necessary to provide those large areas, as they were needed for the supposedly large number of people participating in the annual pilgrimages.

The Dome was not built in a new architectural style and it shows affinities to numerous earlier versions of the same architectural style: for instance, the Chapel of Ascension at the Mount Olives in Jerusalem, the Maria Theotokos Church at Mount Gerizim near Nablus, the Church of the Seat of Mary-Kathisma (which was also built enclosing a rock) which is located about half way between Jerusalem and Bethlehem. Other examples are churches in Bosra and Syria, and in the cities of Caesarea at the Mediterranean coast and Capernaum at Lake Genezareth. The church near Capernaum is said to be at the site of the home of Saint Peter. This architectural church style was found throughout a large area that even extended to Italy (San Vitale in Ravenna) and Spain (Las Vegas de Pueblanueva). The church of Saints Sergios and Bakchos in Istanbul ("Little Hagia Sophia"), which is said to have been used as a model for the great Hagia Sophia, is basically of the same style. It is obvious that this architectural style was very common throughout the Roman-Byzantine world. All of these churches were built during the third to the sixth centuries. They are all characterized by both the same architectural elements and the same basic octagonal shape—just like the Dome of the Rock.

The octagonal shape is derived from religious numerology and symbolizes the resurrection of Jesus after the Day of Sabbath. It therefore represents the eighth creation day which completed the Creation. For that reason, the number eight stood for the theological idea of "Completion" during the medieval period. The believers were on the path to "Completion" with this symbol by their side. It is precisely this same type of octagonal outline in combination with a cupola covering the cylinder which characterizes the Palace Chapel of Aachen ("Pfalzkapelle"), Germany, built by Karl the Great in AD 790. Both al-Malik and Karl the Great were Christian leaders of the Early Middle Ages who viewed themselves as successors of David and representations of Christ. For geographical reasons, it was probably easier for the architect of Karl's Palace Chapel to just travel to Italy in order to study the church of San Vitale in Ravenna, which is of the same style as the Dome of the Rock. However, the fact that he created his church as "the Image of the Heavenly Jerusalem" strongly suggests that he was most likely familiar with the original Dome of the Rock.

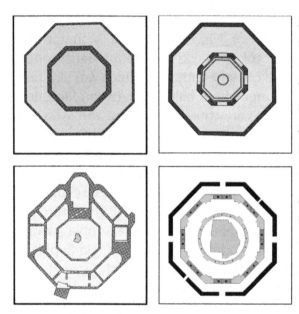

Floorplan of a church near Capernaum said to be built at the site of the home of Saint Peter (2nd/3rd century), left

Chapel of Ascension at the Mount Olives in Jerusalem (4th century)

The Church of the Seat of Mary-Kathisma which was also built enclosing a rock (5th century), left

Floorplan of the Dome of the Rock (7th century)

According to Islamic tradition, it was the Islamic caliph of the Umayyads al-Malik who built the Dome of the Rock as a mosque. Latest research results, however, show that al-Malik was a Christian-Arabic ruler and that consequently, the Dome of the Rock was a Christian sacred building. Oleg Grabar,[32] who is one of the most renowned experts on the Dome of the Rock, rejects the idea that the Dome could have been built as a mosque but rather as "some kind of a sacred building." He refers to it as a "paradox" because the interpretation that the Dome of Rocks represents an Islamic building is too contradicting to him. The contradictions dissolve at once, if the Dome is interpreted as a Christian building.

---

32   Oleg Grabar, *The Dome of the Rock* (Harvard: Belknap Press, 2006).

Jerusalem has been a city of churches for a very long time, back then as much as it is now. But in the eyes of al-Malik, who viewed himself as the representation of the true tradition of Zion, the churches of earlier time periods were the ones of the "wrong-believers." Therefore, he saw it as his duty to build a monumental statement of the rightful belief, a *haram*, located at *the* place—at the Temple. There, he put up his message, his idea of the rightful belief—it is his answer to the *ekthesis*, which is the statement of belief in the Trinity of the Byzantine Imperial Church located in the Hagia Sophia. Although in Islamic tradition this statement is interpreted as Verses of the Qur'an, to modern scientists the testimonial on the 240-meter-band that wraps around both sides of the Octagon is a clear monarchical declaration of a strict monotheistic Christian-Arabic belief.

The level of importance of the *haram* at the Temple Mount decreased with the developing of Islam, and soon the Temple's significance would lag behind the ones of Mecca and Medina. Despite that, Islamic legends emerged that included ties to Jerusalem. In the eleventh century only, the tradition evolved that Muhammad ascended to the heavens from the rock under the cupola on his horse Buraq, the white horse that had a woman's head, and wings. Probably during the same time period, meaning the eleventh century, the *haram* got the obligatory *mihrab*, which in this case was a plate, that shows the direction to Mecca. The *mihrab*, however, was not attached to the hall but it was put up in a cave located in the rock formation below. So far, no plausible explanation for that has been provided.

To the Crusaders, this building was simply *templum domini*, the "Temple of The Lord," which meant a connection with the Old Testament legacy and also denoted a place where Jesus practiced. They (the crusaders) did not consider the Dome to be a mosque but they assumed that it was the original temple of the time of Christ. The Crusaders were not so much interested in it because the other Rock of Jerusalem, the Church of the Holy Sepulcher at Golgotha, was of more importance.

It was in the time period of the Ayyubids (thirteenth century), who replaced the Crusaders, when the Dome of the Rock became an Islamic holy site. The time periods of the Mamluks followed, during which, however, hardly any changes were made. A few renovations were carried out only when absolutely necessary but no changes were made on the structure of the building. During the Mamluks' time, people were of the opinion that the Crusaders had built the Dome. According to legend, the rock underneath the Dome hovered in mid-air and in order to tame the rock the Crusaders built the Dome. During the Ottoman time, namely under Suleyman the Magnificent (regency 1520–1566), extensive reconstructions were carried out. He, for instance, completely changed the outer facade and covered it with tiles. Many repairs were done on the interior as well, but there the original substance was kept. No works at all were done on it during 1875 to 1959. During the years 1959 to 1962, all of the tiles that had been put up during the Ottoman time were removed and replaced with new ones. In 1990, another renovation was carried out.

The Dome of the Rock as we see it is a creation of the twentieth century. We don't know how much of today's version corresponds to its original appearance. Most likely, there is only little resemblance. However, its core structure has never been changed. Up to this day, this represents the only part that still appears exactly the way it was during Malik's time: with mosaic-covered arches that function as support for the cupola and the octagon with the original script band—the statement of belief of Abd al-Malik.

It is obvious that the Dome was certainly not built as a mosque but as a church. However, it was not meant to be a church for day-to-day-life religious activities either. The Dome of the Rock symbolizes a central point of the Christian-Arabic religious tradition as it was built on the place to which the Savior is expected to descend. Numerous coins from al-Malik's time have been found displaying Jesus at the Day of Judgment, indicating that this expectation was of central importance in the minds of the people.

Even during time periods of Islamic rule, the Dome was not perceived as an active mosque. Garnished with many mysteries and myths, the *Haram al-Sharif* was first of all seen as the place where Muhammad ascended to the heavens. The al-Aqsa mosque located across from it was the building commonly used for prayers. Up to recent times, tourists were shown the true location of Jesus' cradle—which is located in the southeastern area of the place—and were told about the secrets of the Biblical and Christian history of this site. But that has now been put to an end. About one decade ago, the Dome of the Rock was turned into something that it had never been in its whole history: an actively operated mosque. And it has become the symbol of the Palestinian nationalism.

❖ ❖ ❖

The Metamorphosis:

From Jesus to Muhammad

It is ink that flows through the veins of the Prophet—and it also contains the ink of Western "Orientalists."
—Karl-Heinz Ohlig, Professor of Religious Studies

The history of the Middle East during the first half of the post-Christian Millennium was characterized by the permanent conflict between the Persian and Byzantine Empires. Some fights were settled on the battlefield directly between these two powers but in general, the conflicts were carried out by proxy wars, as both empires maintained a network of Arab allies who kept changing sides.

Nowadays, the term *Arabia* refers to the Arabian Peninsula. During ancient and medieval times, however, this term denoted a different geographic region: in general, Arabia referred to the region that included Syria, Palestine, and Mesopotamia. But "Arabia" did not involve the Arabian Peninsula except the northwestern part which belonged to the Nabataean Kingdom. Politically and religiously, ancient Arabia was like a pressure cooker. It is no coincidence that three of the five world religions evolved here. Jews, as well as Greek, Babylonian, and Asian pagans, Melkites, Jacobins, Syrian, Egyptian, Greek Christians, Catholics, Nestorians, Zoroastrians, Manichaeans, Gnostics, and many more were competing with each other. Practically on a daily basis another messenger, a new Messiah, an additional salvation preacher, and/or a new prophet was spotted. People were always expecting the apocalypse to be near; the end of the world was always thought to be just around the corner. And they were always busy trying to be prepared for it.

Each individual religious branch had its own religious texts which were discussed, argued over, attacked, and defended. The discussions about the "true teachings" were especially fierce between individual

Christian groups. Among them, the central issue was the question regarding the true nature of Jesus. Besides discussions that were carried out in sophisticated Greek-philosophical styles, some discussions turned into big brawls, whereby even noble Church seniors used their fists or sticks in order to win the arguments about true teachings.[33]

To the Monophysites, Jesus only had one nature, a divine one. Others, like the Dyophysites (from Greek, *dyo* = two), believed that Jesus was son of God and was both human and divine in nature, whereas the Monarchian Christians viewed Jesus as a messenger of God who was just a human after all. Those were the questions with which people in the Middle East were dealing for centuries. And they were doing so at a level of intensity that might be incomprehensible to people today. But according to their understanding, the fate of their souls was at stake. The return of the Messiah was expected at any minute, and with flaming sword in his hand he would hold court over them. Life was overshadowed by a doomsday atmosphere. At several councils these questions were fiercely discussed. Namely in the Council of Nikaea in AD 375 and Council of Chalkedon in AD 451, the Trinity teaching was adopted as the official dogma. Consequently, it meant the separation of the Arabic Christians from the Byzantine and Roman Christian mainstream.   *greek?*

But a certain type of spatial separation had already taken place earlier.

In the ancient Orient, it was common practice of war to kill or deport a defeated people. Survivors of both battles and massacres were deported to various provinces and forced into labor. The well-known story of the deportation of the Israelites to Babylon by Nebuchadnezzar comes to mind. And there were other such events: at the end of each of the three big wars by Shapur I (regency AD 242–272), huge waves of deportations of the local populations in nowadays Syria and Iraq took place; in one of them the Bishop of

---

33   For example at the council of Ephesus (AD 431), known as the "Robber Synod," gangs of thugs were hired to win the argument concerning which teachings were true.

Antioch with his whole community at the Syrian Mediterranean coast were deported to the Iranian Province of Khuzestan and forced into building the newly founded city of Gundishapur. The population of the northern Mesopotamian metropolitan area of Hatra, located between the Euphrates and Tigris rivers, shared the same fate.[34]The inhabitants of this area, which is called *Djasira* ("island"), were known as *Arabi*, which means "the ones who live in the west," and referred to people in the regions located west of the Tigris river. In this context, the term *Arabs* was manifested, but it didn't have much to do with today's meaning of this expression.

The language of the Arabi was Syro-Aramaic. They were Christians and had their own Holy Books, among others the "Peshitta" (Syrian Bible) and the "Diatessaron" (Gospels) which had probably been written in Djasira. It can be assumed with great confidence that they took their Holy Books with them into the Persian Diaspora. Another set of deportations was carried out by Chosroes I (AD 531–579). One of the deportations, which took place in AD 540, resulted in the relocation of the whole population of Antioch to the provinces in the east where Chosroes forced them to build the city of *Veh-Antiokh-i-Chosroes* ("the better Antioch of Chosroes"). But the deported ones carried on with their religious life in Persia.

In the seventh century, the conflicts between Persia and Byzantine turned into clashes that were religious in nature. In AD 613, Persia carried out another incursion, advancing west. Chosroes II (AD 590–628) occupied Syria and conquered Jerusalem in AD 614. He purposely destroyed the Church of the Holy Sepulcher and took the relic of the Holy Cross with him as a trophy. In AD 619 he conquered Egypt. But in the eyes of Heraclius he had gone too far. Byzantium was unwilling to tolerate these actions and, therefore, Emperor Heraclius marched with his army to Persia. Under his personal command—an absolute rarity in the history of the late antiquity—a battle in Armenia (today East Anatolia) was fought in AD 622 which resulted in the defeat of the Persian army. In the following year, Heraclius captured the city of

---

34 Those gaps were often filled by forcefully relocating people from Greece and the Balkans.

Ganjak and took revenge for Jerusalem by destroying the local Fire Temple. The battle of Nineveh in AD 627 eventually led to the total and triumphant victory of the Byzantine Empire.

But Chosroes remained unwilling to consider peace and, hence, was assassinated by his own people. His son Siroes made peace with Byzantine. As a result of the "compensation" agreements, the Byzantine Emperor was nominally given back his former Arabic territories. Those were regions which he had actually never really controlled. But in the process of a complete restructuring of the Byzantine Empire, Heraclius had already decided on giving up Syria and Mesopotamia and just keeping control over of the harbors and some cities. His absolute priority was the consolidation of the central areas of his empire as its western territories were fighting for survival. As early as AD 618, Heraclius, a native-born North African, had considered giving up Constantinople as his capital and using Sicily as his governing residence instead. His mind was changed by the uprising of the people and a disagreeing Church. The Church, however, had to pay now for his war campaigns, which he successfully completed in AD 628. He even topped his victory by personally performing the ceremonious return of the Holy Cross relic to Jerusalem in AD 630.

This war campaign, however, was not of the usual kind—it was the first Crusade in history, the fight of Christians versus Fire Worshippers. Despite some religious differences, the Arabi sympathized with Heraclius and even marshaled significant numbers of troops. Several verified reports prove that, among the public back then, comparisons were made with Chosroes, who was viewed as an Old Testament-type pharaoh who had deported the children of Ishmael, who were later brought back home.[35] Therefore, the Persian Christians regarded Heraclius as their natural ally. After her defeat, the Persian Empire fell apart into principalities. The Arabi principality, which consisted of several emirates, was one of them.

On one side, the authority of Persia as a dominant power had been shattered; on the other hand, by the death of Heraclius in AD 641, the

---

35 In the Qur'an, the Persian King is also erroneously called *Pharaoh*.

arrangement with Arab allies that had resulted in the glorious victory ended. The Arab emirs held the power in Persia now. And they were all Christians, as corroborated by numerous archaeological findings: coins have been found which often show the images of the Arab emirs in connection with symbols that show Christian motifs.

The Persian hegemony in Mesopotamia, Syria, and Egypt had been backed by local vassals. Although the defeat inflicted by the Byzantine Emperor destroyed both the Persian Empire as a powerhouse and the Sassanid Dynasty, the Arab emirs all across from Chorasan to Egypt were unaffected and even strengthened by this event. Byzantine just kept the harbors to ensure their power on sea and a small number of religiously important places like Jerusalem and Damascus. In addition, they signed contracts with local rulers that corresponded to the so-called *foederati* vassal-treaties. Heraclius also tried to come to a theological agreement with the East but all of his compromising suggestions were rejected. The *ekthesis,* the statement of belief in the Hagia Sophia in Constantinople, had even caused uprisings in northern Africa. Attempts by Heraclius" successor, Constans II, to smooth things over by removing the ekthesis from the Hagia Sophia in AD 646, were unsuccessful.

Practically from one day to the next, the Arab emirs became their own bosses. Suddenly, they were part of a superpower—though not a centrally organized one—and they had achieved it without having to go to war themselves. It came as no surprise that the Christians in Egypt or Syria were quite cooperative: finally, they didn't have to deal with Fire Worshippers or representatives of the detested Imperial Church anymore, but were now dealing with people who shared their religion. Suddenly, a region stretching from Egypt all across to Persia's east was dominated by Arabs. Miraculously, they had been freed from the power grips of Byzantine and Persia. The Antichrist was defeated, the end of the world was postponed, and a new era had begun, which would culminate in the reappearance of Christ. That's how the year AD 622 became the most important date in the early history of Arabia. The year in which the Christians defeated the Fire Worshippers and, consequently, gave way to the rise of the Arabs, was considered to be of such magnitude that it was used to start a new calendar. The fact that the Byzantine tax year was maintained anyway would prove to become a very useful scientific tool.

. According to Islamic tradition, an Arabic prophet called Muhammad fled from the city of Mecca to Medina in AD 622. And this date marked the beginning of a new Islamic calendar which, however, was a lunar calendar. But, no one used this lunar calendar back then. The solar calendar "after the time of the Arabs" had been kept and no one mentioned either the name of the prophet or his new religion. According to Islamic tradition, Muhammad sent a letter to Emperor Heraclius in which he called on the emperor to convert to Islam. There is no mentioning about this invitation in Byzantine sources. And that is not surprising: we can assume with great confidence that Heraclius never heard of any founder of a new religion who is said to have conquered half of his empire and allegedly captured his holy sites during his lifetime. Heraclius' writers and the people who would have been affected would certainly have told us about it.

The collapse and retreat of the main powers were followed by unsettling times which were characterized by fights for position among the emirs. Islamic historians have built up these internal skirmishes by the emirs to maintain their positions as glorious, centrally directed Muslim wars of conquest. In historical documents, however, no information about a so-called Muslim victory at Gabitha has ever been discovered. The same applies to the "great decisive battle" of Muslims versus the Byzantine Empire at the Jordan River (Yarmuk): no evidence that it ever took place has been found. In AD 639, which means during Heraclius' lifetime (!), Muhammad's desert fighters allegedly captured Damascus—again, there is not a single piece of historical evidence. According to Islamic tradition, Amr ibn As allegedly invaded Cairo in AD 640 by personally leading a Muslim army carrying the green flag of the Prophet—and again, contemporary history sources remain silent. On the other hand, however, there is an inscription at a bridge in Fustat (old Cairo) from the year AD 690 by Abd al-Malik's brother, Aziz, emir in Fustat, which ends by saying "Amen."

Maavia was the first who took advantage of the chance to create a new superpower that included Persia and former Byzantine Arabic estates. His goal was no less than the creation of a new version of the Persian Empire that included the Arabs. Consequently, the battle between the Sassanid Dynasty and Byzantine had to be restarted.

In AD 662, Emperor Constans II left the capital city Byzantium. Not only had he fallen out with all of the Christian branches in the east, but to make matters worse, his imperial views were called heretical by Maximus the Confessor, who was the most prominent theologian of that time. His remarks, however, came at a high price: Maximus was sent into exile to Crimea for the rest of his life. Constans II's moving to Syracuse, Sicily, led to the neglect of the eastern provinces.

In the same year of AD 662, Maavia was elected as *Amir al-Mu'minin* in Darabjerd, southern Iran. Under this title, he would soon become the ruler of Persia and the eastern regions of the former Byzantine Empire. Following Persian traditions, he started war campaigns against the West in AD 663. Maavia's residence was Damascus, the place where the most important holy site and central point of the pilgrimages of that time was located: the Basilica of St. John with the head of St. John the Baptist. We already know about the most important inscription that was created by Maavia. We also know that it was written in Greek and that it was inscribed on a stone located in Gadara, Israel. We know that it begins with the sign of the cross and that it gives Maavia's title: *Amir al-Mu'minin*. It is the exact same title that was found in Persia in the Persian language. As we already know, the title means "Commander of the Protection Providers." The commonly translated version as "Leader of the Believers," whereby the term "believers" is solely interpreted as referring to Muslims, lacks any basis. Originally, Maavia was an ally and feudal lord of the emperor but became a traitor because, being a friend of Byzantine, he would have lost his support in the Persian part of his empire. Maavia had coins minted in Palestine, too. Those coins display figures that hold the orb with the cross in their hands.

Under the name Muawiyya, Maavia represents one of the few persons about whom historic evidence has been found among the people mentioned in the colorful world of Islamic traditions. There is no scientific clarification about his origins but Islamic historians know better: Muawiyya was born in AD 603 in Mecca as a member of the Umayyad clan of the Quraysh tribe. In AD 630 he converted to Islam and served as the Prophet's secretary. Then he was appointed caliph of Medina and later, in AD 639, he was named governor of Damascus by Caliph Umar. Under his command, the enemies of Islam were defeated in several victorious battles, for which he was rewarded with a caliphate. And that is the exact same caliphate of the "legitimate caliph" Ali, the dispute over which led to the separation of the Shi'a.

The facts: The weak spot of the Persians had been naval warfare. For that reason, they were already doomed to failure at Constantinople, just like they had been earlier at Athens. In ruling over Egypt and the coastal areas of Syria, Maavia now had the possibility to put a fleet into action. After step-by-step capturing of individual islands located along a path to Constantinople, he established a fleet base close to the Byzantine capital in 672 AD. When he started a war campaign in AD 674, he suffered a devastating defeat right in front of the city walls. Despite the fact that this war campaign ended in a disaster, in Islamic tradition their "Caliph Muawiyya" made the Byzantine Empire tributary to Muslims. But the absolute opposite is true. Maavia had to pay a price for the peace with the Byzantine Empire and agreed to an annual tribute of three thousand gold coins, as well as slaves and horses. As a result of the defeat, he lost power in the eastern regions; he kept a few provinces in the west but his influence became meaningless. Nothing is known about his final days (but here, again, Islamic tradition has loads of details).

According to Muslim tradition, the Aramean Maavia was "Caliph Muawiyya" from the desert of southern Arabia. But in reality he was an Arabic Christian from the Persian-Hellenic cultural environment.

One of Maavia's successors, Abd al-Malik, originally came from Marw in the eastern Persian province of Chorasmia (today's Turkmenistan).

Coin inscriptions prove that he came to power in AD 681, but he must have been an important protagonist in the east earlier already. Malik's ruling focus was on internal consolidation. Therefore, the renewal of the tributary arrangements with Byzantium included a higher rate. Malik's ambition was to stand up to the emperor on religious terms, a decision which might have been either due to religious conviction or due to the lack of military options. His period in office was rather peaceful and it was during his time in power that the so-called *Muhammadism* flourished.

In Sassanid tradition, coins always symbolized the ideology of the ruler. In the case of Abd al-Malik it was the *muhamad*, the "Praised One." Beginning with the year AD 670, coins from Persia having the *muhamad*-logo surfaced. These coins showed additional Christian symbols and further terms like *abd Allah* (God's servant) or *nam* (blessed). There is no doubt that the term *muhamad* did not refer to a person but that it was used to denote a title. In his inscription that he put up in his holy site in Jerusalem, the "Dome of the Rock," Abd al-Malik himself clearly stated who *muhamad* was: Isa bin Maryam—Jesus, the son of Mary.

The Byzantine Emperor was the highest authority of the Imperial Church and his holy site was the Hagia Sophia. But Abd a-Malik, who was the highest authority of his Arabic Church, didn't have any such monumental sacred building. Time was running out, as the end of the world with the return of Messiah was expected to happen at the turn of the year AD 699/700. Al-Malik wanted to await the Messiah's return in a new Basilica located at the site where the old Temple of Salomon in Jerusalem used to be. He started the construction project "Dome of the Rock," which he finished in AD 694. This building, which is distinguished by a basic octagonal structure with Christian symbolic character,[36] was undoubtedly built as a Christian Holy Shrine. (The assumption that Karl the Great in Germany copied a Muslim mosque when he built his Palace Church in Aachen ["Pfalzkapelle"] in AD 790 with identical structures doesn't seem to be very realistic.)

---

36 See Chapter 6.

Heraclius put up his Trinity statement of belief in the innermost area of the Hagia Sophia. Now al-Malik perpetuated his belief statement by putting it up in his church, built at the site of the Temple (for complete inscription text, please see chapter 6):

> There is no God but God alone, He has no associate.
> Praise be upon God's servant and his messenger.
> Jesus Christ, son of Mary, is the messenger of God.
> So believe in God and His messenger, and say not "Three."

This declaration represents a purely Christian pre-Nicaean statement (corresponding to the theological standard prior to the first council of Nicaea). Abd al-Malik rejects the Trinity idea ("and say not Three"); he sees Jesus as the *muhamad rasul*, the Praised Prophet, but not as the son of God. On one of al-Malik's coins, the basic religious idea of his Church at the site of the old Salomon Temple is emphasized: the coin displays the seven-branched chandelier and the inscription "There is only one God" (*La ilaha illa 'lah*). He viewed himself as the renewer of Zion in the true tradition of David. This tradition was later also kept in Islam but David was fitted up with the all-purpose title "Prophet." In addition, the seven branches of the chandelier were trimmed down to five branches (from prime number seven to prime number five), probably with the intent to create a detachment from the Jewish complex.

When Abd al-Malik left the eastern region of his empire and moved west to Jerusalem, so did the *muhamad*-motto that had previously been deported to the east together with the *Arabi*. In the following time periods, the *muhamad*-motto would appear on mints in Syria and Palestine. In addition, the *muhamad*-concept was easily spread throughout northern Africa but seemed to have a hard time in Egypt under the influence of the Coptic Church. The "Muhammadism" in the sense of the *Praised One* (Jesus) was the defining characteristic of Malik's time. Its followers became known as *Muhammadans,* which, back then, did not denote what is known as *Muslim* today.

Abd al-Malik's coins are especially used as proof by the traditional interpreters that he was an Islamic caliph. The usage of the term *muhamad* is seen as clear evidence that he meant the Prophet. In addition, the commonly displayed image of a figure holding a sword ("standing caliph") and the inscription *khalifat Allah* are considered as the portrayal of the caliph in office. There is a large number of such "standing caliphs." These images represent standardized portrayals and only occasionally the ruler's name is given, whereas the (word-) root MHMD or, when it is spelled out, *muhamad(un),* is found frequently. As a rule, the figure holds a disproportionally big sword in his hand, the sword of justice. In some portrayals it can be clearly identified as the flaming sword. In reality, the "standing caliph" is the "Praised One," namely Jesus. The image reflects the idea of the role Jesus had during that time: the eschatological Jesus who would soon return as the messenger of God (*khalifat Allah*) in order to hold the Day of Judgment.

According to some interpreters, there is a "ladder" shown on some of Malik's coins. The same image, together with the sign of the Byzantine cross, is found on Byzantine coins. Malik's coins lack the sign of the cross; sometimes it is replaced by a ball or a circle. The traditional interpretation explains that Malik, as an Islamic ruler, had these signs of the cross erased. In more recent interpretations, however, it is said that leaving out the Byzantine cross was part of the ideological dispute with Byzantium but also indicated the spiritual return to old Semitic traditions of aniconic stone idols. It is seen rather as debyzantinisation than dechristianisation. The cross was *the* symbol of Christendom in the west, but not in the east. The "ladder" symbolizes the *Yegar Sahadutha,* which is the stone pyramid of Jacob's legend in the Old Testament. It is the ladder that leads to the Holiest. Malik's coins that were circulated in the western territories of his empire (northern Africa) also showed the *Yegar Sahadutha* together with his antitrinitarian program in Latin: *In nomine domini non deus nisi deus solus non est alius* (In the name of the Lord, There is no God but God alone, He has no associate).

"Standing Caliph"
There are numerous coins with this motif. Traditionally, it is interpreted to represent a Caliph or even Muhammad himself. In reality, however, this figure displays the eschatological Jesus holding the sword of justice, whose return was expected in the turn oft he century (i.e.700). This image always follows the same principle

The figure with the „muhamad"-motto of the „Praised One". Minting place Harran

Coin from the year 696 A.D. in Persian tradition. The front of the coin (not shown) shows the portrait of the ruler, the back shows Jesus holding the flaming sword and the inscription "Messenger of God"

Standing Caliph from Edessa, today Urfa, Turkey

Arabic gold coin, showing Jesus with the flaming sword

The enlargement of an another gold coin of this type (around 700) issued by Abd al-Malik shows clearly the flame structure of the sword of the eschatological Jesus

The question arises of why titles were used (muhamad, abd Allah, etc.) over and over again, but the one they were talking about was rarely named. It has to do with the reverence of that time, which was shown by avoiding the careless mentioning of holy names. Such behavior was demanded as a sign of respect for holy figures. This way of thinking had already been known from the Old Testament, where God never could be addressed by name. The Nabataeans wouldn't even mention the name of their highest God but only referred to the title of *Dusares*.

Similarly, *Christ*, the term commonly used today to refer to Jesus, is a title describing who Jesus is believed to have been—the "*Christus*" ("the Anointed One").

Worldly rulers of that time also preferred the use of titles for themselves but took titles far below their actual status. In AD 629, Heraclius gave up his title of "autocrator" and exchanged it with the modest title of "basileus" (king). Justinian II even adopted *servus Christi* (God's servant) as his main title, just as Maavia and Abd al-Malik did: *Abd Allah*...God's servant. A number of rulers were known only by their titles, expressed by their spiritual mottos, and not by their names.[37]

And after all, the coins of the Umayyads displayed a large number of the most common Christian symbols: fish, cross sign, palm tree, agnus dei ("God's lamb"),[38] and the Old Testament's stone pyramid. A large number of unmistakably Christian coins have been found from time periods and regions that, according to traditional interpretations, are supposed to have been Islamic for a long time already. Though there might be a number of different reasons that this could be so, the one that seems most likely is that the producers of the coins were Christians. It is impossible for Muslims to have been present because of the great importance that coins mean in terms of demonstration of power and ideology—much too important than to give subjugated subjects the minting rights, literally for hundreds of years. It is incredible to see how numismatists in the past tried to make their interpretations match the idea of the religious history instead of trying to adjust the interpretation of the religious history to the facts. The results are often entertaining, twisted stories.

---

37 Maavia was not the real name of the ruler. *Maavia* means "the Picture of Misery" or "the Lamenter" and denoted a person who had characteristics that were highly valued in a devout Christian—a person who was moved to weep over religious acts such as an "unjustified" crucifixion.

38 In a traditional coin description the *agnus dei*, perfectly known to scientists and believers, is called "four-legged animal."

Syrian coin showing the archetypical-Christian symbol of a fish with an extended muhamad-motto „Praised be the Disciple of God" on the back side

Ruler carries a vessel containing the relic of the head of Baptist St. John. On the back of the coin, instead of the commonly shown sign of the cross, there is the Christian-Arabic symbol of palm tree above the declared value. It stands for the birth of Jesus under a palm tree

Figure in Byzantine tradition with the sign of the cross and the inscription Amman. On the back it shows the declared value M (=40 Nummia) with the inscription "muhamad" (meaning "the praised one")

Ruler holding the orb with cross, backside the cross over the denomination

All figured coins are from the time period of the "Umayyads", according to tradition Muslim caliphs. Most of the "Ummayad" – coins display Christian symbols

No relics or documents of the seventh or eighth century, neither Islamic nor non-Islamic, have been found that mention Muslims or Islam in the sense of a new religion in Arabia. But according to Islamic tradition, all of the ancient Orient was supposed to have been Islamic already. Statements by Johannes Damascenus are high in demand when proof of the existence of Islam in the eighth century is in order. But one has got to take a closer look at what he actually said: he did not speak of "Muslims" but about the "heresy of the Ishmaelite." Heretics are the ones who leave the officially adopted belief spectrum—from the viewpoint of the Imperial Church, that was the Arabic Church of al-Malik—but they are never followers of another religion. Despite the fact that there is no historic justification, it has become a common feature to view "Arabs" as a synonym of "Muslims."

The term *Muslim* was first found on a Persian coin from AD 753. These "Muslims," however, were not members of a religion called Islam, as we see them today, but they were the Aramaic *meshlem*, the *Orthodox Ones*, meaning the true believers (a denotation which Greek Orthodox say about themselves, too). In his call for the first Crusade in AD 1096, Pope Urban II spoke of recapturing and starting settlements in the Holy Land. The image he painted of Palestine was that of the land of the Bible in which there was "milk and honey." Many crusaders left with their families and were shocked by the sight of a land that was just a hot stony desert. Urban spoke of "godless ones" in general, but did not specifically refer to Muslims and their religion. Had he perceived them as "Muslims," one expects that he would have called a spade a spade.

Many of the terms that appear typically Muslim today are simply Aramaic or Arabic in origin and had no Islam-specific connotation until the end of the first Millennium:

Allah: very early Aramaic term for "God" in general and still is usage by Aramaic Christians up to this day.

Muhamad (Muhammad): the Praised One, the Arabic understanding of "Christus."

Abd Allah: Servus Dei, God's servant.

Rasul: Prophet.

Bismillah: in the name of God.

Bismillah rahman rahim: in the name of the merciful and compassionate God (*in nomine dominis miseriscordis*), a very commonly used pre-Islamic Christian-Latin expression.

La illah ilallah: There is no god but God alone. It represents the Arabic translation of the Latin expression *non deus nisi deus solus*. Both of these expressions have been found on coins in North Africa but yet have been carelessly called Islamic.

In addition to those expressions, there are many more terms and phrases that originated in Arabic Christendom. One has to realize that the appearance of one term or the other needn't necessarily have anything to do with the religion of Islam; nor does it prove the existence of Islam in any way. It was during much later time periods that those terms assumed an Islamic connotation, often by applying bizarre and twisted procedures as seen in *mahdi*:

Just like back then, the *Mahdi,* the Savior, has always been Jesus to the Arabic Christians. In the Qur'an, *Mahdi* is also referred to as Isa bin Maryam. Despite the fact that Muhammad is supposed to be the last prophet, mainstream Sunni Islam awaits the advent of yet another Messiah without, however, giving any specifics about him, nor providing any clarification regarding the relationship to the prior "final prophet," Muhammad. There have been numerous Mahdis already, none of whom ever made it beyond local significance. In Africa alone, several dozens Mahdis have been known. The most famous of them was Muhamad Ahmed who established a theocracy in Sudan, which was later shattered by the English in 1898. [39] Another well-known Sunni Mahdi was Master Wallace Fard Muhammad, who founded the Black Muslim organization in 1930 in the United States of America.

---

39 This story is told in the movie *Khartoum,* 1966.

It was also a Mahdi who was involved in the storming of the Great Mosque in Mecca on November 20, 1979, that shook the foundation of the Royal Dynasty of the ruling al-Saud family in Saudi Arabia. It corresponded to the turn of the year 1399/1400 of the Islamic calendar, and some hundred ultra-orthodox Muslims stormed and occupied the Great Mosque including the Holy Ka'aba. In their eyes, Arabia had become un-Islamic. By occupying the Ka'aba, they wanted to demonstrate against the atheism of the al-Sauds and called on Muslims all over the world to join the final *jihad* against unbelievers in general. And they had a Mahdi with them: the twenty-five-year-old Muhamad Abdullah, whose appearance corresponded to the handed-down Mahdi description, including fair skin and a mole on his right cheek. He took position at the exact place of prophesy next to the "Black Stone" in order to receive homage, but he was not accepted by the people that were present. Gun battles even broke out. It took the Ulama (Muslim Wahhabi scholars) three full days to come up with a *fatwa* (juristic ruling concerning Islamic law issued by an Islamic scholar). That's how long it took to negotiate with the Royal Dynasty. The outcome was that the Ulama got the Royal Dynasty to make a number of concessions: the Ulama received a billion-figure sum in order to do missionary work. In addition, the reform process that had been initiated by King Faisal had to be reversed. Thus, the demands by the rebels had been met after all. It was the first blackmailing by Muslim extremists—but it wouldn't be the last. In return, the fatwa denied the legitimacy of the Mahdi and at the same time, defined the ongoing military intervention by Saudi forces as being covered by the Qur'an. The Mahdi, who considered himself immortal, picked up a thrown grenade that had landed at his feet. It exploded in his hand, and the Mahdi Muhamad Abdullah of the Uteibi tribe was history.[40]

---

40   In spite of the fact that he knew otherwise, in hate speeches, the Iranian Ayatollah Khomeini claimed that all these events had actually been operations by the United States and Israel in order to get control over the Holiest Sites of Islam. The very next day, the US Embassy in Islamabad was set on fire and several people were killed, and attacks in Izmir (Turkey), Dacca (Bangladesh), and other places followed. From then on, the United States was viewed as the true Satan in the Islamic world. On November 20, 1979, Islamic terrorism was born.

The Shi'a branch of the Twelve Imami Shi'a sees the expected Mahdi in connection with a certain figure—the concealed twelfth Imam Muhamad al-Mahdi who, according to Iranian Constitution of 1979, is the official head of state, but who is substituted for by the ayatollahs until his return. *Muhamad al-Mahdi*…or maybe it is actually the *praised Messiah*?

According to Iranian-Shi'a belief, the Mahdi can only appear during times of chaos. Based on that idea, it could be considered a God-pleasing deed to cause chaos in order to speed up the process of the Mahdi's return. With that in mind, a rocket named "Mahdi" was introduced in Iran in August 2010. President Ahmadinejad has already prophesized several times the appearance of Jesus (!) and the Mahdi Muhamad in the near future. The Day of Judgment would take place seven years (the prime number again) after their appearance.[41]

While Saint Paul carried out the process of transition from the "Oriental" to Romanized Christendom by his interpretations of scripture, and while Byzantium founded the Orthodoxy, Abd al-Malik created an independent Arabic Church. Naturally, he was a Christian, just like all Marwanids (colloquial *Umayyads*) as well as the first representatives of the Abbasids that would follow. The *muhamad* was his head saint, and the Dome of the Rock as the new Temple of Salomon was his *haram*.

According to Islamic historical literature of the ninth century, al-Walid started a war campaign from Mecca and conquered Mesopotamia. In addition, in following the footsteps of Abraham, he invaded and defeated Syria and Palestine, which included the legendary battle at Yarmuk. In Islamic tradition, the expansion under Muhammad allegedly took place from south to north, but in reality, the *muhamad* traveled from east to west. And with him traveled a number of Arabic Christians, who had been either deported by the Persians or forced to leave their country under pressure from the Byzantine Imperial Church during earlier time periods. They moved out and back to their original home

---

41   See Iranian website regarding the preparation for the return of the Mahdi: http://www.mahdaviat-conference.com.

country. This was a *hijra,* and may well have provided the genesis for the idea of a legendary Hijra of the Prophet from Mecca to Medina.

Al-Walid (the "would-be military wizard" in the literature of conquest) was a son of Abd al-Malik. Following Persian tradition, he built himself his own residence—in Damascus. He expanded the quarter of the holy shrine of John the Baptist from Maavia's time and built a new holy district. The building that nowadays is referred to as the Umayyad Mosque was undoubtedly built by al-Walid as an Arabic-Christian worship site. Among other things, he put up the saying: "There is no compulsion in religion." This phrase was no verse from the Qur'an, as traditionally interpreted, but it was later incorporated in the Qur'an—unless one accepts Luxenberg's idea that an Aramaic pre-Qur'an existed, in which case, he may have taken it from that. Apparently, Walid turned against the Imperial religious dictate—and also moved away from his father's fanaticism. His brother Hisham took over the holy shrine of Saint Sergios, a very popular Syrian sacred soldier, in Sergiopolis (Rusafa, Syria). Under Hisham, the reign of the Marwanids in the East ended in AD 750 (but a two-hundred-fifty-year long aftermath would follow in the West, in Spain).

According to Islamic tradition, the *Umayyads*—Marwanids from Mecca—descended from Umar. Again, there is no historical evidence for that claim. But something about the Umayyads must have appeared eerie to Islamic writers, because in Islamic tradition, some of the Umayyads are described as having been less than charming: Abd al-Malik, for instance, is said to have tried to steer Muslims on their pilgrimage, their *Hajj,* away from Mecca to Jerusalem.

Is goes without saying that, during al-Malik's time, the destination of the pilgrims was, besides of Damascus, no other city than Jerusalem, as the Dome of the Rock was the religious center for Arabic Christians. Abd al-Malik's final goal, as was also seen by his actions in his personal life, was dedicated to the return to the Promised Land [42] to wait for the end of the world. In order to be prepared for this event, Christians were <u>urged to</u> execute *islam*—meaning to work on the concurrence

42 Zion (meaning the site of the Temple), Falastin (meaning the Holy Land) on coins.

of the scripts so that they would appear before the Messiah not in dispute but in harmony.

Islamic tradition tells us that it was Umar II, another Umayyad caliph, who left us the set of instructions regarding what, in the presence of Muslims, unbelievers are allowed to do and what is forbidden to them. But, again, as there is no scientific evidence about Umar II, he can confidently be considered as another figure conjured by the creators of Islamic tradition. Currently, at least eight out of the fourteen Umayyad caliphs that are mentioned in traditional literature remain unconfirmed by non-Islamic sources. Among those are, for instance, the Umayyad caliphs Marwan I and Marwan II.

The creation of Marwan I and later Marwan II, who are mentioned in traditional reports, clearly shows the lack of understanding regarding the basic concept of the dynastic model. The Persian word-root MRW (Marw) was either misunderstood, or its meaning was deliberately twisted, because this root first of all refers to the place of origin of the Marw Dynasty in eastern Persia. But the place name was turned into the name of a person called Marwan, who, of course, originated from Mecca and is said to have belonged to the inner circle of the Prophet. One reason for such misinterpretations was the strong desire to have a confirming history—meaning nothing less than falsification of history. Another reason for this was to cover up discrepancies which resulted from later recalculations from the Arab solar calendar to the Hijra lunar calendar. Gaps were filled as one saw fit, a rather common feature of history writing in the early days.[43]

The transition from the Umayyads to the Abbasid Dynasty was also a period of religious transition, whereby the greatest change took place after the time of al-Mamun. The first Abbasid caliph (Abd al-Abbas) built a Holy Shrine in Medina in AD 756. Today, it is known under the name "the Prophet Graveyard." Even this "caliph" still used to put up expressions of Christian belief, but the process of pushing Mary and

---

43 According to many theorists, some personalities in the Bible were only able to "live to a ripe old age" because information about their exact genealogies had been lost. Therefore, those gaps were filled by expanding life expectancies.

Jesus into the background had already begun. According to Karl Heinz Ohlig, the inscriptions in Medina probably show the *muhamad* logo in connection with Christian expressions for the very last time. Gradually, the Holy Shrine of Medina gained importance over the one in Damascus.

The seventh and eighth centuries, meaning exactly the time period of the alleged victorious Islamic battles, were actually the time period during which the Arabic-Syrian Church had its heyday. Numerous new church buildings were created, among which were the famous Dome of the Rock in Jerusalem and St. John's Basilica in Damascus. Missionary work was carried out far beyond the Persian border, even reaching areas as far as China.

Theologically, the Arabic Church rejected the idea of Jesus as being God in human flesh. Consequently, this also meant a separation from the philosophical problems typical of Greek–influenced Christian theology. In the Arab's view, Jesus was just another of God's prophets. The Greek Church was going through a step-by-step process of becoming "nationalized" into a distinctively Arabic form of Christianity.

Arabic Christendom was characterized by Semitic religion and was therefore closely connected with Abraham's tradition. Following the concept of this tradition, a gradual process took place that rejected the Hellenic Christendom including its extravaganza, the image cult, and the construction of philosophical-theological complexes that were simply incomprehensible to some.

To the understanding of the people in the classical world of the Greeks and Romans, it was the minimum that a divine person had at least been born to a virgin. Consequently, Mary's husband Joseph was pretty much pushed out of sight in Christian tradition, whereas Mary herself was elevated to holy status and appointed to "virgin." Similarly, in the Qur'an, as being a product of the late-classical world, Joseph is not mentioned a single time. But there was another problem with which the Arabs had to grapple: according to their understanding, it was absolutely necessary for the importance and legitimacy of a person, to stem from an absolutely impressive lineage. Anything less would be out of the question, and nothing else would be easier to fix: step number one was to reinterpret *abd Allah* as Abd Allah, who was then pinned down as the father of *Muhamad*. In addition, Muhammad was garnished with a most impressive line of ancestors that goes back to progenitor Abraham, then Noah, and ultimately to Adam himself. Now, Muhammad was linked with progenitor Abraham, and the Persian "Ali" was quickly tapped as his son-in-law, the Umayyads were tracked back to an Umar, the Abbasids were tracked back to an Abbas, and they both, of course, belonged to the inner circle of the Prophet.

With breathtaking speed, the interpreters had effected a thorough legitimization of Muhammad by reaching back across time and space.[44] Nevertheless, the historians are still waiting to see a single piece of evidence to support any of their claims.

Syro-Aramaic was the main language, and it served as a connecting element in this culturally diverse region. This language was of such great importance that, even in Persia, numerous official documents were issued in Aramaic. Politically, this region was also diverse but often unstable. Central powers in each region hardly extended beyond the cities; in the provinces, Arab emirs, each having a different level of influence, carried out their power struggles. Simultaneous to the decline of power of the Marwanids, the influence of *muhamad, the praised one*, declined. Or was it the other way around? Was it the frustration over the hope for the return of the Messiah? The *muhamad al-mahdi* never showed up. He did not appear at the Temple Mount for the Day of Judgment as predicted. That disillusionment might have been the decisive moment for the disappearance of the muhamad-Jesus concept—and finally of the Umayyads themselves.

In the some parts of Iran the concept of Jesus as *wali-Allah*, the "representation of God," dominated. The term *wali-Allah* corresponds to the title of "Magnificent" (*ali*) and is seen as an Executor of God's will in the sense of a Persian Knight. Just like the attributive term

---

44 Once, Saddam Hussein caused great upset in the Arab world when he addressed King Hussein of Jordan as "Cousin." This was interpreted as an attempt to insinuate himself into the family of the Prophet, which can be traced back to the Hashemite Dynasty of King Hussein.

muhamad gradually came to be understood as the name of a person, so did *ali*. This was the cause for a dispute which led to the separation (*shia*) of the party of *ali*: they are known as today's Shi'a. Just like Muhammad, Ali was also created in Persia,[45] but has never really made it beyond the Persian borders. The first post-Marwanids ruler was most likely a follower of Ali. We know his coins, but we don't know his name. He never mentioned his name on any coins or in any historical documents that have survived—but Islamic tradition claims to know it, anyway: he allegedly was an Abbas (a member of the Abbasid Dynasty) who, conveniently, descended from the Prophet's family. Just like Umayyads, the Abbasids[46] were assigned both a dynastic name and a historically large (but unproven) succession.

The *muhamad*-motto of the Marwanids was replaced by several different titles of concealed mottos of Jesus. The ruler put his regency, which was often anonymously carried out, under a certain Jesus designation: *al-hadi* (Savior), *mardi* (the beloved Son), *harun* (the Just One), *mansur* (the Victorious One), *mahdi* (the Savior), and many more.

God had sent the articulate Aaron as *kalif* ("messenger") to be at Moses's side; this attribute would now be recycled and put to use. These various terms of attribution referenced mostly Christological and biblical programs and titles, but the founders of Islamic tradition nonetheless reinterpreted them as the actual names of specific rulers.

Most likely, there were no such rulers with the names of al-Mansur, al-Mahdi, Musa al-Mahdi, or al-Saffah—and the first "Abbasids" were definitely Christians.

Consequently, the historic value of the famous Harun al-Rashid—the prototype of all fairytale Islamic rulers—is in danger. As it turned out, it was not a man but a woman, Zubayda, who had coins minted

---

45 It is *ali* in the South and *muhamad* in the East.
46 They referred to themselves as *the Hashims*, "the *Noble Ones*," who were allowed to be the first to resurrect. They ended the tradition of Marw and Jerusalem, and established Mecca as a religious center, where, in the beginning, the tradition of Abraham had priority.

during thirteen years of Harun al-Rashid's alleged reign. Did she rule using the motto *"Harun al-Rashid,"* the "Just Messenger"?

A group of temple keepers, called *Barmakits,* served as ministers and had great political power for generations under the Abbasid caliphs at the Abbasids' Royal Court. They were Buddhist temple priests in Baghdad who had emigrated from the Buddhist provinces in the eastern parts of the Persian Empire. Their name was derived from the title *Parmak,* denoting the abbot of the main Buddhist monastery in Nawbahar (today's Afghanistan). They worked under several caliphs and had high political positions, including minister status; some might have even been rulers themselves. There are still many unanswered questions.

The successor of Zubayda, al-Mamun (AD 786–833), was a remarkable ruler. After having lived in Marw, Chorasmia, eastern Persia, he moved to Baghdad in AD 825. It was probably at a time when he felt politically strong enough, because on his arrival, he disposed of the current ruler, his half-brother Amin. In Baghdad, al-Mamun found an intellectually and philosophically aspiring city. There was a lively Jewish community, Buddhists, Zoroastrians, and Manichaeists, as well as Persian, Arabic, and Hellenic Christians. They also discussed the texts by an Arabic prophet, which had just begun circulating.

A native Persian, al-Mamun had never been to the western regions of the empire. Now was his time to catch up on everything he had heretofore missed. Accompanied by a large scientific delegation, he first moved to Harran, which was both the place of Abraham and the scientific center of the Sabeans. [47] From there, he moved on to Damascus. He visited the Basilica of St. John and the buildings of the Marwanids. From there, he traveled to the Nile River. Theories about the Nile's origin were discussed, and, with his own eyes, he saw the place where the prophet Moses had drifted down the river in a basket as a baby. He traveled to Jerusalem and, together with his delegation, examined the inscriptions by Abd al-Malik in the church at the Temple Mount. And they found evidence that proved that there was a Prophet of the Arabs. Here it was, in black and white: *muhamad abd Allah.* What

---

47 "Star worshippers"—followers of the old Babylonian religion.

used to be the "praised servant of God" had now become "Muhamad, the son of abd Allah" in modern Arabic. In an era of upheaval with new linguistic standards mixed with a portion of goodwill, anything—including grammatical impossibilities—can happen. In addition, it is said that Mamun had al-Malik's name removed and replaced with his own name;[48] but the year 72 *kata Araba*, however, he decided to keep.

Coins of al-Mamun have been found on which he refers to himself as *kalifat Allah*. It was the first time after Abd al-Malik that this title had been used again, but this time it had a different connotation. While al-Malik referred to *kalifat Allah* as *the Messenger of God*, meaning Jesus, Mamun now used this expression reflexively in the way that the title "kalif" and "imam" referred to himself, meaning that Mamun viewed himself as the number-one representative of his god. But which god was it? It must have surely been the one God, Allah, who sent the Prophet Muhammad to the Arabs. Nevertheless, Mamun did not see himself as a "Muslim"—the process of independence of what we today call "Islam" had not taken place yet.

Mamun gathered the most intellectual people of his time at his royal court: scientists of all imaginable fields. There was intellectual freedom; when, for instance, he heard that in the Qur'an the earth was considered to be as flat as a carpet, but, in contrast, Arabic astronomers of his time defined the earth as round, he immediately got to the bottom of it. In order to calculate the circumference of the earth, he sent an investigative expedition to the steppe near Mosul. They put up markers at various angles of incidence so that the sunlight would hit them at defined geographical gradients. His expedition came up with result: the circumference of the earth, it determined, was 40,075 kilometers (the exact number known today is 40,235 kilometers).

At that time, some Qur'anic texts had already become known and were discussed. The first comprehensive text in Arabic known to us was produced in the late ninth century. Mamun was follower of the *Mutazilism*, a spiritual concept that incorporated the use of ancient

---

48 It has not been verified that al-Mamun made the changes himself. It is possible that they were done later.

philosophies. He had the statement issued that the Qur'an, too, had been created, and that therefore, it was permissible to discuss it. By putting the emphasis on rationalism, which demanded the use of logic and openness when dealing with sources of knowledge, the Mutazilites were in total contrast to the Orthodoxy clergy who called for accepting the Qur'an as the only source and following it in literal terms. The Islamic tradition hails the time of al-Mamun as Islam's heyday, but nothing could be further from the truth. Being a Mutazilite, Mamun felt much closer to the Arabic Enlightenment mindset than the Islamic Qur'an doctrine. He fought *Hanbalism*. In other words, Mamun fought against a branch that would become commonly known as *Islam*.

Mamun's time was followed by a great change; *muhamad* and *ali* were heading toward personification, and the caliphate—though by Malik and Mamun only used in a completely different sense—were retroactively stamped on every ruler since "Muhammad," constructing an unbroken theocratic chain that had never actually existed. The Qur'an was compiled and, simultaneously, the writing of the Arabic languague defined. The *Muhamad* got his grave in Medina, while *Ali* had lost in the programmatic dispute and was fobbed off with a martyr legend.

The mysterious Qur'anic *Bakka* (Sura 3:96) was eventually "identified" and manifested as the Arabian Mecca. In reality, however, this constantly emphasized "essential trade center called Mecca located at the intersection of important roads" was completely unknown in "the times of the prophet". Up to this day, there is no evidence that a historic place called Mecca existed in the sixth or seventh century. In the Qur'an, there is only a reference to a *Bakka*, which was supposed to have been located at Abraham's first house of prayer. Because all of the non-Islamic traditions report that Abraham was in Mesopotamia, even in a report from the eighth century, the term *Bakka* was described as a location in Mesopotamia. At-Tabari (again at-Tabari) was the first who spoke of a "Mecca" located in the Arabian desert in the ninth century. According to Luxenberg, however (again Luxenberg), the term *bakka* means "fenced in, enclosed, encircled." From that, it can be concluded that the term *Bakka/Mecca* did not refer to a specific place but that it denoted a general term for an enclosed or fenced-in holy district. The fact is that Mecca was never a city. In the seventh century in this location, there was a church like many others in Arabia, but besides that, the location had no significance. Defining Mecca as the cradle of Islam is a creation in hindsight, put down in literature of later centuries.

Moreover, there is no information about the Prophet's tribe, the Quraysh, before its name was mentioned by at-Tabari. The same applies to other very important names and places. For instance, there is not even the slightest information about Badr, the place at which "one of the most decisive battles of mankind" took place.[49] Despite the fact that a Google search for Badr gives around two million results, including maps and sketches, information about military buildups, photographs of war graves, etc., no one has ever been able to actually find the place.

Scientific evidence does not support the existence of a Badr, and neither—correctly considered—does the Qur'an. Tradition alleges that the town is referred to in Sura 3:123, but this is a misreading. As Luxenberg proves with an old Qur'anic text (BNF 328a, Folio b), *bi-idr* was misread as *bi-badr*. While *badr* makes no sense, this construction was eventually interpreted as a place name, *Badr*, in later centuries. The true meaning of this term, however, is "help/auxiliary force" and its connotation becomes comprehensible when reading the words of the subsequent verse, Sura 3:124, which talks about a heavenly force of three thousand angels.[50] That means that the Battle of Badr is also another story from the collection of inventions.

Other incidents mentioned in the Muhammad legends seem to have been derived from historic events, like Heraclius' Great War against the Persian religious enemy. The victorious "Battle of the Trench" by Muhammad in AD 627 coincides with the year of the Byzantine/Arabic victory at Nineveh, and the subsequent signing of the peace treaty in the year AD 628 corresponds to the "treaty of Hudaybiyya."

49   From: http://www.islamreligion.com/de; 2009.
50   Detailed explanation in Luxenberg, "Keine Schlacht von Badr," in *Vom Koran zum Islam*. Berlin, 2009.

In AD 630, the cross was returned to Jerusalem, and the Church of the Holy Sepulcher was reopened in a festive ceremony; this is the year Islamic interpretation speaks of purification and opening of the Ka'aba. Coincidence?

The first two hundred fifty years of traditional Islamic history consists completely of parts that were legendarily moved to the Arabian desert or were newly created altogether. The possibly first original Mosque (*masjid*) was built in the new seat of power in the city of Samarra (today's Iraq). Its design shows the adaptation of the Old Babylonian-style ziggurat as its symbol and the mother of all minarets. We are now at the turn into the tenth century.

Up to when exactly one should still refer to a "church" and after that to a "mosque" cannot be dated precisely. In Aramaic, the term *masjid* has always denoted a general place of worship, back then as much as today. It was much later that this term acquired the meaning of an Islam-specific house of God. A Christian-Syrian *masjid* had precisely the same features as a Muslim *masjid*, which can only be considered a mosque when it shows a *mihrab* (a niche in the wall or a plaque showing the direction to Mecca, to which worshippers turn their face while praying).

Islam means "concurrence" or "correspondence," in reference to concurrence with the Holy Scripts. These were Christian books: the Old Testament, the Gospels, and apocryphal books.[51] The Arabic-Christian Church began evolving as early as the second or third century and had kept on developing continuously ever since. Initially, Jews and Jewish-Christians probably lived side-by-side without any major theological dividing lines between them. But gradually, individual branches developed that had their own theology. At various councils, for example the Nicaea Council in AD 325, deep segregation lines cutting through "Oriental" Christendom were already apparent. The Arabic Christians refused to follow some of the theological concepts

---

51 The Apocrypha are texts that have not been officially recognized by the clergy. Up to this day, the Copts use a Gospel of Peter which has been accepted by neither the Orthodox nor the Western-Roman Church. A Gospel of Thomas was very widespread throughout the Arabic world.

of the Roman and Orthodox churches and kept to the pre-Nicaean theological model. Their goal was to find the true Christendom. They viewed themselves as the Ishmaelites, the sons of Ishmael in the true tradition of Ishmael that had become distorted. They were searching for *Islam*, the concurrence of the "scripts."

In just a few centuries after Christ, the Hellenic Christendom in the ancient "Orient" had spiraled downward in that it had almost become a religion of the Holy Ones, magical tokens, and miracles. The influence of the classical world was at work here, as could also be seen in the great appreciation they had for pictorial representation; one might certainly detect pagan features in that. In addition, the influence of the Greek-theological style was obvious (e.g., making a cult out of Mary's Immaculate Conception and the Trinity idea). In contrast, the Arabic Christians still showed much closer affinities with the Jewish-Christians. Consequently, they were much more closely related to the world of the Old Testament than to the Romanized or Hellenic Christianity of the Mediterranean culture.

Therefore, the Arabic Christians didn't want to have anything to do with the Byzantine Dictate-Church that kept to the Trinity idea, which, in the eyes of the Arabic Christians, was nothing short of renunciation of the belief in the One True God. As a matter of fact, no other issue is emphasized in the Qur'an more than the idea of "the One True God." Needless to say, from the viewpoint of the Imperial Church, that attitude was clearly "heresy"—it meant the falling away from the rightful belief. And that is exactly what the Arabic Christians were called in contemporary reports—*heretics*. They were called false Christians but were not considered to be followers of a new religion. The feeling was mutual; the Arabic Christians called the others heretics, too, using the Arabic term *mushrikun*. Traditionally—and here we are dealing with another one of these numerous cases of misreading—the rebuked *mushrikun* of the Qur'an are interpreted as "pagans." But the term was derived from the word-root *sarik*, which means "companion" and "accompanying person." And this is to what the term refers: it is the accompanying person, the one who stands by God's side. The Qur'anic *mushrikun* are, in reality, the Trinitarian Christians, those who put God an accompanying person at his side.

During pre-Christian and pre-Islamic times, the lunar culture was dominant on the Arabian Peninsula and was found in an area stretching from Syria to Yemen. Regionally, different deities existed. Lunar cultures are typical of herdsman societies. While the sun was considered to be a destroyer by desert people (in contrast to people of agricultural societies who revered the sun), the moon was interpreted as having a number of positive characteristics. As can be clearly seen even today, those desert traditions largely influenced the developing religion.

The deity siblings, Allat and Uzza, were especially popular in middle and northern Arabia. Sometimes the Goddess Manat was included, who traced out the people's fate. Allat, which is the short form of al-Ilahah, meaning "goddess," was the goddess of the Moon. Uzza was the goddess of the Morning Star, which is the reason why Hellenic sources referred to her as Venus. These goddesses were also responsible for water and fertility. It is said that people made human sacrifices to at least one goddess, Uzza. They used sacred trees, holy springs, and especially rocks to worship their goddesses. Some of Allat's stones were located in today's cities of Mecca, Ta'if, and Petra; Uzza's holy trees and one of her holy springs were also in the vicinity of today's Mecca, close to her sister's holy stone. In addition, *jinns*, evil demons, were on the rampage throughout the desert.

The fact that both moon and star cultures were very persistent among Bedouins can be seen in various places in the Qur'an that refer to idol worshippers.[52] Only Muhammad was finally able to chase the idols off of the Ka'aba, which, strangely enough, did not prevent them from perfectly establishing themselves in his religion after all: up to this day, the black rock of Allat, set in a silver frame, is worshipped, while being walked around again and again, and the spring of Uzza, known to today's Muslims as the Well of Zam-Zam, is a mandatory

---

52 That especially applies to Sura 5:19–23.

part of every pilgrimage. In addition, the jinns, the evil demons, are mentioned in the Qur'an plenty [53] and are still feared by the believers.

The crescent of the moon of the pagan Moon goddess, Allat, has become the trademark of Islam, and can be found on the flags of some Islamic countries together with the symbol of Allat's sister, the goddess Uzza, the Morning Star.

But the dark era of the pagan gods, which were allegedly defeated by Muhammad, was not directly followed by Islam at all, in contrast to traditional claims. There was a Christian intermezzo that lasted for several centuries—but this is completely passed over in silence.

In the seventh century, the Arabian Peninsula was almost completely Christianized.[54] In addition, there were important Jewish communities. Throughout the Nabataean Empire, which stretched so far south that it also included Mecca, the Trinitarian Christendom was distributed. The South, meaning today's Yemen, was influenced by the Ethiopian Church, and the eastern areas of the peninsula were under Persian influence, with its dominating Nestorian Christendom.

All across the Arabian Peninsula, substantial archaeological evidence has been found in the form of churches, monasteries, and sacred buildings, but it is prohibited to carry out research on these sites. And to make matters worse, in twenty-first-century Saudi Arabia, many of the relics that are suspected of being pre-Islamic in age are being relentlessly destroyed.

It seems to be completely forgotten that the Ka'aba itself is of Christian origin. In southern Arabia, "Ka'abas," which are cubic-style buildings, have a tradition that go back to the fourth century BC. In Yemen, a number of Ka'abas have been found that were originally built as temples or churches. The Ka'aba in Mecca represents the

---

53 Sura 72, "The Jinni," Suras 55:33, 56, 74, etc.
54 C. D. G.Müller, *Kirche und Mission unter den Arabern in Vorislamischer Zeit* (Tübingen, 1967).

northernmost of such buildings. This bloc is ten by twelve meters in size and was originally part of a church. In front of the northwestern flank of this cubic building is a plaza that is enclosed by a lunate wall base. This wall structure is the foundation wall of the apse of the former church, which was the additional structure of today's Ka'aba. Following clerical tradition, under the altar room there used to be a crypt used for the dead bodies of very prominent persons. In Arabic, this part is called *higr*, meaning "lap" or "womb"; according to Islamic tradition, the progenitor Ishmael and his mother Hagar were buried here. (Another name for the *higr* is *al-hatim*, meaning "that which was razed to the ground.")

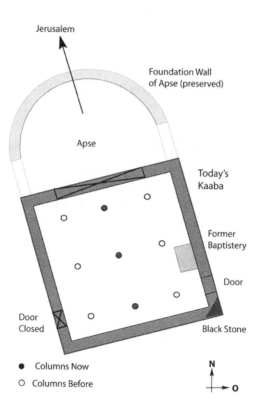

The Ka'aba in pre-Islamic time as church
(Al-Azraqi / G.Lüling)

That means that the Ka'aba formed a constructional unit with the apse of the former church, which included a baptismal font next to the entrance on the right and a number of wall pictures.[55] It is said that the apse was destroyed during the invasion of Mecca in AD 693 by al-Haggag, the deputy of Abd al-Malik. The main part of the building, however, was still used as a church until the early ninth century—well beyond Muhammad's lifetime. Originally, the Ka'aba was a building that had windows and doors, but during early Islamic times the Ka'aba was changed into an empty, almost sealed building with no windows. To researchers it now resembled a large-scale Ark of the Covenant, and they see this as a symbolic return from the Hellenic back to the Semitic Christendom, the latter of which had a distinct relation to the Old Testament. In this connection, the disappearance of signs of the cross from coins and the re-occurrence of the stone pyramid must be taken into consideration. These changes suggest the turning to non-iconic worship, whereby the black stone of Allat, being a non-iconic symbol, probably became acceptable by society again.

An Islamic allegation is that there have never been any Christian communities in the regions of Mecca and Medina, but the existence of the Ka'aba clearly proves otherwise, and the discovery of further Christian relics, presumed by researchers to be located around the church's former site, would provide final evidence of this. These relics, reported by construction engineers, now rest under paving stones in the Mosque district and are, just like all the other pre-Islamic evidence in Saudi Arabia, unavailable for study.

---

55 According to some reports, two pictures (Abraham; Mary and Jesus) were present up until recently. And persistent rumors say that they still exist.

The place of the Ka'aba used to be the place for worshipping the pagan deities Lunar Goddess Allat and the Goddess of the Morning Star Uzza. Their symbols, moon crescent and star, embellish the national flags of several Muslim countries (see below). The foundations of the apse of the former church located in front of the Ka'aba is distinctly visible.

The stone of Allat, who was also Goddess of Fertility, is embedded in a remarkable frame on one corner of the Ka'aba. Kissing the stone is considered to be one of the highlights of the pilgrimage

To many researchers of Islam, the seventh and eighth centuries are a puzzling time period because there are no Islamic texts known from this era. The Qur'an expert Rudi Paret calls it a "transmission gap." [56] Were the Arabic Christians/early Muslims illiterate or incapable of writing? Certainly not—they were capable of writing and proved it many times. They did write—but it was not in classical Arabic. They language and script they used was not the language that Islamic scholars expected them to have used.

Starting in the middle of the ninth century, the production of written works made a spectacular comeback, and a surprising one, as it came somehow from out of the blue. These written works contain reports from the late sixth century in which people are mentioned who, practically overnight, started speaking Qur'an-Arabic and telling us in great detail about events that had taken place two hundred years or more before.

Why hadn't their ancestors mentioned any of this in contemporary reports? The answer by Islamic scholars is that the Arabic culture used to be an oral one with a great storytelling tradition but no writing tradition. And yes, there were many people capable of learning the whole Qur'an by heart, without any mistake or error. We stand in awe of these intellectual giants, but why should the Arabs have produced written works before Muhammad, then remained silent for two hundred years, and then, suddenly, started writing again? The claim that only oral traditions were present has been disproven; we have evidence proving the existence of written transmissions *during* the alleged "transmission gap."—including the Qur'an itself.

The written works that were produced *after* the "transmission gap" contained a lot of material but hardly any variety. This material essentially consisted of two things: texts of a holy book called the Qur'an and a huge amount of information about a prophet called Muhammad. He had not been mentioned at the beginning of the "gap," but at the end of it, there was no other topic. Now, a competition

---

56   Rudi, Paret, *Die Lücke der Überlieferungen über den Urkoran* (Wiesbaden, 1954).

seemed to have started regarding who could write down the most evidence about the Prophet and his new religion.

At the same time, information about a number of lost books surfaced, including fragments of written works, cross-references, and catalogues listing their titles. These were books that did not join the chorus of Prophet cheerleaders. Also, a number of Qur'anic versions disappeared that are known to have existed in earlier time periods. For a long time, Westerners who worked in the field of "Oriental" studies simply believed the usual, traditional explanations—and they did so despite the fact that there had already been reasons to reject those explanations on account of problems regarding orthography or dialects. Even in stories of the Prophet, the burning of books is mentioned.

There is no doubt that censorship and book burnings had reached major proportions. Some authors didn't even bother trying to hide it. The earliest biography of the Prophet was allegedly produced by Ibn Ishaq, but this work is lost—if it ever existed.[57] Later, Ibn Hisham (AD ?–834) referred to Ishaq's work in his description of the Prophet's story but stated in the introduction: "I will omit all the information given by Ibn Ishaq that does not mention the Prophet, cannot be found in the Qur'an…and if it can be used neither as explanation nor as proof."

That brings it down to the point. In all of the early Islamic literature, only historical information that could be used as proof of the Prophet was considered legitimate. That is the traditional Credo: *The Qur'an is a unique work, had no precursor or source materials, and would have been impossible without its transmitter, Muhammad.*

But even despite what appears to have been a severe attempt to eliminate all traces of them from the earth, some early Arabic, pre-Islamic poetic works have survived. We have enough evidence to know a good deal about their prose, the expressions they used, and their formal styles. And it is clear that their contents are, when dealing with religious issues, of biblical and Christian origins.

---

57   Despite the fact that it is listed on Amazon.com.

Why was it considered so important that these pre-Qur'anic works be eliminated? After all, even the Muslims never claimed that Muhammad was the first prophet—only the last and the greatest. The problem for Islamic traditionalists was that both the style and contents of these pre-Qur'anic verses and strophes can often be found reproduced in the Qur'an. This makes it clear that the Qur'an is not a unique work. Therefore, there is no way to reconcile the claim that Qur'anic rhyme prose could have not existed without its interpreter, Muhammad. Qur'anic prose represents just a single link in a chain of Arabic poetry tradition. It did not appear in the Qur'an, introduced by its messenger, for the first time. The Qur'an is a typical piece of work of the late classic period in ancient Arabia, including extensive use of copy and paste.

The allegation by Islamic tradition that the Prophet was illiterate and could neither read nor write is nothing more but an attempt to disconnect the Qur'an from any pre-Islamic poetry and tradition. Under no circumstance should anyone ever get the idea that the Prophet might have adopted anything that preexisted. After all, the Qur'an was said to be derived freshly and exclusively from heaven, not from the past.

According to Islamic ideas, nothing existed before Muhammad, at least nothing that would be worth mentioning. The time before Muhammad is officially called *jihiliyya*, the time of ignorance, the barbaric times. And then, all of the sudden, like a bullet in the blue sky, it was all there: the Qur'an , the Revelation, the Prophet, and a lot of fiction about him. All of the sudden…after two hundred years of silence.

The truth of the matter is that there never was a "transmission gap." The Arabs most certainly produced written works, during that time—a lot of them—namely the Qur'an, step-by-step, version-by-version. We have handwritten documents that prove how this process happened. But in those writings, they didn't say anything about the Prophet. How could it be that they were able to write their Holy Book and not mention its primary source? The reason for that is that there was nobody to write about; there was nothing known about the Prophet.

So what happened during these two hundred years between the alleged events and their eventual heralding? Well, nothing less then the birth of Islam. But there was no forceful angel, no divine inspirations on mountaintops, no first-response teams sent from heaven, and no sand storms sent by God. It was simply a process taking place, but because the Semitic tradition holds that religious truths can only become known by a high-profile revelation, the Islamic historiography practically blinded out the first two hundred years and patched-up this "transmission gap" by filling it with legends called the *Sunna*. In Islamic literature, the seventh century essentially jumps directly to the ninth. This leap has been noticed by numerous historians, but few only would draw any conclusions from it.

As previously pointed out, Luxenberg argues persuasively that many passages in the Qur'an were originally not written in Arabic. So far, he has been able to identify around four hundred Aramaic words in the Qur'an. That seems like a small number of terms. But, as already shown, even these four hundred words have resulted in significant misinterpretations, thanks to which the world now has to deal with the head veil and the blessing of Paradise virgins, for instance.

Originally, the Qur'anic texts were written using a consonant structure consisting of an Aramaic-Arabic mix of languages. The existence of numerous manuscripts proves that the *Arabi* continuously worked on their Holy Book. This work called the Qur'an was the continuation of the Qeryan that had been produced for a specific Arabian community. There is no doubt that it was a Christian text.

If one had asked an Arab around the year AD 700, meaning about a hundred years after Muhammad, about his religion, his answer (unless he was a Jew or a pagan) would have been, "I am a Christian." A public opinion poll would have revealed the presence of various traditions in different regions. That would have included different ideas about Moses, Abraham, or Jesus, the latter of which might have been viewed as God, the son of God, a prophet, or a messenger. We would have mainly found out about various views regarding the role of Jesus. While the emphasis or focus on certain ideas would have been different, these would have been no reason for anyone to see a new religion on the horizon or to change their religion altogether. Over a time period of two to three centuries, there were no clear-cut dividing lines; no one was faced with the choice between Christendom and Islam, between Jesus and the Prophet. Because, again, Jesus *was* the Prophet at the beginning of the development of Islam. Therefore, the Christians in Syria, Persia, or Spain didn't mention anything about the appearance of a new religion. Christendom was very widespread, but gradually, Arabic Christians transformed into Muslims in some areas. However, it is clear that in later legends of conquest, the Islamic traditionalists had to come up with a good explanation why the "subjugated" Christians and all the other peoples of nations conquered by Muhammad and his successors so happily cooperated with their conquerors. Thus, the fairy tale of the tolerance of Islam was born.

In general, the transition from the Qeryan to the Qur'an was—except for the rejection of the trinity—not so much theological. The dividing line was the understanding of Jesus. The moment that Jesus ceased to be the central figure of Arabic Christianity and was viewed as a prophet among others, the Qur'an had become the book of a different religion. Muhammad abd-Allah was only the result of this shift in meaning but not its cause.

Theologically, there was not enough reason or justification for calling out a new religion. But no religion can demand the adherence of followers without justification—thus, a founding myth was in demand, and it would be delivered in the form of Muhammad. The beginning of the Muhammad myth was the beginning of the religion called Islam.

As a result of the change in the political landscape, the seventh and eighth centuries were characterized by both the rise and the expansion of the Arabian Empire. But it was not an Islamic Empire. The *Arabi* had a strong desire to have a gospel of their own. Their wish was finally coming true, but the craving for their own Prophet had yet to be satisfied—after all, a prophet had been promised, over and over again. The Jews had their prophets; the Christians had a prophet of their own, as well; and now, in the ninth century, the Arabs would finally get their prophet, too.

Rumors about the appearence of an Arabic prophet would have circulated. But because, and this was most unfortunate, he had been around at least two hundred years earlier and no written documents existed, oral transmissions had to do. And these oral transmissions would begin bubbling up everywhere, with no end in sight. In addition, these tales provided evidence linking the origin of the Qur'an with the Prophet. After all, at least parts of the Qur'an already existed and could be used as proof. As a result, a package consisting of the holy book and the Prophet was later reinterpreted. This process of essentially creating something new—it couldn't be called anything else—was mainly carried out during the ninth century in Mesopotamia. The authors literally collected every piece of transmission they could find and wrote them down. But as it turned out, they were not in full command of the language of the time period in which the transmissions originated and were thus unable to fully comprehend the former meaning of the terms used. For that reason, they interpreted, assumed, suspected, created, and established meanings from day one—and that is what characterizes the Qur'anic readings ("interpretations") to this day.

They tapped fantasy caliphs and fought imaginary battles, and used the help of miracles whenever the stories seemed to be no more comprehensible for the public. It can be assumed that some stories contained information about real historical personages—maybe a sheikh or a prominent local preacher—but these were later relabeled with the name "Muhammad."

Numerous instructions and regulations, as well as the type of highly detailed regulations that are found in the Qur'an, correspond to the structure of Bedouin societies of that time. Desert-specific elements had most likely been incorporated into this religion at an early stage.

And probably even more of such components were later added during reinterpretations. Just by taking a look at the Meccan Suras (they basically represent the theological part of the Qur'an) and comparing them with the Medinan Suras (they essentially represent implementation instructions), it becomes clear that they differ from each other to such degree that would make it implausible for them to have been derived from just one person during only one time period. They are completely different in nature. The authors didn't even have any scruples in relocating the Old Testament Abraham to Mecca under the name of Ibrahim and appointing him as the first "believer." And, of course, it goes without saying that this "believer" could have only been a Muslim. The Lebanese author Kamal Salibi went ahead and moved the whole Old Testament to today's Arabia in order to completely tie it up with Islam.[58]

Naturally, the language of the new book had to be Arabic, but a comprehensive Arabic language didn't exist at that time. And above all, there was only a rudimentary Arabic script—that meant that a readable and binding script had to be created first. Therefore, the creators of the Qur'an acted as grammarians, and the result of their work was actually the Qur'an-Arabic language. It is assumed with great confidence that the Qur'an was the very first text written in this new linguistic version.

Immediately after the book had been finished, religious authorities were eager to establish it as the only real thing, the all-embracing entity. From now on, this would be the only book that people needed because it contained it all: the whole past, present, and future. It pertained to every aspect of a person's life. Now the seed had been planted that would grow to a network, intertwining private, public, civil, and governmental issues—an all-inclusive system that would become the trademark of Islam. There was even room in the Qur'an for the donkey Luqman from the *Akhikar*, which is the Indian book of Wisdom—a souvenir from the Buddhist-Hindu-influenced area of eastern Persia, home country of the *muhamad*.

---

58   Salibi Kamal, *The Bible Came from Arabia* (New York: Pan Books, 1987).

The authors created a new language, a new script, and a new history—and lost sight of the reality of their past. What else could show more clearly the completely shattered relationship of Islam with its own past than by their using symbols of the detested pagan goddesses on their flags and prayer houses—the Crescent Moon and Morning Star.

Al-Hira plays an important role in the transformation from historic event to legend. It is a town in the southern area of Mesopotamia in which there used to be an association of Arab tribes. Religion was the binding element that connected these tribes beyond their tribal affiliation. The people of al-Hira viewed themselves as a community of *Ibad*, the "servants" (meaning the "servants of God"). In the Qur'an, too, the term *Ibad* is mentioned. That appears rather strange, as in there the form would have to be *Abid* (the plural form of *Abd*) but not *Ibad*. The term *Ibad* represents a word that is unique to the above-mentioned community. Just a misspelling?

As mentioned in an earlier chapter in this book, *Hira* was also the name of the place in the vicinity of Mecca (a mountain or a cave), in which, according to Islamic tradition, Muhammad received his first revelations. Just a coincidence?

As a matter of fact, there is reason to believe that the story of al-Hira, a place that really exists, was used and transferred from one location to another. It is a type of procedure that has been known to have been applied throughout history. Were these Christians of al-Hira the "early Muslims"?[59] (We will be meeting the al-Hira Christians, or Ibadites, again in Chapter 9.)

Because the Arabs grew up with the Judeo-Christian belief system, they were very familiar with the traditions of the Bible and the Torah. Even more, they lived the stories of Moses and Abraham;

---

59   In one legend, a person who was both merchant and preacher is mentioned who is said to have converted to the Arabic Christendom in al-Hira and spread it in southern Arabia. His name was allegedly Qutham, who later became famous under the name Muhammad.

the progenitor's expulsion by the Pharaoh; various prophecies, conquests, and settlements; the inevitable apocalypse; and the hope for the final salvation. They compared contemporary events— political events, natural events, and prophets; searched for parallel incidents; and were on the lookout for signs.

Unsuprisingly, the pattern of Islamic stories greatly resembles the pattern of stories found in the Semitic religions in general: for example, the occurrence of a prophet or messiah is announced; he appears; mystical stories grow around his birth; at the age of twelve, he gives learned talks and speeches; he starts having visions; people misjudge and underestimate him; he gets pursued and prosecuted; he retreats to the desert; he preaches, performs miracles, and rises to heaven. Jesus did so, and the same elements are found in the story of the Arabic Prophet.

Even when hopelessly outnumbered, the right ones are always victorious. And if an ordinary miracle is not sufficient, swarms of angels will come to the rescue. It is the same blueprint in the Old Testament, in the Qur'an, and in the ancient Orient. Whenever they entered a foreign country—fire and sword were at hand. They destroyed, killed, and pillaged—in the Old Testament and in the Qur'an. Everyone knows the story about how the Israelites destroyed Jericho (of course with the help of a miracle) and caused a bloodbath. But from archaeological findings we also know that nobody lived in Jericho back then. And there is no archaeological evidence regarding the stories about bloody conquests of all of Palestine.

The same applies to the stories of Islamic conquests in the name of the Prophet. There is no scientific evidence about invasions and the capture of Syria, Persia, or Egypt by Muslims during these time periods. That is because the establishing of the Arabian Empire was not a result of Islam—the empire had been there already. Only due to its existence was the exhaustive spread of Islam possible. Hence, the conquests of the first two hundred years under the green banner of the Prophet are nonexistent. Therefore, the tradition either made up heroic conquerors out of nothing or fab.. interesting legends and fitted them to historic persons. The autho.. of these traditional reports had an understanding about history that completely differed from the today's concept. Their ideas about history were related to the inspiration that was derived from images and epic traditions of the ancient Orient. We are not dealing with historically accurate reports but with people's desire to meet expectations, express their territoriality, and fulfill the need to form an identity: "Our religion, our superiority, our direct line to the Big Guy—so you'd better listen."

After having gone through a process with many intermediate steps of changing, editing, and adding that lasted for half a Millennium, the Qeryan, the Aramaic liturgical book of the Arabic Christians, had finished its transformation. It had become the book of a new religion. The Qur'an started out as a Christian Book but was converted into the Islamic Qur'an when Jesus had lost his special status. Theologically, this book represents a very much slimmed-down version but still contains the original key features. On first sight, its Arabic Christian nature cannot be detected easily anymore, which is a result of later revisions. It was only during the process of these later revisions that Muhammad evolved and acquired his own profile. The new religion received its special character both by later reinterpretations of the original message and by incorporation of Bedouin traditions.

The birth of Islam and the creation of its Holy Book did not happen overnight. And Islam certainly didn't spread over half of the ancient world within just a few years, like religious legends are trying to tell us. The history of Islam is long and twisted. It originated from the Arabic Christendom. Christendom split off from Judaism, and Islam split off from the Christendom. Signs of an upcoming separation were visible during the sixth and seventh centuries. The separation took place in the eight and ninth centuries. That's when the situation actually occurred that was traditionally described as being already completed in the seventh century. The creation and establishment of what we refer to as Islam today was not completed before the twelfth or even the thirteenth century. The descriptions and stories in Islamic traditions that deal with the Prophet and his Book, especially the ones about the first two hundred years, belong in the category "tales from the East." As mentioned in the introduction of this book, we have only just begun to discover the history of Islam. And thanks to science, the true story is beginning to surface, little by little.

❖ ❖ ❖

Boris Kester

Residential castle in Marw (Turkmenistan), seventh century. Marw evolved from the classical-ancient Antiochia Margiane, and was the ancestral residence of the Marwanids who became known as the "Umayyads"

St. John's Basilica in Damascus, built by al-Walid (705-715), son of Abd al-Malik

Original baptistery inside the basilica, which was later converted into a mosque and renamed "Umayyad Mosque"

Mezquita in Cordoba. Built by ar-Rahman I. in the year 785 as Christian-Syrian "masjid" (foto showing the oldest part), by his successors expanded and later transferred into a mosque

Dymon Lynch

Dome of The Rock, Jerusalem. Built by the Umayyad Abd al-Malik as Christian church (completed 694) in order to await here the arrival of the messiah Jesus

Transfiguration in Hindsight:
The "Golden Age" of Islam

Moses, Jesus, Muhammad—these criminals.
—"Islamic" philosopher ar-Razi (AD 865–925)

The source of all wrongful belief is to have even ever heard of such horrid names like Socrates, Hippocrates, Plato, and Aristotle.
—Islamic "philosopher" al-Ghazali (AD 1058–1111)

People like the former Egyptian President Gamal Abdel Nasser, Saddam Hussein, any preacher carrying out the Friday prayers, a pious journalist of a newspaper, or Osama bin Laden roaming around in the Afghan Mountains all have one thing in common: they all refer to the "Golden Age" of Islam.

But to what, exactly, do they refer?

First of all, the "Golden Age" of Islam stands for the time periods of both the lifetimes of the Prophet and his immediate successors, namely the "Rightly Guided Caliphs."

They were "Golden" time periods because the revelations transmitted by the Prophet occurred, meaning that the time periods during which God's words were the law, were allegedly good ones. The Prophet himself watched over people to ensure they adhered to the law and, in addition, he himself was the shining example—in other words, it was the most ideal situation for a pious Muslim. On top of that, the social situation is said to have been just ideal in every way. These conditions prevailed under the successors who were in charge immediately after the Prophet, so they say. And all of these successors were allegedly members of the Prophet's family. But as we already know, there are no solid facts proving any of this, as all this information, without exception, is derived from religious sources. Therefore, this information has got to be regarded as a matter of belief. It is faith that creates ideal circumstances.

It is said that these pious events happened in the Arabian desert, in a region between Mecca and Medina. But as we already know, this region didn't have anything to do with the development of Islam. Therefore, it would be futile to hold forth on the situation that existed in the Arabian desert back then.

Nevertheless: in general, the conditions in the Arabian desert of the seventh century must have been difficult. People lived at the subsistence level, often even below. Even until as late as the nineteenth century, raids frequently occurred which started from the Arabian desert into Mesopotamia, the Nile valley, and North Africa as a result of poverty, misery, and desperation.[60] It can be assumed that obvious Bedouin robbing sprees were later "re-historicized" and glorified as Islamic missionary expeditions.

Can we image what this society was like? It was a society that suffered privations but it was also a highly ideological patriarchal society with archaic rules like "eye for an eye." According to traditional reports, Muhammad himself is the best example: once he was in power he ordered the killings of unpopular persons and started dozens of massacres and wars. (Today, those activities are either hailed or interpreted as inevitable actions by the *Umma*, the "Community of the Believers.")

The allegedly "Golden" events were supposed to have happened during the Middle Ages—but referring to which Middle Ages? The Byzantine Empire was certainly the most advanced society during that time and the Arabic core regions such as Syria were at a similar stage. Europe distinctly lagged behind those two areas at that time. But in the Arabian desert, despite the use of iron, they still had the Bronze Age—and in some regions people hadn't even made it to that stage.

---

60   Up to this day, villages in Egypt in which nineteenth-century Arabic plunderers used to live are avoided by the locals. No marriages with the people of these villages take place.

Even in the most hostile environment, religious people might consider themselves to be living under ideal conditions spiritually. But it is actually of minor importance to figure out how exactly these conditions used to be back then. The problem arises when situations that are assumed to have been ideal in a different, long-gone epoch that took place in an environment that doesn't exist anymore, try to get transferred into a different time period. In this case it is the Bronze Age society of an Arabian desert environment that finds itself in the twenty-first century of a globalizing world. The desperate clinging to old times can only be regarded as the denial to realize that historic, social, and technical developments have been made. In other words, it is the denial to acknowledge that time and space change. And this is exactly the idea that the rather modern Islamic branch, called *Salafiyya*, follows. The obsession to hold on to a past that took place in an extreme environment in which figures played a role, about whom we actually know nothing, is a millstone round today's Muslims—that at least applies to Muslims who wish for those conditions to come back.

The "Golden Age" also includes all the tremendous conquests carried out under the green flag of the Prophet. The Islamic army allegedly started its conquest from the desert and conquered the Arabian Peninsula, Syria, Palestine, Iraq, Egypt, northern Africa, and Persia—and all that within a time period of just thirteen years. Right after that, successful conquests were carried out in the Caucasus, Spain and parts of France, Russia, India, and China. Yes, they got a lot done, and got it done fast. It allegedly all started in AD 629, when the Prophet's troops invaded Palestine.[61] Just a few years later, in AD 633, another Muslim army advanced from Mecca to Syria. In Islamic sources these events are reported as follows:

The Army was able to advance only very slowly until Caliph Abu Bakr ordered more troops, which were simultaneously conquering Mesopotamia, by saying: "Hurry, hurry, the capture of one single Syrian village comes at a price that is higher than the capture of

---

61 It should be remembered: in real history, Emperor Heracius ended his victorious campaign against Persia in the year AD 628 and restored the True Cross to Jerusalem in the year AD 630.

all of Iraq." With this reinforcement, the army was able to defeat the Byzantine army south of Jerusalem.

The location at which the alleged battle took place is unknown; the year of this alleged event is unknown; yet, surprisingly, all other details are very well-known: the general was Khalid al-Walid, the would-be military wizard of all time. (In real life, he was the creator of St. John's Basilica in Damascus.)

Number of troops: Muslims thirty-two thousand versus ninety thousand Byzantine troops. In order to create the right atmosphere for the battle, al-Walid sent a famous battle-champion to the frontline. He positioned himself before the Roman lines and shouted:

"I am the death of your ashen faces. I am the killer of the Romans. I am the scourge that has been sent to you. I am Zarrar, son of Azwar." When a Roman officer stepped forward to accept the challenge, Zarrar ripped off his suit of armor and threw away his shield. The Romans recognized him. They knew that he had killed dozens of war veterans, including generals from Tiberias and Amman. At the same time, a large group of Romans moved toward Zarrar as well. When al-Walid realized that a dirty trick was going on, he immediately threw himself into the battle; it was truly a most unfair fight, as there were only ten Roman soldiers against the greatest sword fighter of all time. They were no match for Khalid; he killed them swiftly and mercilessly. [62]

In either AD 637, AD 638, or AD 639,[63] the "decisive battle" of Kadesia in Iraq took place. Islamic sources cannot give any precise date about this battle but details about everything else they can provide plenty: one hundred thousand Persian troops with war elephants versus thirty thousand Muslims. It was a tough fight but when a desert storm began blowing toward the Persians, it was the end of them.[64]

---

62   From: http://www.islamreligion.com, 2009.
63   Let's remember: right before that, in several battles between AD 622 and 627, the Persian Empire was completely defeated by the Emperor Heraclius.
64   The interesting feature about the alleged battle of Kadesia is that later, in 1980, the former Iraqi dictator Saddam Hussein would use this event as a shining example

In AD 636, the "all-decisive battle" of Yarmuk (Jordan) happened: two hundred thousand Byzantine troops versus twenty-five thousand Muslims. The Muslims were victorious because "Persians and Romans" were disunited and, in addition, a stiff southerly breeze blew dust into their faces.

In AD 638 (some Islamic sources speak of AD 634), the Muslims conquered Jerusalem. In AD 639, they conquered the Persian province of Khuzestan; in AD 640 they captured Cairo; and in AD 642, Muslims conquered Alexandria. The same year, AD 642, another "all-decisive battle" took place at Nehawend in Iran. Here, one hundred fifty thousand Persians were fighting against less than ten thousand Muslims. No information is given on the direction of the wind this time. But the Muslims defeated the Persians, who were horrified and ran off in all directions.[65]

The victorious Islamic armies marched on in two major formations: one heading for India, the other one heading for China. On the way, at the Talas River, the Chinese were finished off, namely in another "decisive battle in world history" (Wikipedia, 2009) by—and who would have thought—an Abbasid caliph. The surprise over this little piece of information even increases when going through stories by Islamic sources that deal with different subjects of Islamic history: during the same time in the same region, the Muslim leader Abu Muslim had the Umayyads exiled from this region. In addition to that, he suppressed a "Shi'a revolution" and fell out with the caliph. We are looking at a lot of action here: retribution expedition, an internal religious war, and the crushing of the Chinese army—and it all happened at the same time in the same place.

But that's not all: simultaneously, Islamic armies were busy capturing and subjugating northern Africa, Spain, and southern France. At this point, the author wishes to spare the reader from learning about further conquests and invasions like the one in Russia, reaching the Volga River.

---

for the war against Iran.

65   In a seminar speech put on the website http://www.politik.de in 2009 it was stated: "It cannot be considered a coincidence to be defeated all the time but always be victorious anyway."

Under the Caliph Umar ibn al-Chattab (*vulgo*: the pulled-out sword of God), the Muslims turned out to be a successful sea power, as had been predicted by the Prophet. According to Islamic interpretation, Muslims couldn't have picked a better way to hit the "nerve center of Byzantium." And that's how they won the sea battle of Phoinix, also known as the "Battle of Masts," in which the Muslims crushed the Byzantine navy. Apparently, the Byzantine commanders followed a very clumsy strategy in that they positioned their battleships too close together, providing the Muslims with the opportunity to jump from one ship to another. That way the Muslims turned this sea battle into a land battle. And the fact that the Muslim fleet consisted of Christians was no problem, as the Christians were very enthusiastic about the idea of serving under the Muslims. The fleet eventually failed by the "Greek Fire," but never mind, the Byzantine Emperor paid tribute to the Muslims.

Let's recall and make a reality check: the exact opposite situation happened. Muawiyya/Maavia paid tribute and was eventually kicked out of office for his failures. And his successor kept on making the payments to Byzantine, as we know. It comes as no surprise that the author of this sea battle is the storyteller at-Tabari. He wrote this story down around the year AD 900, about two hundred years after the alleged events.[66] Needless to say, there is no historic evidence about the good Caliph Umar ibn al-Chattab; therefore, he must be counted as just another of the numerous members of the Never-Have-Beens Club.[67] Not a single one of these Muslim "decisive battles" has been historically verified.

---

66   It seems that we have to say goodbye to our most favorite fairy tale teller at-Tabari, also. According to recent analysis, the at-Tabari-texts were produced in Cairo in the twelfth or thirteenth century. Future research might reveal that "Tabari" was actually not a person but a collective term for compilations of texts of various origins by different authors.

67   Regardless, there is a PhD thesis produced at the Philosophical Faculty Cologne, Germany, about this Caliph's suprahuman accomplishments: the author Halte Uenal wrote: "Die Rechtfertigung der juristischen Urteile des zweiten Kalifen, Umar Ibn Al-Hattab" (Justifications of the legal decisions by the 2nd Caliph Umar Ibn Al-Hattab); Cologne, 1982. Others have expressed the opinion that Caliph Umar was a really bad guy: In reality, Umar Ibn Al-Hattab was a spy for the Jews, and with him the Jewish infiltration of the Muslims began (http://www.alhaq.de/biografien/, 2009).

It seems clear that after the crash of the Persian Sassanides, claiming new territory or privileges, or trying to get former areas back, would have been sources of conflict. Various independent sources report about skirmishes that took place during these time periods without providing any information about the parties involved in these conflicts. They are believed to be fights for position between former members of Persian and Byzantine parties, or fights between emirs that had become independent, and former landowners. But there is no historic trace of Muslims yet.

After the battle of Nineveh in AD 627 in which Chosroes II was finally defeated by Heraclius, there was no Persian power left that the Muslims could have destroyed on their campaign to China. And Heraclius himself was at the peak of his military power.

As for the whole of early Islamic history, including this case, the great problem is the sources. They are, without exception, Islamic sources, which—on top of that—are later reports, without exception as well. All of the relevant authors,[68] who are referenced over and over again, wrote their detail-loaded reports—garnished with innumerable citations— many years later. All of these stories are based on unsubstantiated sources. The stories deal with events ("decisive battles") or persons ("caliphs") about which no historic evidence has ever been provided. All the dates are as good as incorrect because, for one thing, they refer to legends and, second, the recalculations of timetables in order to adjust them to the lunar calendar were carried out much later and often represent a source of error in themselves. The only sources that these authors are able to provide are the traditional chains of oral transmissions by their celebrated "story suppliers."

There are no Islamic sources that deal with Islam's first two centuries, which include Muhammad's life and the conquests. The idea of accepting history that is written later based on no historic evidence corresponds to the idea of Sayyid Qutb,[69] who claims that history

---

68   *Annals* by al-Tabari (AD ?–922), Hadiths collection by Bukhari (AD ?–870), *This History of Conquests* by Al Wakidi (AD ?–822), *Generations* by Ibn Saad (AD ?–845).

69   Islamic theorist, Egypt, 1906–1966. More about him in Chapter 10.

does not happen in Islam because Islam exists in "dimensions that are beyond history."

The following citation may illustrate the flexible usage of historic facts in Islamic interpretation:

"But also the actual historic events, their portrayal, and their explanations will be different, depending on whether or not the historian allows the idea of divine influences.[70]"
And: *"In Muslim tradition, it has been accepted as the right way that this problem* [the absence of any supporting evidence] *should not be resolved by applying a dogmatic ignorance of all miraculous things but by raising the bar regarding the credibility of reporting and coverage."*

In other words, it means that miracles are allowed to be in history reports and even a part of history science itself. But does this gentleman speak of historians or does he refer to "*quassas*," the storytellers in the ancient Orient? Certainly, rational religious people are aware that, from a logical point of view, such events as described are impossible. It would leave no other way than to postulate the existence of miracles or to generally claim that it is impossible to apply historic processes to Islam. Nevertheless, one should keep to the bad Western habits of applying research methods and basing the writing of history on both facts and circumstances that can be verified.

The Christians who lived during the same time in the same region didn't only leave a vast amount of literature but also developed extensive missionary activities even as far as China. One should just take a look at the compassionate discussions and the topics that moved and stirred their minds, and which they extensively documented. They extensively discussed topics of minor importance but would not say a word about this new religion that was spreading.

Based on how the events are described in traditional reports, Islam blew like a blizzard through half of the ancient world. Why didn't

---

70   Mohammed Laabdallaoui on: http://www.muhamad.islam.de, 2009.

any of the people who were most affected by these events, like the Christians and many members of other religions, mention anything about it? Because they welcomed Muslims as liberators? Because the liberators were most tolerant, as the tradition wants to make us believe?

Many attempts have been made to try to verify these events by using non-Islamic sources. In order to do so, it has become customary to use names like Sophronius (seventh-century monk and theologian in Jerusalem), Maximus the Confessor, Thomas the Presbyterian, Sebeos of Armenia (seventh-century Armenian bishop and historian), John of Damascus (monk and theologian, ca. AD 700), and others.[71]

The texts that can be clearly assigned to both a certain author and a definite time period draw a very specific picture: the reports deal with the "Saracens, Ishmaelites, and Hagarites," which are terms that, back then, were commonly used synonyms for "Arabs." They were viewed as "heretics," but by no means were they seen as members of another religion, least of all Islam. Heretics are deviationists from their own religion, and that is exactly what the Arabic Christians represented in the seventh to ninth centuries. There is a most revealing documented verbal exchange between Patriarch John and an emir that took place in AD 644, which was right after Maavia came to power.[72] What did they talk about? Well, besides some administrative issues, they talked about differences between various confessions, about Abraham, Moses, and Mary—and, of course, the nature of Jesus. The emir could have been Ibn As or Ibn Saad. According to Nevo and Koren,[73] "…the Emir was certainly no Muslim, he showed neither the kind of knowledge nor any indication that he was a follower, he never mentioned Muhammad, the Qur'an, or Islam."

---

71   Karl-Heinz Ohlig, "Hinweise auf eine neue Religion in der christlichen Literatur, unter islamischer Herrschaft?", *Der frühe Islam*. Berlin, 2007.

72   F. Nau, "Un colloque de Patriarch Jean avec l'émir des Agareens," *Journal Asiatique*, 1915.

73   Yehuda D. Nevo and Judith Koren, *Crossroads to Islam* (New York: Prometheus Books, 2003).

In such cases, the Islamic interpretation uses the *taqiyya* weapon. *Taqiyya* is the method of deception sanctioned by the Qur'an,[74] in order to get out of an emergency situation, or to profit from an unbeliever by pretending to be his friend. Applied to the emir's case, the explanation would be that he only pretended not to be a Muslim for tactical reasons.

Realistic and sober-minded analysis of certain figures used should be more than enough to realize certain things. How could armies have been put together in a nearly unpopulated area? Only Egypt and Mesopotamia had millions of inhabitants. They could have easily defended themselves using sticks alone. In the tradition, awareness regarding this issue is certainly apparent, and, therefore, the explanation is delivered in a combo-pack together with the historic events: a naked Muslim, only armed with a reed blade, suddenly faces a heavily armed Persian knight. In state of anxiety, the knight turns his horse around and hides all of his arrows in his coat, giving the impression that they all have been shot already.

Between AD 639 and 641, the countries of Mesopotamia, Persia, and Egypt are said to have been conquered—simultaneously—and it necessarily also included the capture of several forts, for which the use of siege machinery and much time was required. It doesn't take a degree from a military academy to figure out that, from a mathematical point of view, this whole set of conquests is plain nonsense. For this reason, Islamic tradition very officially resorts to miracles and even tries to establish their use as a legitimate tool of historic documentation.

Let's try to imagine that, within just a few years, the religiously obsessed Byzantine Empire lost half of its territory—in the name of another religion. And imagine that the Persians lost their whole empire to someone else. Wouldn't they notice any of this? Both of these empires were characterized by elaborate administrative apparatuses. Both of them had a great tradition of keeping records. And they didn't take down a single note that they had just lost half or all of their empires?

---

74 For instance, Sura 3:28, 29.

Millions of affected people like Christians, pagans, Zoroastrians, and Buddhists, in an area that stretched from the Nile River to the Indus and further to the Volga River, didn't notice anything about having been conquered by a new religion? Monks, priests, bishops, highly intellectual theologians, world-travelling prominent figures—none of them was capable of realizing that there was a new religion? Or should we assume that they were all too cowardly to speak out against it? Most of them would have been more than happy to die for their religion. During those times of keen religious awareness and a highly developed writing culture, a militant new religion achieving a complete victory in just a few years would have not been mentioned? This would be the most absurd idea ever.

The only plausible explanation is that the events mentioned in the tradition never took place. With all due respect, it is impossible to regard the Islamic reports as historic documentations. They are stories, fairy tales like the *Arabian Nights*. But the really chilling thing is that those stories have basically minted the Western public's idea about history. That almost sounds like another miracle.

The "Golden Age" of Islamic conquests? *Never happened as reported.* There were indeed some golden years of Arabic self-determination, during which the separation from the two power blocs of that region laid the foundation stone of both an Arabic Empire and Arabic conscience, but it was not until later that this solely Arabic history was reinterpreted into an Islamic one.

In AD 1377, the Arabic historian Ibn Khaldun sat in a hill fortress in the North African desert and spent his days thinking about both the intellectual decay of the Islamic Empire and its causes.

It was exactly the time period during which the Upper-Italian commercial centers significantly gained economic influence, which led to a tremendous boost of arts and sciences—what we now refer to as the Renaissance.

"We hear that the philosophical sciences are now being cultivated in the land of Rome and along the adjacent northern coasts, in the land of the European Christians. The available systematic documentations are said to be extensive, and people who are familiar with them are said to be large in number, and students are numerous.[75]"

The extensive systematic documentations, to which Khaldun refers, had been obtained by the "northern countries" from the east. To a large extent, they represented Latin translations of Arabic texts, which in turn were translations of originally Greek scripts that had been translated into Aramaic, Arabic, or Persian. Ibn Khaldun viewed himself as a member of a culture in which the entirety of knowledge of passed cultures was united and was then further developed. The idea that these unbelieving barbarians might take over this heritage was confusing to him. He sensed that the great times of Arabic sciences were coming to an end, but he was unaware that he would be the last representative of the guild of his kind.

Around the year AD 750, the era of the Umayyads' power had ended. Their successors, known as the Abbasids, established their residences further in the east, mainly in Baghdad and Samarra. Under the regencies of some of their rulers, sciences flourished. This is viewed by some as the cornerstone of the claim that the Islamic Middle Ages were more advanced than the European Middle Ages, that this was the "Golden Age" of Islamic sciences.

Let's take a look at the most important representatives of "Islamic sciences":

Yaqub ibn Ishaq al-Kindi (ca. AD 800–?)

Al-Kindi grew up in the city of Kufa, the cultural center located in Mesopotamia during the enlightened regency of the knowledge-hungry ruler al-Mamun in Baghdad. Al-Kindi's educational life is unknown, but he was appointed the private tutor of one of al-Mamun's nephews, Mu'tasim, who would later become a ruler.

---

75 Ibn Khaldun, *The Muqaddimah* (New York: Princeton University Press, 1967).

Some of his teaching materials have been preserved (e.g., an essay about why it was possible that the ball-shaped earth could float through space). Another article dealt with calculating methods by using "Indian numbers." This is exactly the number system which we refer to as "Arabic numbers." This system, most certainly, was derived from India and made it to Europe through Arabic works.

Al-Kindi tried to explain the phenomenon of high tide and low tide by the occurrence of frictional heat that resulted from the moon's rotation. In another work, he attempted to forge logical links to Qur'anic statements (e.g., the one in which stars and trees throw themselves at God's feet and pray). In these statements, al-Kindi sees the principle of absolute conformity with a natural law—despite the fact that he attributes to the stars the ability to see and hear. His work on "cause and effect" he dedicated to Mamun. By doing so, he put himself in sharp contrast to one of the main Qur'anic schools of thought, which strictly rejects the idea of causality and replaces it with God's will.

Al-Kindi's approach was based on ideas by Aristotle and Ptolemy and flavored by ancient "Oriental" traditions; he seemed to have been particularly close to old-Babylonian star worshippers. Al-Kindi's legacy contains more than two hundred works. In some places in his texts, he appears confused and his ideas half-baked, but he always propagates free and independent thinking as the central issue. He refers to himself by using the foreign term of "philosopher" and keeps on pointing out the importance of recognizing truth, regardless of its origin. He was the first in a series of Arabic philosophers. His way of thinking represents the exact opposite of traditional Qur'anic teachings.

Hunayn ibn Ishaq (AD 808–873)

Originally from al-Hira in southern Mesopotamia, Ishaq was born the son of a pharmacist. His goal was to become a medical doctor, and for that reason he moved to Baghdad. There, he attended the lectures of Yuhanna ibn Masawayh. Yuhanna was a Syrian Christian, just like Hunayn, and also the private physician of the caliph. Customary teaching materials included works by Greek authors, especially those works produced by the famous physician Galen of Pergamon. For some reason (he was allegedly too cheeky), Hunayn was expelled from attending the lectures. He left and started a journey, traveling from one city to another. He probably also made it to Byzantium. Six years later, he returned to Baghdad and started translating standard scientific works of the classical world of the Romans and Greeks into Arabic or into the language his client preferred. He was quite proficient in classical languages, but also in all of the commonly used languages of the region. Due to his medical education, he was qualified to produce field-specific translations, but his spectrum of knowledge included every scientific field that was known back then. One of his works he extended to his former teacher, Ibn Masawayh, without mentioning himself as author. "The one who produced this work must have had support of the Holy Spirit," Masawayh is said to have called out, deeply impressed.

Hunayn became such a busy man that he would soon teach his son and his nephew how to translate standard texts, while he kept dealing with the scientific part of the job. This included the initial step of searching for old handwritten scripts. A large number of incomplete works were available that consisted of fragments written in various languages or by different copyists. When Hunayn had collected a sufficient number of items, he began comparing them. He was wary of the fact that handwritten products could always contain mistakes and errors: misspellings, erroneous translations, and forgeries. Based on these comparisons, he then produced the most reliable translations possible. He also wrote a catalogue on these translations (the catalogue was just found in 1918). He had the habit of renaming the old gods that were mentioned in the texts, calling them either the One God, or naming them after angels or saints. In contrast to other authors, he was not satisfied with the usage of technical terms in Greek, and therefore, he created Arabic words for them. He would also make sure to order extra heavy paper from Samarkand, a region where the technique to produce Chinese paper was known. At that time, his works were already paid for in silver.

Hunayn ibn Ishaq was what today would be called a scientific publisher and editor. When he died in AD 873, he left a significant legacy in the form of works by authors of the classical-ancient world. He was a great Arabic scientist, but not a Muslim one.

Thabit ibn Qurra, (AD 834–901?)

"Who were the ones who built the harbors and canals, who spread the secret sciences? Who were the ones, to whom Deity was revealed, to whom oracles were given, and to whom future things were taught, if it had not been to the wise ones among the pagans? They are the ones who have studied all that, who have explained the healing of the souls and have spread the word of their salvation. They have also studied the curing of the body, and they have filled the world with wisdom, the most important virtue of all."

The above lines were written by someone who was a pagan himself— the Sabean[76] Thabit ibn Qurra, in Harran, in today's eastern Turkey. And he was a firm-believing pagan. One time, when he discussed the emerging new Islamic religion with some of its followers, they emphasized the omnipotence of God, and he asked back: *"Can your God also bring about that five times five is not twenty-five?"*

To him, this newfangled God had, if anything, omnipotence over creatures, but not over Creation itself. He saw God himself as a creature, an understanding rooted in the old-Babylonian star-cult and influenced by classical-Greek thought. The Sabeans revered and worshipped wise men of the past as prophets, among which there were Greek philosophers as well.[77] One slogan stated: *"Plato said: 'The one who knows his own nature becomes divine.'"*[78]

Passing through the city of Harran, a personality of high social status noticed this well-educated Sabean and took him back to Baghdad.

---

76 Sabeans followed a Babylonian-Chaldean star-worshipping cult.
77 It becomes clear that in the empire of the so-called Caliphs, there was richness in religious diversity even as late as the ninth century. At that time, Islam was certainly not the already established and dominating religion.
78 Inscription on the door knocker of a Sabean house in Harran (after al-Masudi).

There, Thabit produced scientific works for this would-be scientist, under whose name these works were published. In addition, Thabit became some kind of freelance employee in Hunayn's publishing company, for whom he answered astronomical questions. Later, he was admitted to the circle of Royal Court Astronomers, and became confidant and close friend of ruler al-Mutatid.

All of the important scientists and philosophers, without exception, had been at least temporarily appointed to one of the royal courts or that of a local emir. Back then, this was the only way to have a career. Thabit was perfectly fluent in Greek and dealt with issues in the fields of philosophy, mathematics, and medicine. Among other books, he produced a collection of questions that a physician should ask his patient. Also, he was of the opinion that there were actually four people who were behind the name "Hippocrates."

As a Sabean, however, Thabit's strong point was the field of astronomy. He was especially intrigued by the fact that the lengths of each individual year slightly differed. Following Ptolemy's system, he assumed that the spheres of fixed stars performed slight movements, the so-called *trepidation*. This concept was even picked up by Copernicus. Thabit is also mentioned by the poet Wolfram von Eschenbach as Thebit in the major medieval German romance *Parzival*.

Muhammad ibn Zakariya ar-Razi (865–925)

One important Arabic medical authority started his career as lute player: Muhammad ibn Zakariya ar-Razi, born in Rajj, today's Tehran. Only a little is known about his life (e.g., he was in charge of hospitals in Baghdad and Rajj, and was also a friend of the local emir al-Mansur ibn Ishaq). He left an extensive legacy, however, in the form of specialized literature; ar-Razi was the greatest clinician of the Arab world and has been well-known, especially in Europe, as *Rhazes*. He dedicated one of his medical encyclopedias to his patron Mansur. The Latin translation of its ninth chapter, which became very popular in Europe, is *Liber Nonus Almansurus*. It contained cures that were grouped according to individual diseases from head to toe, and was even available in some common European languages.

Another ar-Razi work that became very famous in Europe dealt with measles and smallpox. This work was still being published even in the eighteenth century in England. When he died in AD 925, ar-Razi had left a tremendous number of Greek excerpts about clinical cases, to which he had added his observations and experiences. This legacy was later systemized by students and resulted in the work titled *Liber Continens*, which was published in AD 1486. It filled two large tomes.

As was common for every famous physician at that time, Rhazes, too, had great philosophical knowledge, as medical understanding was largely derived from philosophy. He was very familiar with Greek philosophers like Hippocrates[79] and Galen.[80] Rhazes showed that he largely was a free thinker, but he never introduced innovations without paying respect to the great Galen:

"Indeed, it was painful to me to stand up against the one who, of all humans, showered me with the largest number of charities, who was the most helpful one to me, by whom I was guided, the one I followed step-by-step. But the field of medicine is a philosophy that doesn't tolerate any standstill."

While Galen was of the opinion that the soul depended on the condition of the body, Rhazes said that the soul's condition actually decided the condition of the body. As a practical consequence, he suggested to physicians that they should always be encouraging to their patients even if they weren't sure regarding the exact diagnosis. Ar-Razi also went his own way when it came to philosophy. Inspired by Democritus, he assumed that matter was atomic in nature (earth, fire, air, and water). Besides that, he viewed God, the world's soul, as the absolute order in space and time; to him, the cosmos was apparently multidimensional. The creator of the Bible and the Qur'an was only appointed to the task but not really almighty. Rhazes viewed prophets as necessary connecting links between God and men, but excluded

---

79 Hippocrates of Kos, physician, ca. 460–370 BC.
80 Roman physician, AD 129–216; together with Hippocrates as the most significant physicians of the ancient classical period.

the "three criminals Moses, Jesus, and Muhammad"[81] from this idea because they had only sowed the seeds of discord. His "imam" (he used exactly this term) was Socrates.

Ar-Razi's identification as a Muslim has been the most natural thing, but can we really assume that a Muslim would talk like this?

During his final years, Rhazes lost his eyesight; he died in AD 925.

Al-Farabi (AD 890–950)

Most of the Arabic scholars were also physicians, either in their main profession or in a side job. Al-Farabi was "only" a scientist—he mainly interpreted texts of Aristotle and other philosophers by adding his own versions to them. He purposely separated the field of medicine from philosophy because its purpose was to cause a physical reaction in the body but didn't have anything to do with finding truth.

"Al-Farabi" simply means "the one from Farab," a city in today's Kazakhstan where he was born in AD 890. By his physical appearance, Farabi was most likely an ethnic Kazakh. It is said that throughout his whole life, he neglected his external appearance and always wore a shabby Kazakh-style caftan. Little is known about his childhood. We only know that when he was a young boy, he left for the Persian village of Harran and then moved on further to Baghdad. In Baghdad, several Christian teachers took care of him. As it turned out, he spent most of his time in Baghdad; during his final years, he lived in Aleppo, Syria, at the Court of the emir Saif al-Daula. Right before his death, Farabi traveled to Cairo. He died upon his return to Syria. The Islamic clergy made a point of *not* attending his funeral.

And there were certainly reasons for that: although Farabi always tried to find a balance between philosophy and religion, he taught many things of which the imams could hardly approve. But he mainly worked on his interpretations of Aristotle. He portrayed the world as a unity: its origin is God but not in the sense of his being its creator, as viewed by the Qur'an or the Bible, but as the impersonal source of its

81 This statement has been subject to much discussion. Even if it turns out that ar-Razi didn't invent this statement, he nevertheless made it popular.

being. It is the principle source from which things flow or pour forth, the so-called emanation. It is matter that forms the lowest level of the hierarchy, and it is also the level in which the human being is involved. The human being can only reach higher-level worlds by the process of thinking, mystical contemplation, or death. The foremost task of men is to become one with the Universal Intellect by understanding the world and the universe. But only few people can reach this kind of happiness—for the others, there is religion. Hence, Farabi viewed religion as an artificial product but as one that is necessary for the vast majority of people.

Based on this thinking, he created the concept of an Ideal Nation. Similarly to Plato, he called for a philosopher-king who should, however, have a prophet by his side, in order to provide instructions to the less-reasonable common people.

Despite the fact that his philosophy was antireligious, Farabi still had in mind that clergymen should influence the illiterate masses in their day-to-day lives.

In contrast to others, al-Farabi was never in the spotlight but rather preferred to spend his time at the pond in the garden.

Ibn al-Haytham (AD 965–?)
In Basra, a person called Ibn al-Haytham was born who would later become known in Europe as *Alhazen*. He began his career as a civil service worker but switched careers and started carrying out scientific studies in Baghdad and Persia. One day, al-Haytham caught the attention of the counter-caliph in Cairo. When he mentioned that it was possible to dam up the Nile River and provide irrigation for the fields all year around, he was called to Egypt and assigned to the project. With a large team and a lot of devices at his disposal, he went up the Nile River in order to start the project, but when he saw all the impressive old Egyptian buildings along the Nile River, he began having doubts about the whole idea. If not even those people who were capable of creating such buildings were able to build a dam, how could someone like him succeed? Nevertheless, he kept on and

found a suitable spot in Aswan, at the site of today's Aswan Dam. But soon he would realize that this project couldn't be carried out. Coming back to Cairo without having achieved anything, he was lucky to get away with his life, considering the magnitude of this disaster.

After that, he turned to the kind of job typical of many scientists of that time: he translated ancient scripts. Over the years, he completed translations like the whole edition of Euclid and the *Almagest* by Ptolemy, as well as scripts by other Greek authors. As a result, he became financially independent and was now able to turn to his most favorite field: physics, especially optics.[82] While most of the ancient classical, as well as Arabic, physicists were purely theoreticians, Alhazen focused on carrying out experiments—a great novelty at that time. He produced the first glass lens which, interestingly, he only applied in his experiments but apparently never put to use for any practical purpose such as a hand lens or fieldglass. In contrast to Euclid, he discovered that lightbeams traveled from an object into the eye and that it was not a beam radiating from the eye that scanned the object. Using a concave metal mirror, he worked on a certain mathematical problem which is still known today as the *Alhazen's Problem*, which he himself solved in a rather roundabout way. But it would not be until the mid-seventeenth century that a more elegant solution was developed by the Dutch Christiaan Huygens. Alhazen also discovered the primary laws of geometrical perspective as a result of light beams expanding in a straight line. As a consequence, from his studies on light beams he entered the field of astronomy. He observed the world of stars in a very rational way which was as physical units that can be understood and calculated. Based on the principle of refraction, he erroneously calculated the atmosphere to be five miles in thickness because he assumed that it had a clear limit and did not consist of gradually thinning air layers. The magnitude of his work was best described by Alexander von Humboldt who referred to the Arabs as the actual founders of physics. Ibn al-Haytham *aka* Alhazen was their most significant representative of this field, although only parts of his works are preserved. And it was not before long that his scripts were burnt for being against the Qur'an.

---

82 His main work was published in Latin under the title *Thesaurus Opticus* and was highly thought of in Europe.

Abu Ali ibn Sina (ca. AD 979–1037)

Under the name *Avicenna*, Abu Ali ibn Sina became one of the most famous medieval personalities in Europe. In areas of the old "Orient," he is still celebrated today. Iran, Uzbekistan, Tajikistan, and Turkmenistan compete for the honor of calling him one of their own.

There are still many mysteries about Avicenna's life. The first one has to do with the year of his birth. There are four different numbers regarding his age at death, none of which is clear, not even whether it refers to lunar or solar years, providing scholars with eight dates from which to choose. (According to Lüling, Avicenna most likely reached an age of fifty-eight years. This means that Avicenna would have been born around AD 979.) His family was originally from the Buddhist stronghold Balch[83] in today's Afghanistan. They later moved to the Samanid residence town of Kharmitan nearby Bukhara (Uzbekistan) where Avicenna was born. His father was a high-level civil officer at the Royal Court of the Buddhist Samanid Dynasty.[84] Avicenna came from a wealthy family, which ensured that he could be given the best education possible at that time. The study of Porphyrios's *Eisagoge* and other classical works was part of the basic education. Naturally, he also studied mathematics, geometry, physics, and medicine, the latter of which he regarded as not being a difficult science. He was an extraordinarily busy worker who, at least according to his own words, also worked through the nights.

At the age of twenty-two years, his easy life was over. The Turk tribe called Qara-Khanids destroyed the Samanid Empire and deported the surviving members of the dynastic family. Avicenna ("Distress called upon me to move away") fled to Urgench, the capital of Choresmia Province (today's Turkmenistan).

---

83   The Bactria of Hellenic time. Balch included parts of today's Afghanistan, Turkmenistan, Tajikistan, and Uzbekistan. Here, the classical ancient world and the Buddhist world met and mixed in a very fruitful way. Revealingly, the well-known Buddha statutes of Bamiyan wore Greek robes. Avicenna experienced the collapse of this world.

84   The name was derived from the place of residence Saman/Suman. The term *Sumaniyya* used to be synonymous with Buddhism.

At the same time, the Samanid Prince al-Muntasir tried to win back his power in a five-year battle, but eventually failed. Avicenna was his follower, and doors that had been open to him were now closed for political reasons.

Avicenna next left Urgench and continued his migration from place to place, accompanied by his longtime teacher and companion Abu Sahl al-Masihi who was a highly prominent, learned man and former personal physician of the Samanids.

"Distress called upon me to move away"—this became the trademark of Avicenna's life. Throughout his whole life, he remained a political refugee from a Buddhist world that came under Islamic pressure.

Avicenna moved from Urgench to Nisa, then Abiwerd, and other places, and eventually arrived in Gurgan at the Caspian Sea. His companion didn't survive this journey. During his travels, he occasionally worked as a physician under a false name. His hopes for employment with Sheikh Qabus in Gurgan remained unfulfilled. For that reason, he moved to the Royal Court of Shams-ad-Daula in the Hamadan Province in Persia. Here he was given a ministerial position.

One day, a military revolt directed against him got him into serious trouble. The cause for the revolt most likely had to do with his ministerial essay regarding "the food supply and pay of the army, military slaves, and soldiers, and land tax of estates." He barely survived this crisis but was put in jail for four months soon afterward for allegedly having conspired with an enemy emir from Esfahan. He used his jail time to produce several works. After a long series of detail-rich imbroglios, he eventually retreated in secret to Esfahan disguised as a monk. We can only speculate about what the true political background for this might have been.

During the final period of his life, Avicenna was one of the closest confidents of the emir of Esfahan and accompanied him on his war campaigns as his physician. And it was during one of those war campaigns that Avicenna died in AD 1037. He was fifty-eight years old. The circumstances of his death are recorded: in order to prepare for escape after an expected military defeat, he instructed one of the physicians to mix a reviving medicine. The potion accidently contained an overdose of parsley seeds and opium.

Avicenna lived a very intense life. During the day, he was busy working in various bread-and-butter jobs; in the evenings he gave lectures and produced scripts. But that was not all, as one of his students and coworkers, al-Guzgani,[85] reported: "When we were finished for the day, singers of all kinds appeared, an all-inclusive wine delight was prepared, and we got on with it."

And: "All of the master's strengths were very well developed, that especially applied to the most desiring part of the soul, the sex drive. It was the strongest and most overpowering." It was known nationwide that Avicenna lived a licentious life.

Apparently, Avicenna saw his calling as politics; he earned his living as a physician, judge, and scholar. It was the latter profession in which he produced his philosophical work. His life was strongly influenced by the collapse of the Samanid Empire, which took place simultaneously with the collapse of the "eastern-Iranian Renaissance." Most likely, Avicenna's roots were Buddhist. He never directly made any statements regarding his roots and painstakingly avoided showing any partisan spirit. He never showed any kind of religious inclination and was well-known for living an un-Islamic life. This also included the fact that he, most likely, carried out dissections of cadavers, a practice which is banned by the Qur'an. Avicenna refused to accept that a prophet was necessary for conveying divine revelation[86] (this idea represents the key concept of the *Sumaniyya*, or Buddhists), an attitude that was a continuous source of trouble with the Islamic orthodoxy.

Avicenna's legacy contains extensive philosophical and medical text materials, though his works on arts and humanities might be overrated.

85 The first half of his biography was most likely produced by Avicenna himself. The second half was written by his student and companion al-Guzgani.
86 There is a nice little story from the fifteenth century, according to which the Prophet Muhammad appeared to al-Magribi in a vision and complained to him that Ibn Sina had made contact with God without his [the Prophet's] intermediation.

The *Book of Healing* and the *Canon of Medicine*, a systematic work on medicine, were standard works that made him famous in medieval Europe. He was rather "high-spirited" or arrogant, as one would say today, and had a ruthless character. Accusing Rhazes of making concessions to religious viewpoints, Avicenna wrote that Rhazes had better keep to "investigating skin diseases, urine, and bowel movements." It can be assumed that he edited works of his companion and teacher al-Masihi, and published them under his own name.

In the history of science, there was a great leap that took place from Hippocrates to Galen, but the advancing step from Galen to Avicenna was even more significant. For as long as five hundred years, his works had a dominating influence in the field of medicine in the old "Orient" and Europe—until Paracelsus ushered in a new era in medicine in 1530.

Avicenna was a remarkable scientist of arts and humanities, and the greatest physician of the medieval epoch. But just like the previously mentioned "Islamic scholars," he was not a Muslim, either.

al-Biruni (AD 976–1048)
Regarding the fields of nonmedical sciences, today's researchers are inclined to give yet another Uzbek even greater recognition than Avicenna: al-Biruni. In Europe, he remained rather unknown. That may have been due to the fact that there was no biography of him available for a long time. He was a contemporary and countryman of the slightly younger Avicenna. The two met as well but never developed a friendship—something that was apparently difficult to achieve with Avicenna. Biruni was born in Kath, south of the Aral Sea, and came from a humble background. He owed his career to a local dynastic family that admitted him into their family and made available to him the best education possible. At the age of sixteen years, he carried out a geographic calculation of the position of his hometown and, also at a young age, he created a half globe with the northern hemisphere.[87]

---

87 It would take until 1492 for another model of the globe to be prepared by Martin Behaim from Nuremburg, Germany.

For political reasons, Biruni had to leave his hometown in AD 995, presumably for the same reasons for which Avicenna was forced to flee. Without taking his research devices, he moved to Rajj, nowadays Tehran. There, he met an astronomer who was busy building an instrument that measured the position of the sun. Biruni sent a letter to an astronomer in Baghdad, suggesting carrying out simultaneous measurements on the expected lunar eclipse in AD 997. This would give the distance angle of two positions.

After that, he temporarily moved to Gurgan at the Caspian Sea where he spent time together with Avicenna. Soon after, Biruni was appointed to the Royal Court of Urgench. But the city was captured by an enemy, Prince Masud, who allegedly deported Biruni to Ghazna in today's Afghanistan. But what probably really happened, however, was that Biruni was part of a ransom payment. Ghazna was a Hindu stronghold and Prince Masud was very interested in sciences.[88] Al-Biruni had now a new supporter. He attributed the *Masudic Canon*, which was the largest astronomical encyclopedia of the medieval times, to his name. Another duty was to accompany his ruler on numerous war campaigns, which brought him all the way to India. From this trip resulted his unique work about the cultural history of India: *Verification of What Is Said about India*. In order to understand Indian mathematics and astronomy, he learned Sanskrit. All in all, he reported very sensitively about Indian culture. It was something that came naturally to him as he, just like Avicenna, had a Buddhist background. Biruni was the only one who, at least to some extent, had the intellectual capabilities to challenge the Aristotlean system. He was astronomer, physicist, geographer, and philosopher—but, in contrast to all the others previously mentioned—he was not a medical doctor. And he was no Muslim either. He died while preparing an essay on a legal problem.

Ibn Rushd (AD 1126–1198)

We are now leaving the easternmost area of the Arabic Empire for the westernmost region called "al Gharb"—that is, Andalusia, southern Spain. There, Ibn Rushd was born in Cordoba. As *Averroes*, he became

---

88 Masud was most likely Hindu. The fact that Islamic historians defame him as a "drunkard" corroborates this assumption.

a household name at European universities; in the Arabian world, he remained unnoticed. But his great fame made him known there in the modern age only. He received the best education available back then, which as we know, included philosophy, mathematics, astronomy, and therapeutics, and, as he was a member of the judiciary guild, he also studied law.

In AD 1148, the Almohad Berber Dynasty conquered Andalusia under the command of Caliph Abu Yaqub Yusuf. In AD 1153, Ibn Rushd was called to the ruler's residence in Marrakesh. Though worried about the meeting, Ibn Rushd followed the ruler's call. He was introduced to court by Ibn Tufayl, who was also quite well-known in Europe as the author of the philosophical novel *The Natural Man*, which tells the story of people who get stranded on an unpopulated island in the ocean and, there, come to realize and understand the world as a result of observation and rationalization. [89]

Subsequently, Ibn Rushd began his job as judge (*qadi*) in Seville and Cordoba, but his main focus remained on his philosophical work. He was particularly passionate about challenging the teachings by al-Ghazali because, in his opinion, they were destroying philosophy as well as Islam. In 1195, destiny struck: he had been a thorn in the imams' flesh for quite some time and now the imams eventually incited the public and forced the ruler to formally take proceedings against him. The tribunal's answer was "no" regarding Ibn Rushd's orthodoxy. His books were publicly burned, and the whole of philosophy was declared forbidden by edict. Rushd himself was banned from Cordoba and was denied any teaching activities. He died three years later in exile.

It is no surprise that there is almost nothing written in Arabic about Ibn Rushd. Information about him appeared in Hebrew translations. Even Averroes often used to write in the Arabic language by using Hebrew letters. It was a kind of insider language that he used, which indicates the level of intolerance he experienced in his surroundings.

Rushd's idea about jurisprudence had already been that of a passed epoch. While the Qadi (Judge) Ibn Rushd searched for judiciary

---

89 Ibn Tufail, *Hajj bin Yaqdhan* (Amazon Media, 2000).

principles in general terms, the administration of justice in Spain began changing to one based on precedent cases from the life of the Prophet. In the increasingly Islamic Empire, the fields of jurisprudence, philosophy, and science were declining and eventually spiraling toward their end. North of the Mediterranean, however, his statements were fiercely discussed; Thomas of Aquinas spared no effort in proving Averroes wrong.

On one side, Averroes was hailed, but he was also mocked for his belief in authority. On one hand, he defended the Qur'an because, in his opinion, it demanded rational research, but on the other hand, he called for its reinterpretation whenever statements were in contradiction to scientific evidence. The right to carry out this task could only be in the hands of educated personalities. The common people, he believed, were incapable of carrying out logical argumentation and had to keep to drawing analogies regarding the revelation—only philosophers were capable of getting to the core of things. He must have viewed himself as a Muslim, but his contemporaries saw him very differently—and that was what sealed his fate.

The age of independent thinkers in Arabic intellectual history ended with Ibn Rushd. That only leaves us with introducing the one person who makes it possible to pinpoint the date for this end: al-Ghazali (also known as Algazel in Europe), born around AD 1058 in Tuz in eastern Iran, where he died in AD 1111. His two major works are *The Incoherence of the Philosophers* and *The Revival of the Religious Sciences*. Islamic authors hail Ghazali as a great philosopher. In reality, however, he didn't have anything to do with philosophy whatsoever. His life's work consisted of abolishing it.

And this is what his work *The Incoherence of the Philosophers* is all about. In it, he points out why philosophy has no right to exist. In total contrast to Aristotle and all of his Arabic predecessors, Ghazali rejected the causality principle. Consequently, neither logic nor natural law could exist; everything that happened was only due to a special act of volition of God. As an illustration, Ghazali claimed that it was a mistake to assume that it was oneself who made a piece of cotton burn by holding it above fire, when in reality it was God who ordered the cotton to catch fire. Leaves didn't fall from the trees in autumn by themselves but did so only by a strict order of God to every single leaf. The Prussian scholar on "Oriental" languages and philosophy, Friedrich Dieterici, commented on this in the year 1903: "It would be as if every single letter stamped by the Imperial Postal Service was to be delivered by His Majesty in person."[90]

Because of the lack of natural laws, but with the sole existence of God's will, Ghazali postulated the existence of miracles that can be in contradiction to logic. Accordingly, he denied that men had a free will; every single step of humans was controlled by God. The resulting problem was that if a human had no free will, he could not be made responsible for his sins and crimes. However, Ghazali referred again to the omnipotence of God and the nonexistence of logic. Philosophy and natural sciences could not contribute anything to the truth. Therefore, they are not only unnecessary, he argues, but even harmful because they have the potential to dissuade humans from religion. Therefore, he calls for the death penalty for supporting philosophical issues. In his work *The Deliverance from Error,* he created a list consisting of twenty features according to which philosophers would have to be convicted of heresy. He specifically named Avicenna and al-Farabi as heretics.

The fact that al-Ghazali is still portrayed as a great scholar in the Islamic world is one side of the story.[91] But the fact that he is also occasionally viewed as a philosopher in the West has got to be a misunderstanding: in his work *Directorium Inquisitorium* (ca. AD 1350), the Spanish Dominican friar Nicolas Eymerich listed the "eighteen heresies and errors of the philosopher Algazel." Eymerich had deduced these from the Latin translation of the Arabic work titled *Maqasid al-falasifa (The*

---

90 Friedrich Dieterici, *Über den Zusammenhang der griechischen und arabischen Philosophie,* (München: Edition Avicenna, 2004).
91 "The teachings of al-Ghazali had immense repercussions and exerted considerable influence on the history of thought, in both East and West, among the elite of Europe."—Haim Zafrani at http://unesdoc.unesco.org/ images/0011/001144/114426eo.pdf. Unfortunately Mr. Zafrani does not give us any evidence for the 'considerable influence' of al-Ghazali on Western thinking. Instead he provides us with more of his UNESCO-sponsored historiography in the next chapter.

Intentions of the Philosophers) that had been published under the name of al-Ghazali. But the text actually is an Arabic translation of Avicenna's Persian tome, *The Book of Knowledge*; only the title and introduction of this book were produced by Ghazali. In other words: what was labeled al-Ghazali contained Avicenna's words. It remains unknown how this error happened, but it certainly helped al-Ghazali to get the reputation he never earned. One can expect more texts falsely attributed to Ghazali.

For that reason, with the exception of evaluations by Islamic authors, whenever al-Ghazali's work is assessed to determine whether or not he was truly a scientist worthy of the name, the outcome only shows catastrophic results. In the Islamic world, al-Ghazali's second book, *The Revival of the Religious Sciences*, is considered his major work, and it merely consists of a defense of the literal interpretation of the Qur'an. Only what is found in the Qur'an, he argues, is science. For example, while Avicenna interpreted the legend of the Flood as a symbol for the drowning of ignorance and overcoming the Flood by Noah's Ark as the triumph of knowledge, it had to be taken literally according to al-Ghazali. Anything else would have to be considered heresy worthy of the death sentence. While al-Kindi and Ibn Rushd saw the Qur'an as acceptable only for the ignorant and illiterate masses, al-Ghazali defined it to be the iron rule and the only possible source of all knowledge. It remains completely unclear why Ghazali is occasionally called a *Sufi*. He was definitely not.

His text *The Forged Sword in Counseling Kings (Nasihat al Muluk)* gives insight into how devoted to ultraorthodox thought al-Ghazali was. In this work, he listed eighteen features which, in reference to Sura 4:34, are supposed to prove the inferiority of women:

1. Menstruation
2. Pregnancy
3. Childbirth
4. Separation from her parents when getting married
5. The inability to control herself
6. Receiving a smaller portion of an inheritance

7. The liability to get repudiated without having the right to file for divorce
8. Allowing men to have four wives but for women to have only one husband
9. Getting locked up in the house
10. The rule to cover her head
11. Her testimony that is only worth half of that of a man
12. The rule that prohibits her from leaving the house unaccompanied
13. Prohibition to attend the Friday prayer
14. Exclusion from governmental and judiciary posts
15. The fact that 999 of 1,000 commendable deeds were done by men and only one was done by women
16. Wholesale condemnation at the Day of Judgment instead of individual justification
17. Waiting period of four months and ten days after her husband's death before remarriage
18. Waiting period of three menstruation cycles after divorce before remarriage

That's al-Ghazali all over: he has no problem with mixing cause and effect, with confusing natural law and human law, because he has already compromised his relationship with logic and causality in his work *The Incoherence of the Philosophers*. Calling him a philosopher or scientist would be a great insult to all of his Arabic predecessors, from al-Kindi to Ibn Rushd. And he was not the "Renewer of Islam" for which he is hailed in the Islamic world, either. He was rather a propagandist for the most radical movement of his time and the first person who was prominent for preaching hatred. Starting with al-Ghazali, a development began that Dan Diner referred to as the "sealed time" in *Lost in Sacred: Why the Muslim World Stood Still*[92]: the spiritual standstill of the Islamic world that began in the twelfth century has remained to the present day.

While al-Ghazali was a Muslim in the sense of today's idea of "Islam," the other workers mentioned here were not. Hunayn was a Christian

---

92 Diner Dan, *Lost in Sacred: Why the Muslim World Stood Still* (New York: University Press, 2009).

and Thabit was a pagan. Avicenna and Biruni came from a Buddhist background, and, presumably, so did al-Farabi. Al-Kindi, Alhazen, and Rhazes (this one with the "three criminals") represented the typical freethinkers who were in absolute opposition to the Qur'anic tradition.

In defiance of hostility, all of the mentioned authors were still able to maintain their independence; while Biruni and Avicenna had to be more cautious, for Ibn Rushd it was already too late. Ever since he started his teaching post, he was subject to persecution by orthodox imams, to whom he eventually fell victim.

Although there were some differences, the premises of Aristotle and other Greek philosophers were the common ground of all the mentioned authors. In expressing their fidelity to logic, causality, and scientific methodology, they all positioned themselves in total contrast to the Qur'an, despite the fact that, owing to arrogance, some of them granted the rights to entertain such thoughts only to themselves and a few handpicked others. But what could be the justification for calling them Muslims? Except for Ibn Rushd, whose idea about Islam ran opposite to the orthodox Islamic teachings, not a single one of the main figures was a Muslim in any sense.

In this context, a short note about the poet Omar Khayyam (AD 1048–1123) from Neyshapur, eastern Persia, should be given. As a follower of Avicenna, he was known as a philosopher and mathematician during his lifetime. But his quatrains (Rubaiyat) were completely unknown back then and remained so until they received late recognition in the West.[93] This glory traveled back to his Persian home country, where he was then later turned into an Islamic poet for whom was built a memorial in the Laleh Park in Tehran (where Biruni was also given a memorial). The distinctly blasphemous nature of many of his verses don't seem to be of anybody's concern, but they strongly imply that Khayyam was no Muslim either.

---

93 English translation produced ca. 1850 by Edward Fitzgerald; starting in 1880, several German editions were published.

A letter written by Khomeini and sent to Gorbachev in January of 1989 provides a revealing example about the extent of ignorance in the Muslim world regarding their famous thinkers. In this letter, Khomeini told Gorbachev that Islam was the way to solving the Kremlin's present problems and recommended that he read the works by al-Farabi and Avicenna instead of pieces by Western thinkers.[94] Obviously, Khomeini didn't know that his model philosophers were no Muslims, and that for this reason, they had been condemned by the model-Muslim al-Ghazali, and furthermore, that their texts had been burnt by Muslims. Or were Khomeini's suggestions meant to be a diplomatic gesture since both of the authors used to be citizens of lands later occupied by the Soviet Union (Avicenna was from today's Uzbekistan and al-Farabi came from today's Kazakhstan)? Likely, Khomeini didn't know about either issue and was just disappointed that Gorbachev never responded to his letter.

The above-mentioned personalities achieved tremendous accomplishments during their lifetimes. Alhazen pushed the field of optics, Avicenna did the same in the field of medicine, and others produced further developments based on Aristotle's ideas. But these accomplishments only refer to the most prominent figures. The vast majority of authors remained at the level that matters stood in the classical ancient world. And without trying to minimize their accomplishments, they need to be put into perspective in that the achievement often came by reissuing products by ancient authors by which these works were transmitted and made available. In the West, from early on the Church had done everything in its power to withdraw from circulation Greek and Latin texts written by ancient philosophers. And the same fate happened later to the scripts by Arabic scientists: right after the death of these authors, or sometimes even already during their lifetime, their texts were burnt for being un-Islamic. Only a fraction of their works is available today. Only the material that had been whisked to Europe in time was saved from destruction.

---

94 "If your Excellency would consider initiating research in such fields, your Excellency should arrange for the students to seek advice in the philosophical works by al-Farabi and Avicenna, instead of in books by Western philosophers."

The reason for the flourish of spiritual life in medieval Arabia, especially in Persia, has to be seen in the continuation of classical ancient traditions. Since the time of Alexander the Great, the Greek-cultural influence stretched to central Asia, to the borders of India and China. In those areas, classical ancient spiritual life was preserved longer than elsewhere and came into contact with a culture that is characterized by Buddhism. The central points of the ancient Greek-cultural influences were in Oasis cities of central Asia, in nowadays Turkmenistan, Tajikistan, Uzbekistan, and Afghanistan—an unbelievable idea to us today. But in this rather remote area the classic period managed to survive longest. Up to the eleventh century, Islam was no subject there.

Just by taking into consideration the various ethnic origins of each individual personality, one might, but should not, doubt the existence of an "Arabic" spiritual life and sciences. Because after all, despite the fact that these people came from very different ethnic backgrounds, they were united by the Arabic language, just as Latin was the element uniting the people in the Roman Empire.

In contrast to what the tradition claims, the majority of rulers during this time period were not Muslim caliphs or emirs, but rulers influenced by many different cultures and were therefore a part of a tradition of spiritual freedom and exchange. Most certainly, they carried Arabic titles, but it would be inadmissible to automatically refer to them as Islamic.

The "Golden Age" of Islamic sciences? There never was any. But there was a "Golden Age" of Arabic sciences. This era, however, abruptly ended when Islam got established as the dominant Arabic religion. It drove out the knowledge from the East into the West. And this is where it has remained up to this day.

❖ ❖ ❖

Another Arabian Night
The Fairy Tale of al-Andalus

*Muslims entered Spain not as aggressors or oppressors,
but as liberators.*

—Maryam Noor Beig[95]

It was sometime during the year 89 after the Prophet had fled to Medina, which corresponds to the year AD 711. The commander of the Arabic army Tariq ibn Ziyad got ready on the North African side of Gibraltar or the "Pillars of Hercules," as it was also called back then. From here, Ziyad looked over to Hispania, the country that was to be conquered for the Prophet of the Arabs and his religion.

But it was not that simple, as the script of the play "al-Andalus" called for tragedy, entanglements, and complications. And that was provided by a person named Julian, who was a Byzantine (or Gothic?) governor of Ceuta, a city on the African side of the strait. This Julian sent his daughter named Florida to the city of Toledo to the Royal Court of the Gothic King Roderick to be educated. So far, so good. But things changed when Florida accused King Roderick of having raped her. He denied all accusations but her father was outraged and plotted revenge: he made common cause with the Muslims in North Africa and encouraged them to participate in the adventure "al-Andalus."

But even that would have not been enough to cause a catastrophe, if Roderick had not made a capital mistake: in the Toledo Palace there was a forbidden room. Even the king was not allowed to enter it. Whoever set foot in it would bring great disaster on himself and his empire. The unfortunate Roderick entered the room. There he saw paintings of Arabs—and read the Prophesy that said that these men would invade his Kingdom the very same day and bring his reign to an end. And that's how it happened. Together with seven thousand Berbers in four

---

95   From: http://www.hispanicmuslims.com, 2010.

boats, Tariq landed at the cliffs that, from then on, would bear his name: Gebel Tariq, Gibraltar. Soon after, on the twenty-eighth day of Ramadan in the year 89 after Hijra (AD 711), Tariq completely defeated Roderick and his army in the battle at Guadalete River (or it could have been Barbate River). Apparently, the Prophet's rule that unbelievers are to be killed, just not during the holy month of Ramadan, didn't seem to be of much concern to the invaders. The most unlikely victory happened because the vengeful Julian got a significant number of soldiers of the Christian Gothic army to change sides and join the Muslims. This little piece of information, together with many more details, including speeches by the people involved, is given by Arabic historians.

But there were more events to come. The very next year, together with eighteen thousand troops, Musa Ibn Nusayr, the Prophet's general in North Africa, ferried across the strait and invaded the whole country. From now on, it would be called al-Andalus.

The whole country? Not really: in the very northernmost part, in the cave of Covadogna in the Cantabrian Mountains, there was a Gothic aristocrat called Pelayo who had no intention of surrendering. In AD 718 (or was it AD 748?), this rebellious Christian defeated the Islamic army that was led by Arab commander Qama, whereby one hundred twenty-four thousand Muslims lost their lives and the remaining troops (sixty-three thousand) were finished by a landslide.

These numbers remind us of the equally miraculous stories of the Muslim victories of Yarmuk or Nehawend.

Some believe these stories, some others think that they have a true core, and then there are people who think they are legends. In any case, we don't know whether or not the battles of Covadogna or Guadalete ever took place. They may or may not have happened, but they were essential for the production of the play: a betrayal which, on top of that, even involved a woman and led to the *conquista*, the Islamic conquest of Spain. And a refusal to capitulate and the courage of one single Gothic aristocrat, seemingly fighting a losing battle, formed the germ cell of the *reconquista*—the recapturing under the sign of the cross the territory conquered by the Muslims. One just needs to add the feature of the Umayyad Dynasty whose superior Islamic culture turned al-Andalus into a sun-kissed paradise that was a sanctuary for science and tolerance, and remained as such for the following eight hundred years. With all these details mixed together, one now has the complete set of acts of the play called al-Andalus, and if you believe this, you can consider yourself in conformity with the conventional historic picture.

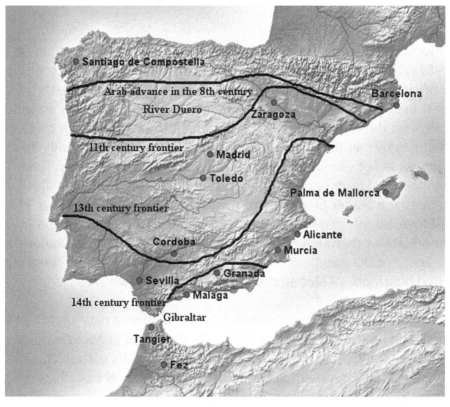

stepmap.de

Spain during the Arab-Islamic occupation. The boundaries are approximate, they were always in flux

But the catch is—as it is for the entire complex of the early Islam— the sources. However, there is indeed a text that consists of a verbal agreement between the earlier-mentioned Julian and Tariq, in which the author of this text gives the impression of having attended this conversion in person. But this script was produced in the fourteenth century.

According to storyteller Ibn al-Kuttiya, Tariq challenged his troops to fight for Islam and Allah, and held out the prospect of martyrdom in paradise for them. Just the Gothic derivation of (the name) Kuttiya makes him a credible source in the eyes of some people—the issue of jihad against unbelievers, however, occurred for the first time in the eleventh century and the oldest version of Kuttiya is from the fourteenth century.

Another frequently mentioned author is the Egyptian al-Hakam (AD ?–870) who never claimed to have been in Spain. To a large extent, his work is only known from a seventeenth-century text. Despite the fact that in such cases the texts had usually been subject to a cosmetic overhaul during later—Islamic—centuries, in Hakam's work there is neither any mentioning of Islam nor a Holy War (his work mainly deals with issues of plunder and the problems regarding its distribution). Muhammad is mentioned only once and just briefly: Hakam viewed him as the leader of a gang of thieves but not as the founder of a religion; he referred to Palestine as the "Holy Land," and the Ibadites (more about them later) he did not perceive as Muslims. Obviously, in Egypt of the middle of the ninth century, the official and currently used biography of Mohammad had not been known yet.

The oldest-known document is the capitulation treaty of AD 713 between the Gothic Theodomir and the Arab Abd el-Aziz. This treaty has been frequently used as an example of generosity of the victorious Muslims. This document, however, is not the original but exists only as an essay from the thirteenth century—that means a five-hundred-year gap.

That's the situation regarding all sources that are used. And interestingly, the wealth of detail and information about verbal exchanges increases with the length of the time period that lies between the events and the reporting. It should be pointed out again that Arabic writings represent a literary genre meant to lift the spirit and be entertaining but never to provide historically correct records. Johannes Thomas, who works on Arabic studies, says: "In general, in Arabic accounts there is little or no interest in chronology or historical facts."

Certain narrative elements, also found in the al-Andalus story, which had been known from the Bible, appeared repeatedly throughout the whole of Arabic literature. That includes, for instance, the story about the capture of Cordoba that only happened because a shepherd gave away information about a cleft in the city wall. The same narrative element is found in the conquest of Damascus, Caesarea, Alexandria, Cairo, and Tustan. Tripolis, for instance, was conquered because the water receded and then started rising sharply, thereby defeating the enemy. Moreover, there are also stories that mention the collapse of city walls due to booming trombones cutting through the dead silence of Jericho, or chronicles like the one about the army leader who obtained water by striking a rock and, by this, saved his troops.

A typical case of name symbolism we see in the name of a troop leader called Tarif. This name is most likely a derivation from the existing place Tarifa, which was then transformed into the name of a person that needed to be created. A similar case involves the name Tariq. The term *tariq* means "way" or "path" and is frequently found in Arabic literature where it is used in wordplays in the sense of "nomen est omen." It is a so-called "talking name" that gradually became independent and eventually the name of a legendary person. In some stories Tariq is an Arab, in others he is Persian, and in some stories he is a Berber. This is a very good example of the level of unreliability of the reports, as there is no evidence that those persons called Tariq or Tarif ever existed. It is more plausible to assume that "Tariq" got his name from Gibraltar than assuming that it was the other way around.

From the non-Arabic domain, there are Spanish Chronicles written in Latin that were produced in AD 741 and AD 754. In neither one is there any mentioning of Islam or any kind of religious conflicts with conquerors. In none of the contemporary sources is there any sign of Islam, Muslims, or the much-asserted Holy War.

As it is typical of all of European countries, Spain, too, has a very complex settlement and colonization history. From the last days of European Neanderthals who vanished from the coasts of the Iberian Peninsula around thirty thousand years ago, we now jump into the first millennium BC and join an unspecified Iberian population. As early as 800 BC, Phoenicians from the eastern shores of the Mediterranean Sea (today's Lebanon and coastal regions of Syria) founded numerous settlements along the Iberian coast with the city of Cadiz as the most important one. Later, the Greeks came and founded Rosas and Malaga in addition to other settlements. Later, starting around 600 BC, Celtic immigrants from the north joined the ethnic groups that had already been present, forming the Celtiberians.

As a result of the rise in power of the city of Carthage, which had also been founded by the Phoenicians, southern Iberia came under Carthage rule. Later, in 201 BC, after the devastating defeat at the hands of the Romans in the Second Punic War, Carthage fell under the authority of the Roman Empire. But it would take another two hundred years for the Roman Empire to get control over the whole Iberian Peninsula. That was achieved in the year 19 BC under the rule of Emperor Augustus. Hispania was divided into three provinces and took on all characteristics of the classical Roman culture. A road network connected individual provinces and cities. They were also linked by an efficient water system that supplied spas, gardens, and irrigation systems. The population grew fast. Moreover, transfer and traffic, trade and business, as well as public life flourished. Under the rule of Emperor Vespasian, the inhabitants of the Hispanic provinces were granted the civil rights which completed the process of becoming Romans. The Emperors Trajan, Marc Aurelius, and Hadrian were all Hispanians, as was the philosopher Seneca.

Mass migrations of the Germanic tribes began which also affected the Iberian Peninsula. At the beginning of the fifth century AD, the Vandals appeared. But they, eighty thousand men strong, moved on and ferried over to North Africa, where they founded a kingdom under the Vandal King Geiserich in AD 429. But in AD 534, their kingdom was destroyed by the Byzantine general Belisarius, and the Vandal aristocrats were deported to Constantinople. The common people, however, stayed and thereby became another facet of the ethnic and religious puzzle of North Africa.

People of the West Gothic tribe were given a territory in Gallia by Rome. But they increasingly felt pressure by the Franks and migrated to Spain after they had lost the battle of Vouille in AD 507. The so-called West Gothic Empire was founded with Toledo as its capital city. Despite the fact that the Gothic people were only a minority in Spain, the Royal Dynasty and the aristocrats were all Gothic. But it wouldn't take long before they were Romanized and spoke Latin.

The situation on the other side of the strait, in North Africa, was not much different. Both sides of the strait were Punic (meaning Carthaginian) and were later incorporated into the Roman Empire and assimilated into their culture. Again, the East Roman Empire (name of Byzantine Empire in the late-classical era) replaced the Western Roman Empire ("Rome") as ruling power in North Africa. In between, there were also some episodes during which Berbers and Germanics played roles. Just like Spain, North Africa, too, had become a melting pot of various ethnic groups. Across the strait, these two regions always remained in close contact by political and cultural association and even family ties. In all, the Mediterranean Sea didn't represent any dividing feature as we see it today, but it was a uniting element.

With the emergence of the Arabian Empire after AD 622, the Arabic influence also became increasingly noticeable. But its influence was restricted to the eastern areas of North Africa that were Egypt and Libya. The western regions of North Africa, generally corresponding to today's Tunisia, Algeria, and Morocco, were occupied by Berbers.

The term "the Berbers" represents a vague collective noun for a number of ethnic groups that include unspecific native populations and immigrated Celts, Phoenicians, and Germanic peoples, as well as native Africans who most likely belonged to the Tubus (peoples of Ethiopian decent who were the former rulers of the Sahara desert). These peoples either mixed or kept to their own tribal communities.

In addition to tribal dialects, the Berber spoke Latin and they were Christians or Jews. On the other side of the strait it was the same situation: there were Christians, regardless whether they were Hispano-Roman or Gothic people. But they were, however, Christians of various branches.

Just like all Germanics, the Gothic people were Arian Christians. That changed when King Rekkared I (AD 586–601) became a Roman Catholic for political reasons. That resulted in a deep friction between the Royal Dynasty and the aristocrats, who, in general, refused to convert and remained Arian. To make matters worse, there were no clear succession rules in the Gothic tradition. The person who had the most powerful lobby became king.

Around the year AD 710, fate struck again. A person called Roderick was crowned king but the aristocrats disapproved of him. And because they also had allies, friends, or even relatives in North Africa which they mobilized against Roderick, they eventually defeated him.

At this point already, the Islamic traditional literature gets into trouble, because the people who ferried over to Europe were, without any doubt, Berbers and not Arabs. For that reason, in order to make plausible the claim of "conquests by the Prophet's troops," the stories talk of "a very few Arabs" or "Arab officers" who were placed at the Berbers' side. Another puzzling issue deals with the question of how the Berbers, all of the sudden, were supposed to have become Muslims. We have no trace of Muslims in the area at that time.

Musa Ibn Nusayr,[96] who was around during the reign of Abd al-Malik, the builder of the Dome of the Rock, and Umayyad, governor of Tripolitania, represents one of the few verifiable figures regarding the scenario about the conquest of Spain. With a regular army at his disposal, he conquered the whole Iberian Peninsula, except its northernmost region. Maybe he followed a call for help or just took

---

96   Musa Ibn Nusayr is also mentioned in the stories of the Arabian Nights (in nights 566 to 578). In these stories, however, he doesn't conquer Spain but searches for the legendary "City of Brass" located somewhere in the southern Sahara Desert. Up to this day, adventurers look for this city in the hunt for the Oasis Zerzura.

advantage of the favorable situation to expand the empire of his rulers, the Umayyads, from Damascus to Europe. However, what started out as a limited military campaign developed into a full-blown conquest. At Musa's side there was a Bishop named Oppa, and Urban, a North African Christian, who was one of Musa's troop leaders.

Musa's complete name was Musa Ibn Nusayr al Lahmi. That means he was a Lahmite and, therefore, a member of the tribal-religious group of Al Hira in Mesopotamia. Under the collective noun of "Ibadites," the people from al Hira belonged to the anti-Trinitarian and East-Syrian branches of Christianity. As an integral part of the troops of Persian King Chosroes II, they had already been Arab allies during the Egyptian conquest in AD 619. Later, they belonged to Abd al-Malik's troops. They built in North Africa numerous places of worship, the so-called "masjid" which, as a matter of course, are interpreted as being "Islamic." But because they were not built facing Mecca, which also applies to the first Cairo Mosque, the Ibn As Mosque, they cannot be called Islamic mosques. They are places of worship of the Ibadites-Arabic Christians.

In a "mosque" in North Africa[97] there can be found the following text:

> We believe in God and in what was sent down to us, and in what was sent down to Abraham and to Ishmael, Isaac, and Jacob, and to the tribes, and in what was passed on to Moses and Jesus, and in what was given to the prophets by the Lord. We do not distinguish between them and are devoted to God.

It is the very same verse that we later see in the Qur'an, but with one difference: the mentioning of Jesus is missing. But it is not surprising, as the text was not from a "mosque" but from a "masjid."

The famous Islamic school al-Azhar in Fustat (Cairo) also goes back to the Ibadites and their Syro-Aramaic roots. The term *Azhar* is certainly not Arabic but Aramaic and means "light." Numerous coins have been found from Ibn Nusayr's time. They all have Latin texts in form of inscriptions like:

97   Sharwas, Gebel Nafusa.

Non est deus nisi unus cui non est alius similis, deus eternus deus magnus omnium creator ("God is only One, He has no equal at His side. God is great and the almighty creator of all")

Non est deus nisi unus cui non socius alius similis ("God is only One, He has no associate")

In nomine domini misericordis ("In the name of the merciful God")

This Latin saying is known already from the fourth century. The version of the Arabic translation is the so-called "Bismillah," which is the opening line of most Suras.

The date on the coins follows the Byzantine tax calendar (*feritus in Africa indictione…*). Why is that? For reasons of internationality? Or are we supposed to assume that, ten years after Tariq's alleged surprise attack, the responsible tax office was still under the authority of Byzantium? Moreover, there is no word about a Hijra-date of an Arabic Prophet; *Africa* had apparently not been turned into *Ifriqiya* yet.

It certainly raises the question why a leading representative of the Prophet Muhammad had Latin coins minted, especially when considering the fact that coins represented a very significant way to show legitimacy, demonstrate power, and state the political agenda of the ruler.

Furthermore, it raises the question why a follower of the Prophet used the Byzantine calendar and not the Hijra system of the Prophet, which was supposed to be the only valid calendar to be used by Muslims since the year 638—not one single contemporary script contains a Hijra date.

And it raises the question why the inscriptions on the coins show the most basic Christian maxims. They are usually Latin translations of Greek or Aramaic originals that were later translated into Arabic, and it was not the other way around as alleged by Islamic tradition.

Defining these coins as Islamic is absolutely arbitrary and completely unsubstantiated. Some North African coins (and later Spanish ones) showed a star. It most likely represents the "star of Bethlehem"; another possible meaning could be that it is of Punic origin. But the star is certainly not a symbol of Islam and could not, therefore, be used as proof of the presence of Islam.

Moreover, as late as the tenth century, two hundred years after the alleged conquests as claimed by Islamic tradition, there were forty-eight Episcopal sees ("bishops") in North Africa. It is therefore out of the question to assume that these areas were Islamized at that time.

There is nothing, literally no facts, relics, or any kind of clearly contemporary-dated scripts that could prove an Islamic conquest of Spain. And actually there wasn't anybody who claimed any of this—until much later. Such allegations were made in secondary literature that was produced afterward, in some cases very much later. And those allegations were repeated by historians of much later time periods, who based their ideas on secondary literature of the Arabic entertainment world which they assumed were primary sources.

That means there never was a Tariq in Africa, looking at the cliffs on the other side of the strait with gazing eyes, and filled with the burning wish that that country over there become Islamic. According to current state of knowledge, the most plausible explanation of the events during the early eighth century in Spain has to do with the siding of Berber tribes amid a succession dispute within the Gothic Dynasty. The opposition party called for help from the powers on the other side of the strait. By that, Arian Christians from North Africa supported their Arian counterparts in Spain against their Catholic rulers. That adds a religious aspect to the events, but it was no Islamic one.

The forces they had unleashed they could no longer control. And that led to the moment when a supporting campaign turned into a war of conquest: it was the moment when Umayyad-Arabic troops under the command of Musa Ibn Nusayr set foot on the Peninsula. Religion was only a very subordinate issue, and it didn't have anything to do with Islam at all. At that time, four Christian factions (minimum) were already in the game: Arian, Athanasian (Catholic), Orthodox, and Arabic Christians.

Those parts of the Gothic and Hispanic populations who felt that it was wise to flee escaped to areas in northern Spain beyond the Duero River that functioned as a fairly stable border. Three-fourths of the southern part of the Spanish Peninsula had already become a part of the empire of al-Walid, the Umayyad ruler of Damascus, in AD 720. Therefore, it was Syria where the points were set for the events that were to come in Spain.

At that time, the Umayyad Dynasty was already in its decline, and was eventually replaced by the Abbasid Dynasty around the year AD 750. A person named Abd ar-Rahman and his family were reportedly among the few survivors who managed to flee to safety in the western part of the empire.[98] At first they were in North Africa and then they moved on to Spain to find protection in a monastery. In Rufasa, Syria, Rahman was raised at his grandfather's Court, the ruler Hisham (AD 724–743), in the location of the Basilica of St. Sergius. He was most likely also very familiar with the Imperial Residence of Damascus. Therefore, he brought with him to Spain the style of Persian palaces[99] with their magnificent gardens as well as the typically Syrian church architecture (combined with Roman architectural elements this style would later be called "Moorish").

In the style typical of his Syrian home country, Rahman built a holy site in Cordoba, called "Mezquita," the Mosque of Cordoba. It has no *Qiblah* (praying direction), strangely enough to some historians, that faces Mecca. But that's not surprising at all, as it does not represent a mosque but a Christian-Arabic "masjid" built in the style of his former home country.

---

98 It should be noted that Rahman's identity as Umayyad/Marwinid is not undoubted either.

99 Keep in mind that the Marw Dynasty (*vulgo Umayyads*) came from Marw in eastern Persia. Their palace concept of Paradise gardens was Persian. From them, the so-called Court Mosques developed.

Ar-Rahman and his successors ruled as emirs for almost two hundred years. In AD 929, Abd al-Rahman III was proclaimed caliph. Under the rule of his successor Hakam II (AD 915–976), the Umayyad Empire reached its peak. Hakam was described as a well-educated ruler; his library is said to have contained four hundred thousand volumes. His son was ruler only nominally; the true power was held by his vizier Abi Amir (AD 938–1002). Under the name of *Al Mansur* (Spanish "Almanzor"), Abi Amir became the epitome of the detested foreign ruler. He boasted of carrying out one war campaign each year against the unbelievers. Indeed, he carried out fifty-two such campaigns, in which he covered the northern areas with war, and pillaged and plundered. Special attention was given to the pillage campaign of Santiago de Compostella in AD 997 when he ordered the inhabitants to carry the Basilica bells and bring them to Cordoba on foot as an act of humiliation.[100] Al Mansur had the library of Hakam II burnt down, as the credo that says that just only this Book was all that was needed, gained acceptance.

The fact that there were six caliphs in the thirty years following the ruthless tyrant Almanzor, made clear the condition in which the empire had already been. In AD 1031, just one hundred years after the proclamation of the Cordoba Caliphate, the time of the emirs and caliphs of the Marw Dynasty from Turkmenistan, commonly called Umayyads, was over for good.

Their ruling time in al-Andalus is described as a very unstable period: revolutions, upheavals, intrigues, disputes over throne successions, forming of splinter groups, and wars. There were always acts of those kinds happening somewhere in their empire. In what could almost be called an act of desperation, the Swiss Andalus-glorifier Arnold Hottinger[101] accused the chroniclers of exaggerating and said in an appeasing statement that the areas of unrest were often separated by such great distances that all of the areas were not affected by acts of violence at the same time...

---

100   In AD 1236, after the conquest of Cordoba, Ferdinand III had the Moorish inhabitants carry the bells back to Santiago de Compostella again.
101   Arnold Hottinger, *Die Mauren* (Paderborn: Wilhelm Fink, 2005).

In any case, these unrests were of such magnitude that they eventually caused the empire to fall to pieces in AD 1031.

Curiously, through all the Arabic texts it is always greatly emphasized that these conflicts were never between "Muslims" and "Christians" but that they had to do with ethnic and tribal issues among the invaders, mainly between Arabs and Berbers, but also between the Arabic tribes. Though there may have been troubles between the different factions, religious conflicts became increasingly important. But at least for the first two centuries, these could have not been conflicts between "Christians" and "Muslims," as the situation during the eighth and ninth centuries, and even in part of the tenth century, was much too complex for such simplicity.

Which branch of Christians are we supposed to consider? The eastern Arians? Or the western Arians? Or are we talking about the Roman Catholics? Or is it the Orthodox Byzantine branch? The Manichaeans or Donatists, which were very popular at that time, or what other of the numerous different "Oriental" Christians?

Which branch of Muslims are we supposed to consider? The Ibadites? The "Muhammadans"? The Malekites, the Ismailites? Or are we talking about the Qaramita or Kharijites? These groups and many more romped around the Iberian Peninsula as well as on the other side of the strait. They were characteristic of that time.

Who would dare speak of "Christians" and "Muslims"?

The main inner-Christian blocs, consisting of Catholic and Orthodox Christians, and Arian and Arabic Christians, "only" disagreed on the key question of five centuries—the issue that had divided families, split tribes, and set empires against each other: what was Jesus's nature?

That's the reason why anti-Trinitarians like the Germanic and Arabic Christians were closer to each other spiritually than they were to the Catholics and the Orthodox groups. And, as previously mentioned, that's how it was possible that North African invaders and locals were able to share one place of worship in Cordoba. In the beginning, their theological differences were only minor.

In AD 850, strange incidents were reported: Christians allegedly cursed Muhammad and Muslims because they wanted to die the martyr's death. As a matter of fact, there were almost fifty executions carried out in connection with this incident. But what had happened?

Already in the late seventh century, a series of councils began in Toledo that focused on the issue of the true nature of Christ and, as a result, turned against varies heresies. The term *manichaean*[102] was frequently used and, like the term *nestorian*, gradually acquired the meaning of a collective term denoting deviants. In AD 839, Abd ar-Rahman II called a synod (council of the church) because, like the bishops, he was worried about the religious developments that were getting out of hand. According to council documents, the *Casians* were condemned based on a number of offenses: Manichaeism, living in a cave, refusal to worship the Saints, polygamy, unusual fasting rules, and many more. The *Casians* had something of everything. They combined features of religious traditions that were Arabic in nature with aspects of Roman religious traditions, but they also had elements that differed from either one and, therefore, neither the "Orientals" nor the "Westerners" knew what to make of them.

But there was no doubt that these were *Akephals*, meaning they were believers who only accepted the authority of God but no human government. Therefore, they were considered intolerable to the establishment. From the council documents, it becomes clear that in the al-Andalus of AD 839, nobody had heard anything about a founder of a new religion by the name of Muhammad. This is the only sensible explanation for the fact that the bishops failed to discuss what would have been seen as a highly threatening religion—why they never even mentioned the name "Mohammed," or the term *Islam*. They would eventually talk about these issues some decades later.

---

102 *Manichaeism* was named after the Persian Mani (AD 216–277). This religion was widespread and represented a mix of Zoroastrian, Christian, and Buddhist elements, and was based on the classical-ancient gnosis.

ⁿ̣ council documents, the so-called *Arures* are also mentioned. In Arabic literature, they trade under the name *Haruri* and are referred to as inhabitants of the Syrian town of Harura. It is the place where, according to the Qur'an, the dead will rise again on the Day of Judgment. And, of course, the Haruri are Muslims. But in reality, this term is the result of another misreading, whereby the Syrian term *hrora*, meaning "cave," was misunderstood. The *Arures/Haruri* were simply cave inhabitants, namely eremites. Eremite living was a very common feature at that time as another "end of times" was expected to be near. But such a lifestyle was disapproved of by the rulers because these eremites represented "Akephals," meaning they were difficult to control.

The Kharijites were also disparaged as *Arures*. In Islamic tradition, however, the Kharijites are considered to be the first Muslim sect, regardless of the fact that they lived a rather un-Islamic eremite life and managed without a Prophet Muhammad.

The so-called "Islamic gnosis" also played an important role in Spain. But how Islamic could these Gnostics and their closely related Ibadites, Nusayrians, Alevi, and Karmathans, have been in reality, since their traditions deeply rooted in Greek Neo-Platonic and Zoroastrian-Zurvanian Iranian concepts? They knew Qur'anic tradition either only fragmentarily or not at all, and, for that reason, they were viewed as Christian heretics by theologians during the late-classical ancient period. Because their surroundings increasingly became a Mecca-oriented, intolerant environment in later centuries, they more and more decided that it was wise to change sides to the Muslim territory, where they have remained as either crypto-Christians or small-time Muslims to this day.

According to Tradition, the first philosopher of al-Andalus, Ibn Masarra (AD 883–931), was, naturally, referred to as a Muslim. But in reality, he was a Gnostic and, therefore, no Muslim. Just as it was for the first Abbasid rulers in Baghdad, the Mutazilism played a certain role in al-Andalus, too. The Mutazila used Qur'anic Verses as well as the New and Old Testament, and, above all, cultivated rationalism.

Just like in the "Orient," the religious situation was also very complex in al-Andalus. There were plenty of different religious views and communities, which defined themselves in ways that are different from how they are perceived today—provided that their individual characterizations and affiliations have been sufficiently clarified.

The Arabic invaders were Christian Ibadites. But during the middle of the ninth century a transformation took place—one might call it a transitional phase between Christianity and Islam. Or in other words: starting in the middle of the ninth century, Islam began developing its own religious identity. The invaders arrived as Christians and changed into Muslims. This change corresponded to the historical development in the "Orient," with which Marwanid Spain was associated. In the second half of the ninth century, some Hadith literature was introduced in Spain. That set off fierce disputes in the emirate because the Malekite judiciary system rejected the Hadiths. Muhamad I (AD 852–886), however, took the side of the Sunna, meaning that he imported the Meccan Islamic mainstream based on Mohammedan Hadiths which increasingly gained power. During the time of Muhamad I, the first records of unequal treatment and harassment of religious dissenters surfaced. Eulogius of Cordoba wrote to Bishop Wilesindus of Pamplona:"this year (AD 851), the raving fury of the tyrant against the Church of God inflamed, and tore down all, devastated everything, scattered all things around, imprisoned bishops, Presbyterians, abbots, deacons, and the whole clergy."

The exhaustive establishment in al-Andalus of what we call "Islam" today was most likely not finished until the caliphate was created in AD 929. To assume a dividing line between Christianity and Islam before the tenth century would be unhistorical, as it does not reflect the situation that existed back then.

The Umayyad caliphate was only fated to exist for one hundred years. Corresponding to the events in the East, there was an organized revolution against the Umayyads in Spain as well. The different ethnic groups might have had problems with each other but it was probably the spiritual divide that was of greater consequence. This, together with the increasing feeling of being under both occupation and religious coercion, eventually caused Arabic-Islamic-dominated Spain, which included about three-fourths of the Iberian Peninsula, to burst apart. The official date for this event is AD 1031; it was the dissolution of the caliphate.

Al-Andalus ended up being quite fragmented into the *Ta'ifas*—the "little kingdoms." The dwindling of the Umayyad Dynasty as a central power, a process that began during their final years, made it possible for numerous small, and even the tiniest, kingdoms and duchies to emerge. At times, there were as many as sixty of them, but their number as well as their size kept constantly changing. Their rulers were Arabs of different clans, Berbers of different tribes, Romans, Normans, Gothic people, and pirates from all over the medieval world, to name just a few. In addition, every religious branch and their various sub-branches were present. It becomes clear that there were no factions of "natural" allies but that everybody made pacts with as well as against everybody. In a continuous state of war, these small empires tried to keep or to expand their territories. Amid this confusion appeared the Knight Rodrigo Diaz, who became the national Spanish hero under the name El Cid. By most skillfully applying the Ta'ifa-tradition, he changed sides several times between the Spaniards, Arabs, Berbers, Christians, and Muslims, and was also active as warlord on his own behalf.

While the small empires of al-Andalus continuously weakened each other, the Christian Empires in the north became more and more powerful. Subsequently, a number of Ta'ifas were now unable to maintain their existence without the support from the north. But neither support from nor truce with the north was free. It came at the price of a protection fee or tribute. Moreover, the explosion in the cost of the official households of the rulers of the mini-empires, most likely a compensating reaction to their insignificance, certainly resulted in the flourishing of art, but also resulted in their ruin. Al-Andalus was bled white and it was the north that gradually gained importance.

But that was only a part of the problem. One of the small-scale rulers with the great name al-Mutamid of Seville called for help from the North African rulers. In this case, it was the Almoravids, a dynasty of militant Muslims from the Sahara Desert. They were opposed to everything that was not in accordance with their idea of religion. They of course fought against Christians but they also made a clean sweep of their Muslim allies. The Princes Mutamid and Mutawakkil were unceremoniously killed the moment they showed signs that they would rather cooperate with their Spanish religious enemies than with their fellow believers from the desert. For Cordoba, Granada, Seville, and other places, a dissolute lifestyle, the life of wine binges and dance numbers, was over.

And again, the forces they had unleashed, the Spaniards, or rather the Andalusian people now, they could no longer control. The Almoravids were no longer interested in providing help. Now they wanted to rule over al-Andalus and over the adjacent Christian Kingdoms as well. Al-Andalus was brought under the Almoravid yoke during the years AD 1090 and 1094.

Strictly speaking, this was already the end of al-Andalus and it seems that some contemporaries were very much aware of it.

The fundamentalists from North Africa introduced a completely new type of conflict to Spain: the religious war, called *jihad*, combined with the Africanizing of Andalusian Islam. While forging of pacts across religious boundaries used to be a common feature during the Ta'ifa times, they became a rarity; only conquest in the name of Allah counted.

But on the Christian side, too, things changed. In AD 1071, the Clunian Movement[103], which was started as the "Clunian Reform" by monks in the French city of Cluny, was established in Spain. Consequently, the Spanish Church was now under direct influence of Rome, and the

---

103   This movement goes back to the Benedictine Monastery Cluny in France. Cluny stood for a rigid type of organization of the monkhood and was one of the most influential and religiously devout centers in Europe until the twelfth century.

Gothic rite was replaced by the Roman one from AD 1076 onwards. In AD 1095, Pope Urban II called for a crusade; in AD 1099, Jerusalem was captured. Almost simultaneous to this event, the Jihadists from North Africa got control over Granada, Seville, Valencia, and Mallorca.

The turn of the eleventh to the twelfth century saw serious conflicts between East against West in the "Orient," and South against North on the Spanish Peninsula.

Against this background of events, the Africanizing of Spanish Islam was taking place while the Europeanizing of Spanish Christendom was going on. Both of these major changes were due to imported influences and they eventually caused the end of any development that could have become a uniquely Spanish way. The Jihad on one side was facing the Crusade on the other. Strictly speaking, only now the moment had come that could be called a *conquista* versus *reconquista* movement in the sense of *Islamic conquest* versus *Christian counter-conquest*.

Almoravid rule didn't even last one century and led to the development of numerous little duchies, the second Ta'ifas. In North Africa, however, a different movement gained power: the Almohads' influence. Their name stood for their program, namely the defending of the *belief in only one God* (*al-muwahidun*, which derived from *wahad*, meaning "*one*"). They have often been associated with "basic Islam." Their central agenda was the extreme monotheism of the early Islam; the Mohammedan traditions only played a minor role. The year AD 1147 marked the date when the Almohads achieved final control over North Africa. In AD 1161 they landed in Spain for the first time. In having carried out their governmental business in Marrakesh and having had to deal with constant resistance and uprisings, they shared the same fate with the Almoravids before them. They were able to put down the major uprisings led by Ibn Mardanish (an Arabized "Martinez") and Geraldo sem Pavor ("Gerald with no fear"), but on July 16, AD 1212, the great showdown took place, which was the battle at Las Navas de Tolosa. Under the command of the Kings of Castile, Navarra, and Aragon, a huge army of knights from all across Europe marched up and faced a pan-Muslim army that was about equal in size, consisting of Jihadists from an area that included North Africa and spanned all across to central Asia. All in all, around half a million troops were supposed to have been involved. The Islamic army suffered a complete defeat and the Almohad caliph fled to North Africa—the Muslims had lost their power in Spain. But it would take another forty years before major parts of the Iberian Peninsula, including the Balearic Islands and Portugal, were under the rule of the Christian kings.

Yusuf Ibn Nasr was the ruler of the miniature state called Arjona. During the conquest of Cordoba, he had supported the Castilian King Ferdinand III and for that, he was granted power over Granada in AD 1236. With this new territory, Ibn Nasr's kingdom consisted of an area that stretched from the coast of Almeria to Tarifa. In AD 1246, King Ferdinand officially recognized Ibn Nasr as ruler of Granada—the last chapter of Muslim rulers began which would be finally closed two hundred fifty years later. It was absolutely clear to Ibn Nasr that there could be no useful resistance against the powerful empires in the North, as they were more than a match for him. And, therefore, he signed a vassal-treaty which actually was the agreement of AD 1246. The Muslim enclave of Granada bought its right to exist by paying tribute and providing services; they were in a total dependency relationship to the Christian feudal lord.

Regardless of major external difficulties, the rulers of Granada never got tired of persisting in carrying out internal disputes. The reason why this didn't lead to their early demise was only because their Christian counterparts were in no hurry to kill the golden goose called Granada as long as it kept on laying golden eggs.

Because Granada's situation became increasingly unsafe, their rulers started looking for allies in North Africa, Egypt, and Istanbul, and began applying risky seesaw politics. Meanwhile, the Hafsids in Tunis had become the controlling power of the lucrative trade between inner-Africa and Spain, and maintained close trading relationships with Castile and Barcelona. And these relationships were to be kept by all means—Granada became only a nuisance.

The marriage of Ferdinand of Aragon and Isabel of Castile in AD 1469 tipped the balance regarding the end of the last Muslim Empire in Spain, as it led to the merging of their kingdoms ten years later and thereby resulted in the uniting of Spain.

Immediately, they began the conquest of cities and forts of the Granada Kingdom until, in AD 1491, their troops finally reached the city gates of Granada. According to traditional belief, the very orthodox Roman-Catholic Isabel pushed Ferdinand into conquering Granada for religious reasons. But Ferdinand's decision to liquidate the enclave was of rational nature: Granada's harbors had always literally remained a safe haven for Muslim pirates, the plague of the Mediterranean. In addition, the tribute payments were coming in more and more slowly. But the most worrisome issue was the fact that Granada had repeatedly initiated contact with the frightening power in the east, the Turks. The "Turkish Danger" was *the* topic of the time and being worried about it was certainly not a result of overreaction: in AD 1481, an Ottoman campaign landed in southern Italy and caused such great panic that the Pope fled Italy. The Turks evolved into a serious threat and, therefore, Spain wanted to make sure that Turkey would remain unable to fulfill possible alliance obligations on Granada territory. That was the end for Granada.

But it was an end that was more or less unparalleled in history: because King Ferdinand's conditions were tremendously favorable, Emir Abu Abdallah didn't have any other choice but to accept. On January 2, AD 1492 he handed over the city keys to the Spanish royal couple. King Ferdinand promised physical safety for the emir, for Granada, which now almost exclusively consisted of Muslim inhabitants, and their properties. Everyone who wished to leave could so do freely. They could either leave with all their belongings or sell them within two years. Just about everyone who had property chose the selling option and left Spain as wealthy people, heading for Morocco.

The Alhambra is the castle of Granada. Its architectural features, cultural aspects, and artistic elements are highly praised. And all these features have been preserved for later generations. A city of even greater, unparalleled architectural, cultural, and artistic significance, however, had a different fate: thirty-nine years earlier, in AD 1453, Sultan Mehmed II captured Constantinople. Emperor Constantine XI was not as lucky as emir Abdallah was. He didn't get the benefit of the kind of conditions that Abdallah had received for Granada. Mehmed's troops committed a bloodbath and wrecked havoc of unimaginable scale. Only a few walls and one large building suitable to function as a great mosque were saved for posterity. The whole world was shocked about this terrible event. And Abdallah probably had this incident in mind when he turned over the city.

With the surrender of Granada, the era of the Muslim Empire on Spanish soil was over for good, but the history of Muslims, however, was not. Already in AD 1507, a law regarding forced conversion was passed: all adult Muslims were left with the choice between getting baptized and leaving. But complications occurred due to the fact that in Islam, arrangements are made for Muslims that allow for the deliberate deception of the non-Muslims, called *taqiyya*. But among the Muslims who decided to stay, how were the real converts to be identified and distinguished from the "crypto-Muslims," the Muslims who only pretended? This task was taken up by the Spanish office of *"santo Oficio,"* the Holy Inquisition in AD 1529. Measured by what was customary at the time, their job was not considered cruel but it was incredibly ineffective. As a consequence, the last one hundred thousand Moriscs (Muslims) were banished from Spain in AD 1609.[104]

Generally, when referring to al-Andalus, the talk is of eight hundred years under Muslim rule during which the flourishing of arts and sciences skyrocketed, where religious tolerance was *the* imperative, and where there was nothing but love, peace, and harmony

---

104   Trials were opened in 10 percent of the cases, 30 percent of which ended in acquittals; in less than 2 percent of them, the verdict was the death sentence. Imprisonment could include labor camps but also house arrest and were then generally restricted to three years. With a few exceptions, the infamous "burnings at the stake" or so-called "autodafes" were restricted to the burning of "effigies," meaning straw dolls. Regarding torture, breaking bones and injuries that would have resulted in permanent mutilations were prohibited. The Spanish Inquisition was in fact extensively regulated.

altogether. In some reports, the talk is even of nine hundred years of Muslim rule, and certain Muslim circles use this to justify real claims for possessions.[105] Because such a claim would consequently form the basis for demands by the Christian world for Turkey, Syria, Palestine, Egypt, and North Africa that would be by far more justified, we had rather not start this useless discussion.

But where is this claim of eight hundred years of Muslim rule in Spain derived from? Even if one has only very limited knowledge regarding this particular issue, it can be regarded as common knowledge that an eight-hundred-year period of uniform conditions has never existed in history.

The seizure of southern Spain by the Berbers and Arabs in the early eighth century was not religiously motivated. A religion called "Islam" had not spread out yet at that time. The conquerors of Spain were Arian Berbers and Ibadite Arabs of Christian belief. Simultaneous to the developments in the "Orient," a religious process began in the middle of the ninth century in al-Andalus by which Arabic Christendom became an independent religion. But it was not until the tenth century that this process had reached the point where the existence of a new religion called "Islam" in al-Andalus could be assumed.

With the arrival of North African Dynasties of Almoravids and Almohads (AD 1090–1248), the Andalus Muslims soon became very aware of the fact that there were different ideas about the right religion—not only that these fundamentalist movements fought the unbelievers but that they also taught the local Muslims what's what. They brought the jihad with them to al-Andalus, where thoughts of a crusade were developing. Only now the religiously motivated *conquista* confronted the religiously motivated *reconquista*. Due to the great success of the *reconquista*, in Spain by the middle of the thirteenth century, only one Muslim Empire, Granada, remained. Granada was a vassal-state, completely at the mercy of the Catholic rulers in the North. In AD 1482,

---

105 The terrorists who caused the March 11, 2004, Madrid train bloodbath, which killed 191 people, referred to the demand that Spain must become a part of the Dar al-Islam again.

King Ferdinand initiated the step-by-step liquidation of Granada, a process which ended with the triumphant entry in the Alhambra.

As becomes more and more obvious, the nature of history is anything but a steady continuation, and the presence of an eight-hundred-year Muslim rule or dominance is certainly out of the question. In hindsight, it becomes clear that the process of political demise of the Muslim-branded Spain already began with the death of Hakam II (AD 976)—it means it happened at the moment shortly after Islam had just been established. That condenses the time period of Muslim rule over al-Andalus to two hundred fifty years, corresponding to the short time periods of the Umayyad Caliphate and the rule of North African foreign powers. Granada was always a shrinking enclave. Its significance was inversely proportional to the view of it today.

Much of the literature dealing with al-Andalus is full of praise regarding the cultural accomplishments of the Mores. According to these reports, the conquering Arabs must have been invading a developing country and were the ones who gave the underdeveloped Spaniards a wake-up call in terms of culture and civilization. The "sons of the desert," famous for their agricultural skills and water management expertise, would have set an agricultural-based economy in place that would have to be called unprecedented. In addition, the spa and thermal culture, apparently totally unknown to people in Roman provinces, would have been introduced by the Arabic Bedouins. And as one can learn from a tourist guide, the same would apply to the Arabic Baths which were covered by these "typically Arabic air bricks" (these are, however, the pan-Mediterranean bricks that can be seen in Pompeii as well as in much older cities anywhere around the Mediterranean). We would have to assume that Spain back then was at the architectural level of a clay-hut culture and that it was only due to the stately buildings by the Mores like the Alhambra, that would have to have been produced instantly and out of thin air, that culture could be established in Spain. And, as the UNESCO website informs us, the conquerors also had tolerance and rationalism in their luggage. The Spaniards must have had the greatest moment in their history.

But in reality, the conquerors came from Africa, the marginal areas of the Roman World, to Hispania, which represented a central province of the Roman Empire. And therefore it had infrastructural accomplishments from the classical ancient period, like the best road network and best water supply system in the world, as well as temple complexes, palaces, spas, theaters, and lavishly outlined cities with fresh-water and wastewater systems. Despite the fact that the Roman Empire had officially ceased to exist, there were still many useful features.

Oleg Grabar, the brilliant expert on Islamic architecture and building historian, has pointed out the similarities of Andalusian palaces with classical ancient architecture. Their style was not the result of some infamous "Islamic" palaces taken as basic examples but it was derived from stately buildings like Nero's "Domus Aurea" and Hadrian's Villa. Architecturally very closely related earlier models were the palaces of Roman provincial rulers in Spain and North Africa. In having arcades, arched columns, double windows, and atriums, they set the trends for the style that was typical of Andalusian palaces. The feature of water gardens, like the Alhambra garden Generalife, is very typically Persian. The walled-in yards that consist of gardens and water parks are regarded as miniature displays of Paradise—a rather extravagant, pre-Islamic, Persian idea of Paradise. These "Paradise gardens" were very widespread. They were found originally in an area stretching from Syria to Afghanistan, and were possibly introduced to Spain by the Umayyads.

The quality of Andalusian stonemasonry was neither a match for the Gothic masonry nor for the masonry of the classical ancient period. Instead of carrying out elaborate work on the stone itself, the supporting substructure was covered by stuccowork. Their typical ornamentations were the so-called *Muqarnas* (corbel-like structures used as decorative devices with shapes like stalactites, bee hives, etc.), which also originated in pre-Islamic Persia.

The Andalusian architectural style of stately and magnificent buildings was predominantly derived from the classical Roman design; Persian models were used to a minor extent. "Islamic" predecessors—

whatever those are supposed to be—do not exist. Today's Alhambra, which by many people is viewed as the most Islamic building of all, was created in a time period during which Spain by no means could be considered Islamic anymore.

The situation regarding the sacred buildings is similar. We know that the North African invaders used the church of San Vicente in Cordoba together with the local population until the Syrian refugee Abd ar-Rahman built his Holy Shrine right on top of it. This shrine was in the style of the churches in his home country and included the characteristic element of arches that rested on classical ancient-style columns. Typically, arches were segmented by alternating ocher/red elements, which was a result of the colors of the original materials, namely bricks and stones. For more than one hundred years, the *Mezquita* of Cordoba was used as an Arab-Christian church until it was gradually transformed into a mosque. The building was permanently expanded but its basic elements stayed the same. The outcome of the building by Abd ar-Rahman I (AD 756–788), and its expansions by Abd ar-Rahman II (AD 822–852), was large halls that contained a forest of various classical ancient columns and red-white double arches above.

The addition by Hakam II (AD 961–976), who was the first caliph, is in a completely new style and of an unequal artistic quality. While the design and finish of the praying booth are very impressive, they are, at the same time, rather surprising as they also include the cover of a magnificent Byzantine cupola. As is well-known, the structure of the Byzantine cupola is based on a layout of a cross. This addition was a gift by the Byzantine Emperor Nikephoros II Phokas who sent artists, their equipment, and all of the materials needed to Cordoba. What could have been the reason for that? It was probably an act of good will and public relations: Byzantium used to be present in Hispania and repeatedly sought to win the caliphate as an ally. The last addition to the building was carried out by Al-Mansur and represented a fallback to the forest of columns style, but this time it was of a much lower class. It was probably for the lack of materials that poor-quality and damaged classical ancient columns had been used and that the arches were not made of bricks and stones anymore but had this design simply painted on. The style of the Mezquita, the Roman-Syrian architecture of the arches, and the Byzantine addition by Hakam II were not of the Andalusian type. In Islamic Spain, the origin of the architectural design, including that of sacred architecture, has got nothing to do with any "Islamic" style, as there had just never been any Islamic models.

In general, both the significance and influence of Andalusian philosophy and science on Europe have been greatly overestimated. As was already pointed out in a previous chapter of this book, it is absolutely inappropriate to speak of the presence of Islamic sciences during the late classical ancient times. In the Arab Empire, there were numerous scientists of various nationalities who had a range of mentalities. Because their connecting element was the Arabic language, it certainly would be fair to call them "Arabic scientists." But only in a very few exceptional cases, however, were they Muslims. Moreover, the establishment of Islam brought the flourishing of the Arabic sciences to an end within a very short period of time.

The flourishing of the Arabic spiritual and intellectual life took place mainly in the Persian Orient. But, without trying to diminish the accomplishments of the Arabic scientists in any way, these were foremost just acts of passing on knowledge like, for instance, Indian ("Arabic") numbers, or ideas of classical ancient philosophers. Passing on information happened without the existence of al-Andalus. In contrast to the often-made claim, Andalus was never the center of science. Regarding this, the story about the medical book by Dioscorides, which was given to Abd ar-Rahman III (AD 912–929) by the Byzantine Emperor as a gift, might be a good illuminating example: this work was written in Greek, which was the language of scholars at that time. But as it turned out, nobody in Cordoba was able to read it; therefore, the emperor had to send a monk who was educated in languages as well.

The burning down of the library of Hakam II (regency AD 961–976) by al-Mansur (AD 938–1002) was already a deed carried out as a Qur'anic act. Almost all the works destroyed were those by Eastern authors because, with the exception of Ibn Masarra, al-Andalus hadn't yielded a single leading author in the fields of science and philosophy. That didn't happen until Ibn Rushd, Ibn Maymun (Maimonides), and a few others appeared in the twelfth century. But these were the only names that connected al-Andalus with the fields of science and philosophy for a short period of time. In the East, Al-Ghazali had entirely asserted himself. From this time on, the Qur'anic word decided about what was to be known and to be thought.

Pierre Phillippe Rey[106] enlightens us by stating that Europe actually acquired rationalism from "North and West Africa, and al-Andalus." Unfortunately, he fell short of giving us any reason for his most interesting proposition. But for now it can be assumed that al-Andalus was neither a connecting link nor the cradle of European rationalism itself.

But the greatest accomplishment of al-Andalus, which is hailed in unison, was supposed to be tolerance: the tolerance for other lifestyles, other ways of thinking, and other religions. And this created an unprecedented form of communal life and coexistence, the legendary *convivencia*.

Among other texts found on the UNESCO Homepage,[107] there is a passage by Mohamed Benchrifa:

> *"Throughout the period of Islamic rule, al-Andalus was a remarkable example and outstanding model of tolerance... It can be said that al-Andalus was home to forms of tolerance that were not seen again until modern times. It was a genuine land of dialogue, dialogue that was at times serene and at others lively."*

Let's take a look at one of those serene and lively dialogues between two of al-Andalus' most significant thinkers, Ibn Rushd and Maimonides, which Maimonides put in words like these:

---

106   Pierre Phillippe Rey at http://unesdoc.unesco.org/ images/0011/001144/114426eo.pdf.
107   http://unesdoc.unesco.org/images/0011/001144/114426eo.pdf.

"The Arabs have severely persecuted us and have enacted banning and discriminating laws against us. Never before has there been a nation that has tortured, humiliated, degraded, and hated us like this."

In another "serene and lively dialogue" which Ibn Rushd had to carry out before the Court of Law in his home city of Cordoba, he was faced with a matter of life and death. It was only due to his relationship with the ruler that Ibn Rushd was given a "light sentence" of being granted banishment, and he was restrained by a lifelong speaking and writing ban, his works were banned, and he was kept under wraps in the Islamic world. His work was only appreciated later, when Christian Europe discovered his accomplishments publicized under the name Averroes.

In AD 1126, Ibn Rushd was born in Cordoba as a son of an esteemed family of *Qadis*. The term *Qadi*, meaning judge, did not only refer to the profession of judge itself but also denoted a rank of honor. His bread-and-butter job was a medical profession but his main occupation lay in the field of physics and philosophy. In AD 1153, he was called to the Almohads Dynasty Court in Marrakesh. On behalf of the prince and later caliph Yusuf Abu Yaqub, he carried out various physical studies and produced translations of Aristotle's works. He spent most of his time in Spain where he was commissioned by the ruler. And that's the place where disaster loomed for him. The times of free speech and free writing had passed. Everywhere, Al-Ghazali and the ultra-orthodox ones were gaining ground, and it was these Ibn Rushd fought with all his might. In his causality teachings, Rushd opposed Ghazali's doctrine that included the word-for-word compliance with the Qur'an and also accused Ghazali of not only destroying philosophy but also Islam.

And that had consequences. A formal charge against Ibn Rushd in AD 1195 denied that he was a rightful believer and banned not only his texts but the field of philosophy altogether. It was only his close relationship to the ruler (he had been his personal physician) that spared his life. Instead, he was exiled from Cordoba and died soon after, in AD 1198.

It was his medical expertise that saved Averroes' life, a fate shared by the second great thinker of al-Andalus, Maimonides. In AD 1135, nine years after Rushd's birth, Maimonides was born as Moshe ben Maymon, son to an esteemed Jewish rabbi in Cordoba. He grew up in an atmosphere of Jewish scholarliness which, however, abruptly ended in AD 1148. The Almohads ruled in al-Andalus and forced every non-Muslim to convert or leave—if they were not threatened with worse things. The migratory life of the ben Maymon family began which would take them all over Spain. There was no place for them to feel safe. So they eventually sailed over to North Africa and settled down in Fez around the year AD 1160.

This relocation "into the lion's den" spurred many speculations. The true reasons for this undertaking are unknown but it seems clear that Morocco must have meant a safer place for them than al-Andalus. Or was it that Maimonides felt safe because he had converted to Islam? There are indications for his conversion but no evidence. Remarkably, Maimonides pleaded for conversion in several reports he wrote, but he suggested a *taqiyya*-like manner.[108]

Maimonides dealt with metaphysics, astronomy, and, of course, Aristotle's ideas. His main works, however, were texts about Jewish belief and law. Maimonides' main occupation was physician.

But the religious persecution eventually reached the ben Maymon family after all. When the chief rabbi of Fez was executed for refusing to convert to Islam, the family fled to Palestine in AD 1165 and later moved on to Egypt. In Fustat (Cairo), Moshe became a respected member of the Jewish community and a popular physician at the Sultan's Court.

But the shadows of the past caught up with him at the peak of his career when a former co-worker appeared who claimed that the Rabbi Moshe used to be a Muslim in Fez. In the end, Maimonides also managed to get out of this life-threatening situation. The close

---

108 *Taqiyya*: the practice of deceit that is sanctioned by the Qur'an in order to gain an advantage against the unbeliever.

relationship to the Sultan as his personal physician probably saved his life. Maimonides died in Fustat in AD 1204. His dead body was moved to Tiberias in Palestine. There, he was buried in the place where his forefathers had been laid to rest.

Today, Maimonides and Ibn Rushd are celebrated as the most significant thinkers of al-Andalus. Both of them were chased and persecuted, lived under deadly terror, and were forced to leave the "oh so tolerant" al-Andalus. And their cases were no exceptions—they were the rule in al-Andalus. It almost seems grotesque that it was exactly that religious branch of Muslims that threatened Ibn Rushd's life which now, after having ignored him for centuries, welcomes him back into their ranks. Ibn Rushd cannot act against it anymore.

Ranked according to population, Spain had Ibero-Romans, Gothic people, Jews, 'new" Berbers, "old" Berbers, and Arabs. But on the regional level, the composition of inhabitants varied significantly, as majorities might have been formed by different groups. The reason for that lay in the continuous conquests, banishments and displacements, enslavements, and translocations that occurred. The maps only show borders in forms of snapshots in time. There were ethnics groups that spoke High Arabic, popular Arabic, various Berber dialects, different Roman dialects, Hebrew, and Latin. During the ninth century, the Arabic language transformed into a day-to-day-like language among the individual groups. In addition to Christians and Muslims, there were also special kinds of groups during this time period in these areas: Christians who converted to Islam (*Mulades*), Christians who lived under Islamic rule (*Mozarabs*), Muslims who converted to Christianity (*Moriscs*), and Muslims who lived under Christian rule (*Mudejars*).

Conversions were never voluntary. People were forced into converting by being subjected to various kinds of maltreatments, ranging from legal disadvantages to physical abuse. Whoever refused to convert became a second-class citizen (*dhimmi*). For them, there was only the choice between flight, tribute, and death. It is amazing to see that this certainly undeniable situation could be interpreted in a different way. That such is even possible was shown by Professor Maria Rosa Menocal, who wrote[109]: "*not only that the Islamic politics made the survival of Christians and Jews·possible but, according to the Qur'anic mission, these Islamic politics more or less protected them.*"

During the period of the Ta'ifas mosaic, the situation, however, was completely different. In general, religion didn't seem to be the most important issue but, nevertheless, the first major massacre of Jews was carried out in AD 1066 in Cordoba. This massacre was preceded by an "expose" by the pious legal expert Abu Ishaq:

> "These Jews, who used to look for shreds of colored cloths in the garbage piles in order to bury their dead…have now divided up Cordoba among them…They collect tributes and dress most elegantly….and the ape Josef covered his house in marble stone…Hurry up to slit his throat, he is a plumb ram. Take away his money, for you deserve it more than he."

During the time periods when the foreign Almoravids and Almohads (twelfth and thirteenth centuries) ruled, there was no quarter for other religions. These sectarists fought unbelievers as mercilessly as they fought Muslim dissenters.

Starting in AD 1237, al-Andalus consisted of not much else than the emirate of Granada. And it kept on shrinking until there was nothing more left than the castle of Granada itself. Due to its growing dependence on the Christian nations, Granada couldn't afford to carry out religious conflicts anymore. At the same time, the growing power of the Christian regimen increasingly put the Muslims under pressure. But pressure was more or less applied by every party that was in the position to do so.

Tolerance as a trademark of al-Andalus is simply a fantasy. The kind of tolerance that corresponds to the idea of tolerance today was found nowhere during the Middle Ages, not in Spain nor anywhere else

---

109   Maria Rosa Menocal, *The Ornament of the World* (Boston, New York, London: Back Bay Books, 2003)..

in Europe. The concept of tolerance is a product of the Renaissance period.

The basis of this concept is truth and freedom. Because it is the nature of revealed religions that they all claim to represent the only truth, their tolerance only goes as far as they are unable to politically enforce their idea of it. Freedom and tolerance pretty much end where religious dogmas begin.

Not only was al-Andalus far from being a tolerant society, it was not even a pluralistic one. The nature of pluralism contains the agreement that all cultures are equal. But the reality of al-Andalus was far from it. The degree of both tolerance and pluralism depended on the degree to which people were forced to give in and put up with things they couldn't change for the moment—but "one worked on it" (or, as it is called by the worshippers of the fairy tale of al-Andalus tolerance, it is "pragmatic tolerance").

The concept of religious tolerance never existed in al-Andalus. The individual religious groups always followed the policy of either taking over or separation, and their pursuit was only interrupted by periods during which the enforcement of neither one was possible. These were the time periods that later became known as the legendary *convivencia*, the happy co-existence of three cultures. It became the pretended trademark of al-Andalus because, in reality, it was the exception. The most promising time period of the *convivencia* was probably during the short interval of the Ta'ifas and in the Christian city of Toledo, when Christians, Muslims, and Jews escaped the assault by the North Africans. In large numbers, they fled to Christian strongholds where they peacefully created a common culture, at least temporarily, until the death of Alfonse the Wise in AD 1284.

At the same time, Islamic fundamentalists destroyed all traces of Christian and Jewish construction activities like churches, synagogues, cemeteries, schools, and community buildings in the south. Therefore, the tourism that focuses on visiting ruins gives a pretty good idea about the superiority of the Moorish culture. In addition, it is unfortunate for some historians that archaeological proof of the *convivencia* got lost under Islamic rule.

Coexistence can only work when there is a certain concurrence between all of the cultures involved, which means they have to live in the same slice of time regarding their states of development in order to see eye-to-eye. Until the tenth century, most of the Iberian Peninsula was influenced by the Syrian-Arabic culture, which was, recall to mind, basically a Greek-Roman one. And, with some reservation, this situation continued during the time of the Ta'ifas.

The first frictions regarding the "time concurrence" appeared with the arrival of the fundamentalist Almoravids and Almohads. They came from Africa's past to the modern age of Spain and didn't know what to do with it. In the end they vanished, but the next event was already on the horizon: the new, radical interpretation of belief that had already been established in the East and was about to befall al-Andalus.

Al-Andalus was cut off from modern times not only by the activities of the bigots from North Africa themselves, but by the developments in the East which also had a significant impact on al-Andalus.

The time period that started when the Almoravid foreign rule took over and lasted until the end of the Granada Emirate was not characterized by a time concurrence. One might be misled by looking at the magnificent stuccowork in a small part of the Alhambra. But this must be compared with the fact that at that time the Dome of Cologne was under construction, the Cathedral of Burgos had been finished, and ostentatious churches and glamorous *palazzos* had been created in Florence which had been decorated with Pisano's sculptures.

It is the spirit that creates inventions. But the elimination of Ibn Rushd marked the beginning of the spiritual petrifaction of the Islamic world.

The discrepancies between different levels of modernity in Spain during that time couldn't have been any clearer: AD 1492 was the year in which Ferdinand and Isabel accepted the capitulation of Granada and the last Muslim ruler left Spain, and they sent off a captain called Christoph Columbus to go on an expedition to the New World on their behalf. It was the New World that was suspected to be somewhere beyond the horizon of the round globe.

Once it had been the Arabic (not Islamic) ruler al-Mamun, under whose orders the globe was measured and its precise length, off by only a few kilometers, was calculated. Now it was the Europeans who sent off ships to circumnavigate the globe, whereas in the Islamized Arabic-world people were forced to imagine that the earth was flat because it was the Holy Book that commanded it. By moving into the Alhambra, the Royal Family from the North was first of all taking up the Castilian state business. But with them, modernity moved in, too:

> "The Alhambra can surely be viewed as a symbolic example for a new, united Europe, where, like never before, different religions and cultures can and must converge."[110]

Why would it have to be especially Alhambra? Which cultures and religions were supposed to have been the ones converging there in a model-like way? If one really likes to choose a symbol that represents the co-existence of the three cultures, it will have to be Toledo. If one really likes to choose a building that symbolizes al-Andalus, it can only be the Mezquita of Cordoba. The Mezquita is a bizarre building. It began its story on the site of a plundered Temple of Jupiter and a Gothic Church that used to be a rather unspecified "place of worship," rebuilt in a style of Syrian church. Mosque additions followed, with the artistic highlight of one addition which was completely foreign and was obtained from Byzantium. This was followed by a relapse into artistically inferior work as seen in the last addition. And then a cathedral was put in the middle of the mosque. It goes together like chalk and cheese, however: in contrast to what one would have to expect, the mosque was not destroyed by the conquerors but was "supplemented" by a cathedral in the middle of it. Certainly, the cathedral represents the dominating element and the minaret is enclosed by the church steeple—but what could more impressively

---

110 Lubisch, (Frankfurter Allgemeine Zeitung), August 12, 2004.

epitomize the historic rollercoaster than this building which combines the basic elements of the (his-)story of al-Andalus?

Appeals and reminiscences regarding the time period in Spain of the "oh so tolerant" Islam are predominantly made from the Islamic side itself. A more careful handling of this issue would be appropriate, since non-Muslim citizens were charged with extra taxes everywhere and at all times and, in addition, were denied full rights. All of the non-Muslims in al-Andalus had the dhimmi-status of second-class citizen. This is what we want to call tolerance?

Not much has been said yet about the third group, the Jews. They immigrated to Spain in the sixth century BC. Because they called Spain *Sefarad*, the Spanish Jews were later called the *Sefarad Jews*. By the Alhambra emotionalism, they were "mediators" between cultures. That is a euphemism for someone who sits between the chairs. Most of the time, members of the two main cultural groups either alternately or simultaneously ostracized them, deprived them of their rights, and robbed, exiled, or killed the Jewish people.

There are examples of Jewish people who reached high social positions, like for instance, Ibn Shaprut of Cordoba or Ibn Negrela of Granada. But they were just downright exceptions. Ibn Negrela, who built the first Alhambra and had the world-famous Lion's Fountain commissioned, was brutally murdered on the occasion of the *pogrom* (organized massacre of helpless people) carried out by Muslims in AD 1066. The fate of Maimonides was already talked about earlier in the chapter.

In the pogroms of AD 1391, two-thirds of the Jewish communities were eliminated. In AD 1492, right after the takeover of Granada, all of the Spanish Jews were ordered to either get baptized or leave the country. The majority left and thereby just about completely closed the chapter of the history of the Jews in Spain.

And here, again: the *convivencia* was the exception to the rule and, after all, was only dictated by political necessities, but neither was it the result of tolerance nor the longing for pluralism.

Finally, let's take a look at what else the UNESCO homepage (see footnote 107) has to offer:

> *"Jews, Christians, and Muslims were most fully and freely able to engage in a wide range of common activities. They include… theological and even religious fields, law and administration…"*
> —Haïm Zafrani

And:

> *"Al-Andalus was a remarkable example and outstanding model of tolerance. It emerged at the time of the conquest, when the Muslim conquerors undertook to preserve the freedoms of their subjects, protect their fortunes and their property, respect their churches and ensure their defense".*—Mohamed Benchrifa

One is anxious to visit the churches that were defended and protected by the Muslims. But—where are they?

These are the fairy tales of al-Andalus. The historic reality is different. There was no tolerance in al-Andalus. Instead, there was apartheid implemented by whichever side had the political power to do so. The hailed happy times of *convivencia* only happened when the enemies were in a deadlock and had no other choice. That's how it was in al-Andalus.

❖ ❖ ❖

"Who Has Done This to Us?"

Reality in Retrospect

We only pay them back a fraction of what they have done to us.

—*Osama bin Laden about his terror activities*

The Islamic world is in bad shape. This especially applies to her key countries, the Arab nations. Regarding all sociological data, they rank among the countries on the bottom of the list. And that is in spite of the fact that they are rich in oil. Only some African countries fare worse.

In contradiction to the general cliché-like notion, the Arab countries are economically poor. When leaving out oil-production, all of the Arab nations combined have the economic power of Spain, which is a significantly smaller region. All production that is carried out in their own countries is essentially based on foreign licenses. Original production is almost non-existent. During the years 1980–2000, the whole Arab world combined just managed to develop 370 patents. During the same time period, Israel produced 7,650 patents, and South Korea, which is often used for comparison because of its similar stage of development, created 16,300 patents. Excluding oil production, during those years, Korean workers have produced a GNP that is four times the production of the whole Arab world combined.

But why would they have to work at all, when they have all that oil, one might think. This might seem obvious but it also represents a part of the problem. There is no doubt that oil nets huge profits but the wealth doesn't make it to the people. The extravagant and ostentatious lifestyle of Arabic billionaires is legendary. But even countries like Iran, which is not known for having a lavish upper class, are not making much headway economically. The only exceptions are some small Gulf States and exotic countries like Brunei.

Regarding education, which is a key factor in every country's future development, all of the Arab countries are far behind. The very high percentage of illiterate people—dramatically high among women—has a logical consequence regarding book production: while 5 percent of world's population lives in Arab countries, in 2005, only 1 percent of all books were published there. Moreover, the vast majority of these were religious titles. Those numbers can be found in the *Arab Human Development Report (AHDR)*, where regular updates are presented by Arabic authors regarding the situation in the Arab countries. These reports are remarkably frank but they also contain clichés. For instance, they explain that the problems in the Arab world are the result of the Middle Eastern policies of the United States and Israel. It is certainly true that Israel represents a psychological trauma for this region. But was the situation any better before the founding of Israel? Not really. The fact that the whole Islamic world, and that especially applies to the Arab nations, is in a crisis is obvious to everybody. And it is certainly obvious to the affected people themselves. When something of that magnitude goes wrong, the questions should be:

"What went wrong?"

"Why did it go wrong?"

"What have we done wrong?"

But that is not how the Islamic world handles this. There, the central question is:

"Who has done this to us?"

Up to this day, the answer to this question is the same: the Franks, the Crusaders, the Mongols, the French, the English, the missionaries, the Soviets, and, currently, the United States, Israel, and the West.[111]

---

111   The region's four hundred years as an Ottoman colony, during which the whole are was extremely repressed, is itself suppressed and only mentioned marginally in Arabic history lectures.

These questions and statements are found in every publication in the Islamic world. At the same time, the Golden Age of Islam is invoked. Muslims are puzzled by what caused the downfall of the golden past and led to the dreary present. Has Allah abandoned them, and if so, why?

The constant evocation of the Golden Age of Islam denotes the time period of the Arabic Empires beginning in the year AD 622. As we know, the time of the Prophet, including all its detail-rich stories, is nothing more than a white-lie legend. The same applies to the miraculously rapid expansion of Islam. In reality, the political development during the seventh century resulted in the establishment of a Great Arabic Empire, but not an Islamic one. Moreover, it had absolutely nothing to do with Mecca, the person of the Prophet, or the creation of the legendary dynasties of early caliphs which were later connected to him by fictitious genealogy. Cultural, religious, and ethnic diversity in the Great Arabic Empire led to the flourishing of society and sciences, especially at the Royal and Noble Courts of Baghdad, Samarra, Damascus, and Tehran, and even in regions of today's Kazakhstan, Uzbekistan, Turkmenistan, and Afghanistan.

The fall of the Roman Empire in the West resulted not only in the disappearance of the classical-ancient culture but also in the vanishing of its intellectual heritage. The "Occident" drifted into the "dark medieval times." But the "Orient" took a different path—Middle Ages in fact did not exist. Here, scientists picked up the concepts of Greek philosophers, discussed them, and tried to further develop them; this was the "East Iranian Renaissance." New domains were entered in the fields of astronomy, medicine, physics, and especially optics. The reason for this was the extended classical period in the Iranian east. The end of this era was reached when Ibn Rushd (Averroes) was declared un-Islamic, his works were publicly burnt, and he died an ostracized man in AD 1198.

The "Mutazilism" of al-Mamun was nothing less than Arabic humanism. That means that during his time, the basis for a "Renaissance" period had already been developed. But things turned out very differently:

al-Ghazali succeeded in getting both reasoning and free thinking outlawed, the Ultra-Orthodox got the upper hand, and Islam became the state religion. Any kind of intellectual activity that went beyond that of dealing with religious books was now subject to punishment—and, a bit further geographically, though delayed, the Renaissance happened in Europe. The spiritual flourishing of the "Oriental Middle Ages" was Arabic but not Islamic. Moreover: the establishing of Islam brought the period of Arabic accomplishments to a very quick end.

The fall of the Arabic Empires began with the deterioration of their spiritual and intellectual life and continued by affecting all other spheres. Three centuries later, the Arabic Empire had become unrecognizable. Their cities were run down, the fertile surrounding the countryside lay unproductive, and the people had deserted the former cultural centers in mass.

How could this happen?

A very popular explanation for this is that the plague struck. But that happened in Europe just the same. Another reason given is the Mongols' conquest in AD 1258. Without a doubt, the Mongols wreaked havoc but, then again, they also went away very soon—as Muslims.

The Crusades? The first Crusade, which took place in AD 1096, was a rather naïve and idealistic movement, meant to free the Holy Land where streams of milk and honey were supposedly waiting for them. The region was plagued by Arabic, Armenian and Seljuk tribes of different religions, the central power in Baghdad had begun deteriorating. The majority of Jerusalem's inhabitants were Christians and Jews, and together with some Egyptian troops, the Jews were the ones who defended the city. Jeruslalem belonged to the Egyptian Fatimids at that time and these were Ismailitic Gnostics rather than "Muslims".

In AD 1106, after the Norman Prince Bohemund returned from the Holy Land, he had a meeting with Pope Paschalis II. In this meeting, the Prince told the Pope who the real enemy was: Byzantium. Immediately, the Pope ordered preaching in favor of a crusade against the Byzantine Empire: this marked the turning point in the history of the Crusades.

The following Crusades developed into a strange mix of agendas, including religious, political, and economic ones. The main goal was the destruction of the great religious enemy Byzantium, still—or again—the biggest power in the region. Islam was only marginally of interest. With the help of the Venetian fleet, Byzantium was finally captured in April of AD 1204. The annihilation of the Byzantine Empire was the basis for the rise of the Ottoman Empire. An additional effect of the Crusades was that they united the Muslims, which, according to Morozov, was actually the moment when they began developing their own identity.

The Crusades, as well, are completely useless when trying to explain the fall of the Arab Empires. The phenomenon of deterioration was seen in every formerly flourishing Arab area from central Asia to Morocco. Back then, Syria, Mesopotamia, Egypt, and North Africa used to be the granaries and cultural strongholds of the world. There were no external influences that could provide a rational explanation for the crash of the Arabic world. Therefore, the cause must have been internal in nature.

Although Islam developed by sprouting off from Christendom in Persia and the Arabic core regions (e.g., in nowadays Iraq and Syria), Bedouin traditions began taking over the Hellenic environment, and with these the laws of the desert came back. As a result, Bronze Age traditions that were long thought to have been overcome were reintroduced.

Astoundingly, European travelers frequently reported that the wheel was not used in the "Orient"—while its usage had already been a matter of course for people in the classical ancient world. There were hardly any carriages in operation, or any carts or chariots, but almost exclusively pack animals were used. As a matter of fact, the occurrence of the desert culture in the rich agricultural countries between the Tigris and Nile Rivers also brought the camel into these areas, which increased its significance.[112] The camel remained important until cars and trains were introduced by Western engineers. One can imagine the impact that just this single step backward must have had. The road network that had been built during the classical ancient period deteriorated; the lavish colonnades and wide avenues of the ancient cities were eventually replaced by narrow roads where only two pack animals would fit side-by-side in accordance with the Islamic judiciary. The lavish Greek city, the *polis*, became the *medina*.

The more the Qur'an was established, the more other books were suppressed until they eventually were banned and disappeared. While al-Mamun had destroyed the classical-ancient scripts only after they had been translated into Arabic, his successors vigorously wiped out everything that was non-Islamic. The tolerance that is said to have existed is purely legendary. Over centuries, the elimination of both non-Islamic ideas and differing cultures was a significant part of the policy. Especially in India, cultural assets of unimaginable dimensions were destroyed. Suppressed works of Arabic authors made it to Europe only fragmentarily. They, however, still contributed to the European Renaissance movement.

For a long time, reading non-Islamic books was punishable by death. At best, possession of those books was "only" despised. The Qur'an was God's word and contained the perfect answers to all questions. Therefore, additional knowledge was harmful and blasphemous. Due to the lack of any influx of new information, knowledge eventually ceased to exist—it meant the intellectual standstill of the Islamic world.

Non-Muslim subjects, the "unbelievers," became second-class citizens. They often had to pay horrific taxes that were so high that they only had the choice between conversion and emigration, especially since they were denied many jobs that were only open to Muslims.

---

112   For three thousand years, the camel was the epitome of wealth for people who lived in the desert. But for the last two decades, it has been the symbol of poverty and has been replaced by pickup trucks produced in Asia.

Not only did this desert-specific ideology, which includes contempt both for different cultures and for knowledge, find its way into the Qur'an, but it became the nature of the Qur'an. Within just a few generations, science and innovation came to a complete standstill. Productive industry and even agriculture were significantly affected. Trade was the only field left.

What happened to the agricultural areas that had supplied the world back then? What happened to the flourishing of the Roman-Greek-Arabic Orient? How was a collapse of such magnitude of the ancient Bactrian possible that it could result in conditions as they are in today's Afghanistan? There was no climate change that could be blamed—it was the Bedouin mentality of the new religion. When the infrastructure was destroyed, that was the moment when cultural and economical "rigor mortis" set in.

The calendar represents the best tool to get a clear picture regarding the regression of the Islamic world. The year AD 622, or the "year of the Arabs," *kata Arabas*, as it is called in the Gadara inscription where it is preceded by the sign of the cross, was the year in which the Arab Empire began. This is the year that was defined as the beginning of the Arab calendar and, naturally, followed the solar calendar that was commonly used back then. But suddenly, we see this date reused and turned into the Hijra year, the year when Muhammad allegedly left Mecca for Medina. It was the beginning of the Islamic calendar, which was based on legendary events that included the Bronze Age traditions of central Arabia and their lunar calendar. That's how the lunar Goddess Allat returned to her original calendar.

It is a completely useless calendar. A person who is born in June will celebrate his next one or two birthdays in May, the following one in April, and so forth. Eventually, the monthly difference adds up and stretches into year-long time periods. For that reason, events like Muhammad's birthday or the fasting month of Ramadan are celebrated on different dates each year. Because in the lunar calendar the scheduling of reoccurring events is indefinable, it is useless for developed societies. For that reason, it had already been abandoned during Roman times.[113] The Muslims now have the lunar calendar back but they generally have no choice but to comply with the solar calendar, which is often demonized as the "Christian" calendar.

The largest Islamic Empire was the Ottoman Empire. After it was founded in 1299 AD, it kept expanding continuously. In AD 1453, Constantinople was captured. After that, the Ottoman people conquered the whole Arabian Peninsula, parts of Russia, the Balkans, Romania, and Hungary, and even made it twice to the city gates of Vienna. In AD 1683, they were eventually defeated at Vienna. After that, it was all downhill for them. The Habsburgs won back almost the entire Balkans, the Russians recaptured all of the regions beyond the Black Sea, and the Ottomans lost Yemen and the whole Arabian Peninsula. In AD 1918, the "Sick Man of the Bosporus" (as the Osman Empire had been called then) had shrunk down to its core areas, the region of today's Turkey.

How could such a total collapse happen? One reason lay in the overstretching of power. But the real reasons are found deeper. The empire's military and economic capabilities couldn't keep up with the developments of their European counterparts. They went on shopping sprees, buying cannons, muskets, and even those watches about which people in the Orient were crazy. But their own commercial productivity developed very slowly and mostly only consisted of producing copies in the standard of the previous century. This situation applied to every field in economy, science, and engineering.

Traveling back then occurred only in one direction and that was from west to east; only in exceptional cases was it the other way around. Europeans traveled to the "Orient," but Muslims almost never went to Europe. The Islamic world had absolutely no interest beyond conquest in the "Occident." They basically only knew that unbelievers lived there.

---

113   The Julian calendar was introduced under Julius Caesar and, in 1582, slightly modified under Pope Gregory XIII. Up to this day, it is in use under the name Gregorian calendar.

The European Renaissance's new ideas regarding national concepts, inventions, advancements in science, and new pictures of the world and the universe—the Islamic world remained ignorant of all that. According to the Qur'an, the earth is shaped like a spread carpet and has seven layers of heavens above it. Even in the era of Google Earth, this view remains their official dogma.

The economic link between Europe and Asia had been a profitable income source for the Islamic countries—and soon it became the only one. The discovery of the Americas, the new seaway around the Cape of Good Hope, the push to the Far East—all of that remained almost completely unnoticed in the Islamic world. They only wished for the newly discovered people that they might find their way to the "right" religion as soon as possible.

Centuries of arrogance, combined with the outdated idea of being superior, would soon come back to roost. The fact that the Europeans had opened their own sea-trade routes to the New World as well as to East and South Asia remained unnoticed in Constantinople and the Islamic world. The Islamic world had lost its trade monopoly, which had connected Europe with Asia. And it had severe consequences, as can be seen just by looking at something as simple as a cup of coffee. Originally, coffee came from Ethiopia, was cultivated in Yemen, and then was introduced to Europe as a delightful drink by Arabia and Turkey. The sugar that was exported to Europe, for the very same coffee for example, came from Mesopotamia or Egypt. But when the Europeans began importing the same items at a lesser cost from Latin America, the tables were turned. Now the Arabs and Turks drank coffee and used sugar from Europe that was imported from Latin America. The only thing left was their water—and even that cannot be said to be true unconditionally anymore.

Every field has been affected in such a way.

A few Muslims, mainly diplomats who knew about Europe, warned about this situation, but nobody would listen. The Islamic world certainly became aware of their deficiencies but, up to this day, they have been trying to eradicate them by returning to the values of Islam and the old Ottoman times. The few attempts to establish European technology in the Islamic world, by the Egyptian viceroy Muhamad Ali at the beginning of the nineteenth century, for example, failed because back then, just like today, the people just kept to consuming and reproducing, but didn't produce any original items.

Nevertheless, the Islamic world still viewed itself as vastly superior and refused to even just take a look and evaluate for themselves the knowledge of the despised unbelievers. It took an unbelievable three hundred years for printing to find its way into the Islamic world, and even then it was only accepted very hesitantly. And it was a European who, practically by using force, installed the first printing press in the Islamic world—namely Napoleon Bonaparte. Up to this day, the Muslim countries have been unable to make up for their backwardness, as is clearly mentioned in the *Arab Human Development Report*.

There is no other reason for this self-destructive, catastrophic approach to education but Islam itself. Its Holy Book, they say, includes and regulates every aspect of human life; it was transmitted by the Prophet, derived directly from God; nothing is to be added, and not one single word is to be changed. The possession of books other than the Qur'an was generally prohibited; and little heed was paid to nonreligious books. Even today, the lesson plan of medical students in Saudi Arabia must contain 30 percent religion classes; in some study branches, it is 50 percent.

This policy has had consequences of unimaginable magnitude for the Muslim world, for it limits the acquisition of knowledge to "allowed" subjects (unfortunately including the construction of nuclear weapons) and consequently, badly affects development and innovation. But the Qur'an claims to be the authority for regulating every aspect of life, including the legal system and education—and such a way would have been ideal for the time of the Prophet. Therefore, both the Islamic mindset and system are still cast in the time of the Prophet and his successors. It is as if there had never been a fourteen-hundred-year history between then and today.

Arabic language and script represent significant technical barriers when it comes to the spreading and teaching of knowledge. "Arabic" as such does not exist. There are colloquial Arabic languages and there is even a so-called High Arabic, the *Arabiya*, which is binding upon the people. But only to a minor extent is it actually comprehensible to the common people. It is a formal language which is not used in day-to-day life. Therefore, *Arabiya* has not undergone the process of adjustment of a living language. But because written products are created in High Arabic, there have been catastrophic results, about which the *AHDR* complains. High Arabic and its script are believed to represent the language and script of their Holy Book and even of God himself. Therefore, High Arabic is not a day-to-day language; it has no profanity, but always represents something sacred.

But this concept doesn't work in a modern world. In order to function as a transmitter of knowledge and information, spoken language and script must be available to every citizen regarding every field. The *AHDR* explicitly points out these issues and difficulties but shies away from clearly naming what consequently would have to be done, namely to restrict the usage of their script to religious matters. And accomplishing this will probably remain an impossible dream for a long time. After all, the Latin script is called the "English script," regardless of the fact that, in addition to other cultural assets, the Latin script originated in the Middle East. Only the Islamic countries of the former Soviet Union and Turkey, as a result of Ataturk's reforms, have made the step from the Arabic to the Latin script.

An Islamic country must be a theocracy. Otherwise, according to definition, it is not an Islamic country. Because one of the most important prerequisites, the separation of powers, does not exist in an Islamic state, it could not be a republic, as, strangely enough, Iran refers to itself. All state authority is derived from the Qur'an, meaning God, and the clergy act as God's deputies in executing this authority. Therefore, the concept of a civil society does not exist. There is only the community of the believers (*Umma*) that lives in the "House of Islam" (*Bayt Islam*). For unbelievers, there is no rank in this house, other than that of a barely tolerated domestic servant (*dhimmi*) at best.

Their rank is right below that of slaves, the latter of which are explicitly provided for in the Qur'an. Only women have less legal rights than male dhimmis or slaves, because the latter still have the chance to change their fate by converting to Islam.

Control and legislation are carried out by the Qur'anic scholars (*ulema*), but the caliph is above all of them. Except by Allah, the caliph is not subject to any control and has free rein as long as he acts according to the Qur'an. Therefore, Islamic society is a perfect breeding ground for all kinds of despots. By their traditional self-image, they are not answerable to their citizens with the exception of following the rule of the Qur'an (or at least they have to claim they do). The idea of resolving problems simply by exchanging people is very widespread in the Islamic world. But fundamental elements cannot be changed without striking at the root of this evil. And this root is represented by the all-controlling position of the Qur'an over every public issue. Striking at the root would mean to separate state and religion.

Until that happens, there cannot be any civil rights but only religious rights which are derived from the Qur'an. That is the so-called shari'a, which in no way corresponds to a defined legal system to which we are accustomed. It does not consist of paragraphs, but it is essentially the commandment to make legal decisions solely based on the religion and its books. The system simply consists of looking for precedent cases in the life of the Prophet or his descendents. The so-called "law schools" practically differ only by which reference sources they admit for usage. As has been shown in most Islamic countries, in order to establish the shari'a system, the existing legal system needn't be changed at all. It simply requires including the addendum that no legal ruling be allowed that contradicts the Qur'an or the Hadiths. In practical terms it means that most civil cases could be ruled according to existing civil laws. But the defeated party could then turn the verdict upside down just by referring to the appropriate Qur'anic passages. The final ruling is carried out by the court of last resort, which is always the mosque. In recent years, Muslim countries have established shari'a courts in addition to the existing civil courts. That means they have two different legal systems existing side-by-side, which has led to a completely confusing judiciary situation. In Malaysia, the Indian and Chinese parts of the population resisted being treated according to shari'a law. As a result, there is a different legal system in each region, depending on ethnic composition. There is no legal security in any Islamic country.

But it is even taken further than that: Muslim countries only recognize international treaties (e.g., by the UN Human Rights Committee) as long as they are shari'a-compatible. In other words, they are not accepting them at all. A special problem of shari'a is that it decides legal cases based on the Hadiths, which are the compilation of deeds and sayings of the Prophet. In basing their decisions on the Hadiths, Muslims believe they are following the perfect system of justice. But this ignores both the completely obscure origins of the Hadiths and the long time period that has passed between the conditions back then and now.

Taken together, all of the above-mentioned features correspond to nothing else but the concept of a desert community that lived fourteen hundred years ago—and this concept is used to handle the present and the future. And this is the concept that is essentially still (or: again) in use in most Islamic countries. The caliph may be called President today—regardless whether he was elected, manipulated the election which he won, or got in power as a result of overthrowing the previous government. None of this really matters as long as he is, at least by appearance, a pious ruler following the Qur'an. And therefore, the term "freedom" in Qur'an Arabic does not denote civic freedom but simply means the opposite to being a slave. That explains why the vast majority of Muslims lack basic understanding regarding the concept of an open society, not to mention democracy. The concept of democracy is said to contradict the teachings of the Qur'an, and therefore, it is considered un-Islamic. The revolutions for democracy in some Arabic countries were not only inspired by "democracy." What we see, in fact, is the establishing of Salafiyya light..

Both the opposing of free acquisition of knowledge and the keeping to medieval concepts, which may not necessarily be Qur'anic teachings but certainly were the established mainstream teachings, have been the millstones round the Muslims' necks and have prevented them from making progress. These days, Qur'anic passages are increasingly emphasized that call for acquiring knowledge. But this only refers to knowledge that is in accordance with the Qur'an, meaning knowledge that is allowed. Biology, for instance, does not belong to this group. Consequently, Muslims in Western countries ask that their children be excluded from Biology class. Therefore, in unison, the Islamic world rejects the concept of evolution. Islamic media generally just state that the concept of evolution has been debunked already anyway without, however, providing any evidence to support this allegation. But then again, how could they, since dealing with such fields is either ostracized or prohibited, just depending on the country. And dealing with knowledge in this way applies again even to twenty-first-century Turkey.[114]

Up to the mid-1920s, Turkey used to be an Islamic country just like the others in this region. But today, when compared with other Islamic countries, Turkey is far ahead in all fields, even without having oil. Beginning in the middle of the nineteenth century, opposition movements began forming in the Ottoman Empire. It was the group called the "Young Turks" that demanded fundamental reforms. The movement peaked with Kemal Pasha. He realized that Islam was the reason for the deterioration and backwardness of his country. In 1924, he abolished both sultanate and shari'a, stripped the clergy of all their privileges, and closed down all Qur'an schools. He combined various systems of government, administration apparatus, and constitutional concepts of different European countries and created a modern state. The key issue of his reforms was the separation of religion and state. It meant changing the ill-fated union that is established in every Islamic country. In order to point the way, he prohibited men from wearing turbans typical of their culture and, for the first time, opened access to schools and universities to women—and banned head veils and head scarves in schools and universities. He led his country from the

---

114   In March 2009, the well-known Turkish science magazine *Bilim ve Teknik* was pressured by a governmental branch into withdrawing a story about Darwin and his theory on evolution.

lowest level of underdevelopment to modern times. His name, *Ataturk* ("Father of the Turks"), was certainly deserved.

A hardly noticed but very important feature of his reforms was the substitution of Arabic scripts by Latin letters. Ataturk also replaced the Ottoman-Muslim identity with a Turkish nationalism which, at times, goes over the top. Nevertheless, as a result of Ataturk's reforms, Turkey accomplished a major leap in development. The current government of Turkey under Prime Minister Erdogan, however, pursues a program of undermining principles of basic civil rights, and those achievements are now threatened.

According to the *AHDR*, the Arabic-Islamic world lags behind in just about every field.

In the Islamic world, the question is frequently asked: "How, after such a glorious past (the "Golden Age of Islam"), could this happen? Who has done this to us?"

And the answers have always been the same: "The Franks, the West, the United States…"

"But," and this is usually the second part of the answer, "this could only have happened to us because we have left the path of the original Islam. Everything will be alright; we just need to reestablish the conditions that existed during the Golden Age of Islam." This is how the Salafiyya puts it, which represents the attitude that is increasingly gaining popularity in the Islamic world and is already shared by many: looking back to an idealized past that never existed.

Sayyid Qutb was a member of the Egyptian Muslim Brotherhood and executed in 1966 by former Egyptian president Gamal Abdel Nasser. By putting it into clear-cut words like no other modern Islamic theorist, he called for the return to the Salafiyya, meaning the obedience to the literal interpretation of the Qur'an, because this was the only way to solve all problems in the world. And he even topped it by stating: "The contents of the Qur'an must not even be thought about and certainly never be subject to discussion. Because Muslims live in a timeless world, a comparison with other cultures is neither possible nor permitted. It is timeless because, during the time of the Prophet and the caliphs, the perfect society existed. And this society must be reestablished again. History is a European invention, which does not apply to Islam." Qutb saw as "undeniable fact" that modern civilization was founded upon the transmitted *Islamic* knowledge, which in turn was the result of the word-by-word following of the Qur'an. The separation of religion and Renaissance-based civilization were the "results of adopted knowledge by the Europeans that they fundamentally misunderstood."

Such statements certainly raise not only eyebrows but also questions regarding this man's level of knowledge and whether it wasn't rather he himself who actually misunderstood some fundamental issues. Qutb was the prototype of a backward radical and did nothing less than abolish and even prohibit reasoning, acquiring knowledge, and using rationalism. He was just another al-Ghazali. Qutb acted this way because he was very aware of the fact that Islam, when interpreted in the traditional way, was no match for the modern world, neither intellectually nor philosophically. Therefore, any comparison had to be declared as inadmissible, and historic processes had to be defined as fabrications.

And as usual, only foreign powers were responsible for the admittedly present misery of the Islamic world: Europe, the United States, the Soviet Union, Israel...the usual suspects. And only by keeping to the literal interpretation of the Qur'an could there be a way out of this misery. And mind you, the Salafiyya is considered a modern movement and Qutb is not just anybody. It would not be fair to claim that the majority of the Muslims were Qutb followers, meaning radicals. But nevertheless, his system of thought represents an important movement in the Islamic world.

Sayyid Qutb (left) and Mahmoud Muhamad Taha

Sayyid Qutb's mentor was the Pakistani al-Maududi (1903–1979), who, like no other, was responsible for the chaos in his country, which was spurred on by his speeches and publications. And that was simply because he had more influence on the public's feeling than any of Pakistan's presidents, who were viewed as aloof politicos. Qutb's way led directly to Bin Laden.

Pressured by persecution under the Nasser regime, numerous members of the Muslim Brotherhood emigrated from Egypt to Saudi Arabia. Among them was Sayyid Qutb's brother Muhammad who left after his release from prison in 1972. In Saudi Arabia, they came in contact with the Saudi-Wahhabi system. The founder of the Wahhabi branch, Abdel Wahhab (1703–1791), had an agreement with the al-Sauds clan, according to which the Wahhabi *Ulema* (religious scholars) agreed to support the Saudis, and in return, the Saudis agreed to accept the validity of only the Wahhabi Qur'anic interpretation. Over time, the Saudis gradually obtained such great power that their land even received the name of the Saudi Dynasty. At the same time, Wahhabism became the all-dominating movement. The result was a very closely intertwined relationship between the interests of the dynasty and the Wahhabi Ulema. But it also resulted in a huge feeling of discontent by the people who felt connected to neither party. Those people found themselves attracted to and inspired by the immigrated members of the Muslim Brotherhood who, as proposed by Sayyid Qutb, preached an even more radical version of following the example of the Prophet.

In 1979, an event shook the Saudi Kingdom: it was the storming of the Great Mosque in Mecca by an ultra-religious Salafist group which wanted to challenge both the dynasty and the Wahhabi Ulema. The same year, the Iranian revolution and the Red Army invasion of Afghanistan took place. Hence, rivalries were spurred between Wahhabis and Qutb followers which resulted in an escalation of ruthlessness among these two groups.

Then, the worst-case scenario for the Saudi Kingdom happened: on August 2, 1990, when Saddam Hussein invaded Kuwait. Because nobody expected that the occupation of Kuwait would be satisfactory enough for Saddam Hussein, panic broke out in Saudi Arabia. On August 7, King Fahd called the United States to the Saudis' aid and asked them to station troops in his country. The idea of having troops of unbelievers stationed on holy ground caused a political test of endurance; it was clear that such an undertaking could not be carried out without the consent of the Wahhabi Ulemas. The dynasty had no alternative if they wanted to survive, but at the same time, the downfall of the Saud Dynasty would have ended the state-supported influence of Wahhabism. For that reason, the Ulemas agreed to the stationing of foreign troops. But this agreement came at a high price in the form of billions of petrodollars, which the Sauds had to pay to the Ulema and which were used to sponsor worldwide missionary activities of unprecedented scale.

This did not satisfy the young, radical Salafists, but there was another option for them on the horizon: a Jihadist-scene had developed in Afghanistan, and, furbished with millions of dollars as seed money, these radical religious warriors were sent off. And that's how the Saudis exported their problems to Afghanistan.

Once "exported," the radicals were immediately stripped of their Saudi citizenship. One of them was Bin Laden. In contrast to the *Umma*, which is the Muslim community, Bin Laden and his Egyptian ideologists were very aware of the situation in the Islamic world. Bin Laden chose to deal with the situation by picking up arms because he saw himself in the role of the defender of the religion against the West—especially the United States—which, in his view, was responsible for the Islamic misery. Again, he was showing a correct understanding of the current situation, but drawing wrong conclusions regarding the cause.

Who has done this to them? *They have.*

The primary, most basic reason lies in the rejection of knowledge. From the beginning on they have twisted it; prohibited, banned, and abolished it; and punished in order to fight it. The reservations regarding knowledge, often indeed even criminalizing it, became a part of the system. Criticism was reduced to a matter of personal insult, blasphemy, and crime.

Therefore, in order to set the record straight, the question—or is it the exclamation?—can only be: "What has Islam done to us!"

Yes, the Islamic world is really in bad shape, but there is hope. One ray of hope is seen in a union of small emirates on the Persian Gulf, the "United Arab Emirates." On maps produced not too long ago, this area is still called the "Pirate Coast"; but now, it is a place where people from all over the world meet. Once a completely insignificant region at the outskirts of the Arabian Peninsula and endowed with a comparably modest amount of oil, Sheik Maktoum Rashid bin Maktoum (1943–2006) turned this area into an Oriental wonderland. In 1971, the emirates were created by the merging of Dubai and Abu Dhabi. Later, more sheikdoms joined. These miniature countries took on the process of modernizing.

For this purpose, they invited foreign experts who created a country on the drawing board. The countries started their own airline that was especially built to connect them with the world. Within a short period of time, favorable economic conditions turned this little spot in the desert, called Dubai, into a popular shopping paradise and encouraged just about every high-class corporation to build a branch there. That has created jobs and has attracted people from all across the world, by now even in their second generation, to settle there. This area has become a mix of cultures, races, languages, and religions. Mosques are found next to churches, temples, and pagodas.

This is what Baghdad must have once looked like during the time period of Arabian prosperity. But just like Baghdad, the success story of the Emirates is an Arabic but not Islamic one. The foremost reason for their flourishing lies in their keeping to secularism.

For people in the Arabic world, the Emirates are very attractive. In larger numbers, Saudis travel to the Emirates in order to indulge in— often rather un-Islamic—activities. Yemenis make up large parts of the police forces; Lebanese very successfully engage in the gastronomical sector; Palestinians, Jordanians, and Egyptians are doing well in the field of business. In addition, there are non-Arabs from almost every country in the world. In the Arab world, the Emirates are envied and are seen as the bar against which the other governments have to match themselves. Qatar has taken the first step in the same direction. It started in 2007, when an inconspicuous little announcement was made that a church was being built there. The country has the ambition to establish itself as an internationally recognized scientific center and is putting a lot of effort into achieving this goal. That is simply a breathtaking development.

But all that glitters is not gold. Time will tell whether the Emirates can stand their ground and how they will deal with the increasing religious pressure from outside. The case of Lebanon comes to mind, once a model country of the Arab world that has now spiraled downward into chaos. But, generally too often, negative issues have been exaggerated and maliciously commented on. As a matter of fact, those Islamic rulers from the once behind-the-times Arabia have overcome themselves. It is a process of truly historic dimension.

Another glimpse of hope for the Muslim world might lie in a rather unspectacular feature that could have, however, great potential: it is the Western Diaspora.

Traditionally, almost all of the Muslims used to live in a country in which they formed the majority and in which their legal system was in place. But nowadays, many Muslims live in non-Muslim countries in which they form the minority, like for instance, Turks in Germany, Algerians in France, and Pakistanis in England. Living as a member of the minority in a non-Muslim country is a relatively new experience to them and, actually, there are no guidelines for this kind of situation. Since the defeat of the Spanish Caliphate, there have been discussions among Qur'anic scholars about whether Muslims should be allowed to live in a non-Islamic country at all. The answer derived from the Qur'an is a clear *no*. A Muslim is not allowed to live in a country of the unbeliever. But if they do so anyway, then it is their obligation to act in the interest of Islam. When Bin Laden was asked about the Muslim victims of 9/11, he answered that Muslims had no business there anyway. Their presence there was in contradiction to Qur'anic commandments and, therefore, they deserved to die.[115]

The believers are especially warned of the so-called tolerant countries because they represented the greatest danger for them. Only in the *Dar al-Islam*, the communal empire of the Muslims, could Qur'anic commandments and shari'a be executed. If a Muslim has to live in a non-Islamic country, he can only do so in the interest of Islam. And this belief is not only pursued in theory, as seen by events since 9/11. To the average Muslim worker in the United States or Europe, such issues are probably rather academic in nature, and they do not overly engage in them. But the Qur'anic demands are always in the back of their minds and work like a hidden poison, which results in a continuous feeling of guilt. As a consequence, this compromises their chance of successful integration. It is a matter of fact that no other

---

115   Interview in the Pakistani newspaper, *Dawn*, November 10, 2007.

group has such great difficulties in adjusting to the host country as Muslims.

There are close affinities between Islam and Judaism in that they are both derived from the same roots and make high formal demands on their devout members. Nevertheless, Jews have always managed to splendidly adapt to their host countries. The reason for this lies in the Jewish precept of *dina demalkhuta dina*: "the law of the state is the law." In addition, Judaism experienced in the ninetheenth century its reformation, the *Haskalah* ("enlightenment"), which could well be a model for the inevitable reformation of Islam.

Jesus expressed this in a similar statement: "Give to the emperor what is the emperor's, and give to God what is God's." This statement basically expresses the idea of privatizing of religion and represents the fundamental idea which later led to the separation of state and religion in Europe.

According to Islamic understanding, however, religion is a public matter to which every aspect of life is subordinate. The "true" right is the religious law. It is a system which excludes the concept of separation of state and religion. Therefore, Islam is a political system. And that is the reason why its followers have these tremendous difficulties in adjusting to a non-Islamic environment and in accepting the non-Islamic world. Muslims who live in a non-Islamic country, in which they form the minority, are left only with the option to leave the country. But if they decide to stay, they will have no option other than to adjust and integrate in order to lead a peaceful and successful life. It will be the duty of the host country to be very insistent regarding their integration. Successful integration requires the adoption of both the host country's legal system and its customs. And, ultimately, this means the privatizing of religion. If the Diaspora is to a Western country, it will lead to the increase of the educational level of the Muslims by, for instance, their attending public schools. In the future, it may not be satisfactory enough to just recite and repeat the centuries-old interpretations of the Qur'an without understanding them. By making the contents of the Qur'anic texts accessible in an educated environment, the language of the host country will have to necessarily become the language of the religion, too.

In general, Islam is considered a religion that cannot be reformed. That might apply to the classical countries of its occurrence. In the Western Diaspora, however, Islam is pressured into reforming itself or, depending on the country, is at risk of dwindling to a sect that people either sneer at or fight.

It is the author's hope to have made clear that historic evidence on one side and the traditional picture of Islam on the other are two completely different things. In the Islamic world itself, little to no information is known about its own heritage and origin. The ideas regarding the origin of Islam still follow the ninth-century dogmatic view. But the Islamic world cannot keep evading the advance of knowledge. Sooner or later, it will no longer be possible to avoid the reevaluation of the Qur'an and other texts. And to take the train of thought even a step further: one of the focal points could become the effort to separate theological issues from regulations regarding proper conduct and subsidiary oral transmissions that were added later, and which have caused nothing but distraction from the basic essentials. This would require focusing on Meccan Suras, that are of theological relevance.

Subsequently, it would end the obligation to follow the codes of a medieval Bedouin society as a central part of religious life. Furthermore, it might be revealed that both the theological concept and the purpose of the Qur'an had been made invisible by adding conduct regulations that completely obscured them. Up to this day, Islam lacks a coherent theology; instead, this gap is filled both by strictly keeping to literal reciting of the Qur'an and by using partly unrecognizable sources. Considering the current situation, even for Islamic scientists those are untouchable issues. But research won't stop at taboos.

The Sudanese theologian Mahmud Muhammad Taha called for the setting aside of the "Medinan Suras" because they only applied to the seventh century. For vocalizing this statement, he was executed as an "apostate" in Khartoum in 1985.

The classical, bearded Qur'anic scholars have served their time and have failed. Most of the problems that now beset Islam arise from its ever-closer integration into a globalized and knowledge-based world. So who else could be the driving force towards solving these problems if not the educated, knowledgeable Muslims of the Western Diaspora and elsewhere? Islam has come to a point where it must either reform itself into a new model, a 'Reformed Islam', a 'New Islam', or it will face a very troubled future.

❖ ❖ ❖

Further Reading

Al-Buhari, Sahih, *Nachrichten von Taten und Aussprüchen des Propheten Muhammad*. Stuttgart, 2006.

Allebrand, Raimund (Hrsg.), *Terror oder Toleranz?* Bad Honnef, 2004.

Bayard Dodge, *The Fihrist of al-Nadim* (New York: Kazi Publications, 1979)

Barth, Jakob, *Studien zur Kritik und Exegese des Qorans*. Strassburg, 1915.

Bartsch, Gerhard (Hrsg.), *De tribus impostoribus (Über die drei Betrüger), herausgegeben von G. Bartsch*. Berlin, 1960.

Bossong, Georg, "Das maurische Spanien," München, 2007.

Burgmer, Christoph (Hrsg.), *Streit um den Koran. Die Luxenberg-Debatte*. Berlin, 2007.

Crone, Patricia, "What do we actually know about Mohammed?" 2008, http://www.opendemocracy.net/faith-europe_islam/mohammed_3866.jsp.

Dieterici, Friedrich, "Über den Zusammenhang der griechischen und arabischen Philosophie," Leiden 1903. Nachdruck München, 2004.

Diner, Dan, *Lost in Sacred: Why the Muslim World Stood Still*. Princeton, 2009.

Finster, Barbara, "Arabien in der Spätantike," *Archäologischer Anzeiger*, München, 1996.

Finster, Barbara, "Cubical Yemeni Mosques," Seminar for Arabian Studies, London, 1991.

Gericke, Wofgang, "Wann entstand das Buch, Von den drei Betrügern?" *Theologische Versuche* 8. Berlin, 1977.

Goldziher, Ignaz, *Muslim Studies*. New Jersey, 2006

Gopal, Jaya, "Gabriels Einflüsterungen," Freiburg, 2006.

Grabar, Oleg, *The Dome of the Rock*. London, 2006.

Grabar, Oleg, *Die Alhambra*. Köln, 1981.

Groß, Markus and Karl-Heinz Ohlig (Hrsg.), *Vom Koran zum Islam*. Berlin, 2009.

Groß, Markus and Karl-Heinz Ohlig (Hrsg.), *Schlaglichter*. Berlin, 2008.

Henning, Max, *Der Koran*. Stuttgart, 1998.

Hottinger, Arnold, *Die Mauren*. Paderborn, 2005.

Ibn, Tufail, *Hajj bin Yaqdhan*, Bloomington, 2000.

Ibn, Warraq, *Why I Am Not a Muslim*. New York, 2003.

Ibn, Warraq, *Which Koran?* New York, 2009.

Kepel, Gilles. *The War for Muslim Minds*. Harvard, 2006.

Kerr Robert M. Von der *aramäischen Lesekutur zur arabischen Schreibkultur*. Inarah Volume 6, Berlin 2012

Kerr, Robert M., Annus Hegirae vel Annus Agarorum, *Etymologische und vergleichende Anmerkungen zum Anfang der islamischen Jahreszählung*. Inarah Volume 7, Berlin 2012

Kolter, Bonifatius (Hrsg.), *Die Schriften des Johannes von Damaskus*. Berlin, 1981.

Lewis, Bernard, *Islam and the West*. New York, 1993.

Lewis, Bernard, *What Went Wrong?* New York, 2002.

Luxenberg, Christoph. *The Syro-Aramaic Reading of the Koran*. New York, 2007.

Lüling, Günter, A *Challenge to Islam for Reformation*, Delhi, 2003

Lüling, Günter, *Die Wiederentdeckung des Propheten Muhammad: Eine Kritik am christlichen Abendland*. Erlangen, 1981.

Lüling, Günter, "Avicenna und seine buddhistische Herkunft" in "Zwei Aufsätze zur Religions–und Geistesgeschichte," Erlangen, 1977.

Malik, Muhammad Faroog-i-Azim, "*English Translation of the Meanings of Al-Qur'an: The Guidance for Mankind*," The Institute of Islamic Knowledge, Houston, 1997.

Müller, C.D.G., "Kirche und Mission unter den Arabern in vorislamischer Zeit," Tübingen, 1967.

Nagel, Tilman, *Mohammed Leben und Legende*, Oldenbourg Verlag, München 2008

Nöldeke, Theodor, "Geschichte des Qorans," Leipzig 1909, Nachdruck Elibron Classics, New York, 2004.

Ohlig, Karl-Heinz (Hrsg.), *Der frühe Islam*. Berlin, 2007.

Ohlig, Karl-Heinz/Puin Gerd-R, *The Hidden Origins of Islam*. New York, 2009.

Mezzomorto, Mavro, *Mohammed auf Abwegen*. Mainz, 2002.

Muir, William, *Mahomet and Islam*. General Books, 2009. (Reprint of the 1895 version.)

Nevo, Yehuda D. and Judith Koren, *Crossroads to Islam*. New York, 2003.

Paret, Rudi, *Der Koran*. Stuttgart, 2006.

Paret, Rudi, *Die Lücke der Überlieferungen über den Urkoran*. Wiesbaden, 1954.

Qutb, Sayyid, *Milestones*. Chicago, 2007.

Runciman, Steven, *A History of the Crusades*. Cambridge University Press, 1987.

Salibi, Kamal, *The Bible Came from Arabia*. New York, 1987.

Sivers von, Peter, *Christology and Prophety in the later Umayyad Arab Empire*. University of Utah, 2012.

Sprenger, Aloys, "The Life of Mohamed from Original Sources," Nabu Press, 2010.

Strohmaier, Gotthard, "Denker im Reich der Kalifen," Leipzig, 1979.

Strohmaier, Gotthard, "Avicenna," München, 1999.

Thomas, Johannes, *Araboislamische Geschichtsschreibung und ihre Auswirkungen auf Geschichtsbilder von al-Andalus* (8. Jh.). Saarbrücken, 2010.

Tibi, Bassam, *Fundamentalismus im Islam*. Darmstadt, 2002.

Torrey, Charles C., *The Jewish Foundation of Islam*. New York, 1933.

United Nations Development Program, *Arab Human Development Reports 2002–2009*, New York.

Waldmann, Helmut, *Die Entstehung des Zurvanismus im alten Iran gefolgt von einer Skizze seiner Einflussnahme auf den heutigen Islam*, Tübingen, 1994.

Wansbrough, John, *Quranic Studies*. New York, 2004.

Wansbrough, John, *The Sectarian Milieu*. New York, 2006.

Weil, Gustav, *Mohammed der Prophet, sein Leben und seine Lehre*. Stuttgart, 1843.

Wieland, Rotraut, *Offenbarung und Geschichte im Denken moderner Muslime*. Wiesbaden, 1971.

Werner, Helmut, *Das Islamische Totenbuch*. Köln, 2009.

Index

Made in the USA
Middletown, DE
20 August 2019